How To Change Your Drinking:

A Harm Reduction Guide To Alcohol

2nd Edition

by

Kenneth Anderson, MA

Executive Director - The HAMS Harm Reduction Network

*To the memory of Andi Emerson
who inspired me with the courage
to go it on my own, and to Electra
Weeks for always being there*

CONTENTS

PREFACE by Alan Marlatt

If you are a drinker who is looking for a change in your use/abuse of alcohol, this is the book for you. Ken Anderson (himself a former problem drinker) and The HAMS Harm Reduction Network have provided us with a helpful manual telling us how to follow through on whatever choice we make about changing our drinking behavior: either to give it up altogether (abstinence), to enhance moderate drinking, and/or to practice harm reduction strategies to avoid negative consequences of excessive drinking. As such, this manual is similar to a driver's training program for safety on the road (whether to slow down, drive safely, or get off the road altogether).

Most people with drinking problems are similar to drivers who end up at an intersection on the highway: the traffic light can be Green (keep drinking at your usual speed), Red (stop drinking), or Yellow (slow down and proceed with caution). Most alcohol treatment programs show nothing but Stop signs, and drinkers are confronted if they run the Red light.

The Yellow light represents a harm reduction, middle-of-the road approach that gives the driver a signal to Yield, given the risks involved of not stopping. Drivers get to take caution and proceed with safety for themselves and other drivers at the intersection.

Readers will be guided in how to make the right choice in terms of choosing your new drinking goal and learning new coping strategies to keep on track and follow the safe road. You will always have control over the choices you make, and this manual will give you the skills and direction you need to make a safe trip. Happy travels.

G. Alan Marlatt, PhD
Professor and Director
Addictive Behaviors Research Center
University of Washington
Seattle, WA

INTRODUCTION by Patt Denning

HARM REDUCTION

Two small, gallant words. Simple, easy to understand.

HARM REDUCTION

Let's see. What kind of harm might we want to reduce?

The harm from driving a car? (seatbelt and helmet laws)

The harm from global warming? (emission standards)

The harm from childhood illnesses? (vaccinations and well baby clinics)

The harm from tooth decay? (fluoride in the water supply)

The harm from icy sidewalks? (salt, sand, or shovel)

The harm from alcohol and drug use? NOW HOLD ON A MINUTE!!

HARM REDUCTION

All of a sudden these two words have become the enemy, the symbol of an irresponsible, nearly evil, intent to cause harm to people. Because the media bombards us, everyone now knows that the only way to reduce harm from alcohol and other drugs is to Just Say No! Of course, alcohol is legal again, so it must be relatively safe. So we're not quite so sure about how harmful it is. Tobacco is legal too, but it's not very good for us. Hmm. This is getting confusing…

Other drugs though, the really dangerous ones like marijuana, are illegal for that very reason- they are harmful! Right?

In any case, at least we've all been convinced that people who are alcoholics or drug addicts can't ever use drugs again if they hope to get better, if they hope to reduce harm to themselves and others. It's been proven, after all! Medical professionals, researchers, everyday people know that addiction is a disease that cannot be cured. The 12 Steps of Alcoholics Anonymous were created to help people whose drinking was causing harm. And everyone agrees- you have to stop. And despite not such great success, 12 Step still is the go-to method.

Just Say No. Go to treatment and do what the experts say: 28 days in rehab and a lifetime of 12 Step meetings if you want to have a prayer of not dying from your disease.

And if your father, cousin, daughter is addicted?? Don't help them if they won't stop!! You'll just make it worse. Don't give them advice, money, or shelter, or even much love. Tough Love is the only kind that helps. Be tough. Don't let them manipulate you. Addicts lie and steal and never can be trusted.

Drugs are illegal. People who use them, people who provide them, are criminals. They belong in jail. It'll teach them a lesson. A felony conviction that insures that they won't get public housing, can't get student loans, aren't acceptable to work, and can't ever vote again will teach them. Well, but people with addictions have a medical disease, though, right? How will jail help? It gets confusing sometimes, but you just have to keep remembering that drugs are bad, evil, harmful and people deserve to go to jail for using them. Simple.

HARM REDUCTION

Over the past 20 years an increasing number of people have dared to challenge these ideas. First, drug users themselves advocated for more sensitive medical care and access to clean syringes. Then public health educators became involved in helping stem the tide of HIV infections by offering people information, condoms, and other infection control methods. Grass roots organizations formed to bring people together in order to strengthen an urgent message: Drugs use is a public health, not a moral or legal issue.

WHERE DOES ALCOHOL FIT IN THIS PICTURE?

Despite the fact that alcohol is a legal drug, it has not escaped the hysteria surrounding addiction. Americans have a decidedly ambivalent relationship to this drug that has been a part of human civilizations since the beginning of time. Responding to real harms of excess drinking in the late 19th and early 20th centuries, the Temperance Movement evolved from advocating moderation in alcohol consumption to a belief that alcohol was evil in any form, in any amount. Prohibition lasted only 13 years, but returning alcohol to legal status did not totally cleanse it of its evil reputation. Instead, we have created a 2-tiered view of alcohol: some people can drink in moderation and that's fine. Others, though, drink too much and too often, causing harm to themselves and others. They are alcoholics. They must not drink. Those who challenge this wisdom run the same risks as those who challenge the Just Say No mentality towards other drugs. We are considered ill informed at best, and dangerous at worst.

HARM REDUCTION FOR ALCOHOL PROBLEMS

If we look at alcohol (or any drug problem) as occurring on a continuum, rather than an all or nothing affair, we can begin to design public health, public policy, and treatment guidelines that can truly help people. We can take a pragmatic and respectful approach, listening to the people we want to help rather than telling them what to do. Studying the science in a way that looks at the grey areas as well as the certainties. This book offers such a pragmatic and respectful approach. The author started a self help group called HAMS: dedicated to Harm reduction, Alcohol abstinence, and Moderation Support. This network currently provides peer support and education both on line and in person. The members of HAMS refer to themselves as HAMSters! A breath of humor in a field of long faces. It is this sense of humor, coupled with the serious understanding of the dangers of alcohol misuse, that propel this book forward.

There are more and more people across the country who are helping people overcome alcohol problems by using client centered, and harm reduction informed, practices. This book belongs on the shelf of therapists, case managers, peer advocates, families, and, of course, people who drink alcohol. This book will most likely get a lot of play! Ken Anderson has created a manual that can be used every day by anyone wanting to learn more about guided self change. He presents the complicated science of how our bodies process alcohol with enough detail to show his immense knowledge, and in language that is accessible to many. He takes the reader through self reflection, self assessment, and self direction by offering a logical and sequential manual that covers all the bases. Throughout the book, Ken communicates a deep respect for each person's autonomy, power, and choice. There is plenty of useful home spun wisdom gathered from the people who comprise the network, the people who really know what works. And there are a lot of suggestions and interventions taken from what we like to call "evidence-based practices", those methods that are professionally developed and subjected to research studies. This combination of street wisdom and empirically derived techniques makes this book the best guide available to helping one overcome alcohol problems.

Ken's consistent message is one of choice, empowerment, and optimism. Change is in the hands of the user.

Patt Denning, PhD
Director of Clinical Services and Training
Harm Reduction Therapy Center
San Francisco, CA

ACKNOWLEDGMENTS

The book which you hold in your hands could not exist without the contributions of many, many people, including:

The Hamsters--the members of HAMS who over the years have shared their individualized alcohol harm reduction strategies which help to form the backbone of this book.

The harm reduction pioneers who got the harm reduction movement started in the United States, sometimes risking arrest by operating clandestine needle exchange programs out of the trunks of their cars.

Particular thanks to Access Works--the Minneapolis needle exchange--where I cut my teeth working in harm reduction. It was by working here that I took the principles that I knew in my head and fixed them firmly in my heart as well.

Finally I want to thank the authors and researchers like Alan Marlatt, Patt Denning, Stanton Peele, Andrew Tatarsky, and many, many more. Your words helped to save my life and continue to help save the lives of many, many more who are failed by more conventional approaches.

The day of the revolution is now.

PART I: BETTER IS BETTER - THE NUTS AND BOLTS OF HARM REDUCTION

"Never discourage anyone who continues to make progress, no matter how slow." --Plato

Did you ever hear people complain that you aren't perfect? Maybe you make some positive changes but they still yell at you that it isn't good enough? Perhaps some people have told you that you have to get worse to get better--that you have to "hit bottom".

These people are wrong. The research shows that it is essential to support EVERY POSITIVE CHANGE. Better is never worse. Better is ALWAYS better!

CHAPTER ONE: Introducing Harm Reduction for Alcohol

"Everything that I like is either illegal, immoral, or fattening" --W. C. Fields

1.1) Why We Need a Harm Reduction Approach for Alcohol

All too often when people seek help for an alcohol problem they are told that they have no alternative but AA and the 12 steps, that one size fits all, and that AA is good for everyone. Although we applaud anyone who manages to beat a drinking problem by going to AA and quitting, the National Institute on Alcohol Abuse and Alcoholism tells us that only 7% of people with an alcohol problem ever seek treatment. And clinical research such as that of Dr, Jeffrey Brandsma shows us that over two thirds of those who enter 12 step treatment programs drop out. Why do so few people succeed with 12 step programs? Perhaps this is because 12 step programs require the following:

- Labeling oneself as "diseased" and "alcoholic"
- Total abstinence from all addictive, mood altering drugs except nicotine and caffeine
- A confession of "powerlessness" and a reliance on a "Higher Power" (i. e. God) to cure one's "disease"

The majority of people find these demands unpalatable and 12 step programs unapproachable.

By way of contrast a harm reduction program:

- Meets people "where they are at" with their drinking
- Does not label people as "diseased" or "alcoholic"
- Empowers people to choose their own goal--safer drinking, reduced drinking, or quitting
- Engages people with realistic goals which they can actually accomplish

Harm reduction programs owe their success to their approachability. Some highly successful harm reduction programs in the United States include:

- Seatbelts to reduce the damage from automobile accidents
- Condoms for safe sex
- Clean needles to stop the spread of HIV

Isn't it time that there was a harm reduction approach to alcohol problems, too?

Harm reduction works on the premise that it is easier to get people to make small changes than to get them to make big changes. Because of this it is possible to have a far greater positive impact on society by getting a large number of people to make small positive changes than by getting only a few people to make big changes. It is easier and far more effective to get people to use seat belts than to eliminate the automobile and driving entirely. It is easier and far more effective to get people to have safe sex than to attempt to make people stop having sex entirely. And it is easier and far more effective to teach people how to plan their drinking and drink safely than to try and eliminate recreational intoxication entirely. Prohibition and coerced abstinence do not work. Harm reduction does.

At HAMS we see people who have been failed by standard treatment approaches to alcohol whose lives have been shattered by drinking. These people turn their lives around completely after learning simple, approachable harm reduction strategies. We also see people who have never suffered any major consequences from drinking who find the disease label unhelpful and unacceptable. These people come to HAMS and turn their drinking around before it ever harms them. It does not matter how much or how little you drink, the miracle of harm reduction can work for anyone who wants to change his or her drinking for the better.

1.2) What Is HAMS

The letters H, A, M, and S stand for "Harm reduction, Alcohol abstinence, and Moderation Support". HAMS is a free-of-charge, lay-led support and informational group for people who want to change their drinking for the better. You can use this book to do self-change on your own if that is how you are most comfortable. Or you can join in on a HAMS live or online support group if you find that to be helpful.

HAMS has found that people are most successful at achieving goals which they have chosen for themselves. HAMS supports goals of safer drinking, reduced drinking, or quitting. In HAMS you choose your own goal and you are also free to switch to a different goal at any time.

At HAMS we do not refer to overdrinking as a "disease". We do not find that stigmatizing people by calling them "diseased" or "alcoholic" or "powerless" or other bad names helps people to change their habits and get on with a happy life. HAMS views excessive drinking as a maladaptive coping strategy. Different people choose different coping strategies to deal with life. If you have decided that drinking is not working for you or if you feel that you rely on drinking too much then you have come to the right place.

HAMS strongly believes in individual liberty. We agree with John Stuart Mill when he said, "The only freedom which deserves the name is that of pursuing our own good in our own way, so long as we do not attempt to deprive others of theirs, or impede their efforts to obtain it. Each is the proper guardian of his own health, whether bodily, or mental or spiritual. Mankind are greater gainers by suffering each other to live as seems good to themselves, than by compelling each to live as seems good to the rest."

1.3) How to Use This Book

You can read this book in sequence if you want to, but you can also dip in at any place that works for you. If you skim through the table of contents and see something that seems particularly relevant to you, then please feel free to read that first. All the elements of HAMS are optional--you really can take what you need and leave the rest.

1.4) How Much Alcohol Is Too Much

There is an old joke about the man who goes to the doctor and asks what he has to do to live to be 100 years old. The doctor tells him to give up eating meat, drinking alcohol, smoking, and sex. The man says. "If I do all that will I live to be 100 years old?" The doctor replies, "Maybe not, but it will sure as hell feel that way!!"

Some folks today want to say that everything fun is an addiction and that everyone had better spend their lives in 12 step meetings talking about their "Higher Power" and holding hands and saying the Lord's Prayer instead of ever doing anything fun. We beg to differ with these people. Prohibition does not work because there is nothing essentially evil, sinful, or diseased about having fun. There is nothing evil, sinful or diseased about drinking alcohol moderately, and for that matter there is nothing sinful, evil or diseased about engaging in recreational intoxication either.

There is not some specific magical quantity which we can say is too much alcohol--free individuals have the right to make up their own minds about how much they believe is too much for them personally. Occasional intoxication is not a symptom of a disease; it is a choice.

Research tells us that men who drink two standard drinks[1] per day and women who drink one will be healthier than those who abstain totally or those who drink more than these amounts. Research also tells us that people who drink a fifth (750 ml) of whiskey or more every day will tend to have health problems, alcohol withdrawal syndrome, cognitive impairment, employment problems, family problems, school problems, and be more likely to suffer from falls and other accidents than those who drink less--even if they do not drive.

If a person really enjoys drinking a fifth of booze every day and has no desire to change then it is not our job here at HAMS to try and change that person--to each their own. HAMS is here for those who don't like their current drinking habits and want to change them. It does not matter at HAMS how much or how little you may drink--if you desire to make a change then we are here to give you the tools and the information and the support that you need to make that change.

So how much is too much? When alcohol starts to interfere with the things that you personally value, then it is too much. Things like your family, your job, your school, your recreation, your health, or your life's dreams. When alcohol starts stealing time away from things that are more important to you than drinking, then it is too much. When you wake up with the shakes and sweats and are sick and tired of being sick and tired, then it is too much. Any time that you are unhappy with the way that you drink, then it is too much.

Some people will find that quitting alcohol completely is their best option. Quitting is straightforward and clear-cut and for some people it is easier than attempting to control their drinking. Other people will decide that they no longer like to become intoxicated--that they prefer to drink moderately instead. Still others will decide that they like to indulge in some

---

[1] See Chapter 13 for the definition of a standard drink.

occasional recreational intoxication so long as they do it safely and don't let it interfere with the more important aspects of their lives.

This book will give you tools to help you determine what the best drinking goal is for you: safer drinking, reduced drinking, or quitting. We will give you information to help you rationally determine the risks associated with various levels of drinking. We will help you to decide how much alcohol consumption is right for you, and we will also give you tools to help you to achieve the drinking goal which you have chosen for yourself.

Physical dependence is not the real essence of a bad habit--what some people call an addiction. Even the DSM-IV says that. From our perspective any behavior can be an addiction if it interferes with your values, harms others, or takes you away too much from what you really want in life.

1.5) Why People Overdrink

The old-fashioned model of alcoholism as a progressive, primary disease which can only be arrested by attending AA meetings and which can never be cured has pretty much been discredited as mythology by contemporary research. Currently most people in psychology subscribe to a **vulnerability-protective-factors-stress theory** (a more modern development by Liberman of Zubin's diathesis-stress theory) to account for many disorders from schizophrenia to depression to alcohol use disorders.

The **vulnerability-protective-factors-stress theory** posits that some people are more susceptible to alcohol problems than others both as a result of their genetics and their upbringing--this is the **vulnerability** part. It also states that genetics or upbringing can confer **protective** factors on individuals. Finally, it states that individuals with **vulnerabilities** and lacking **protective factors** may develop an alcohol use disorder in response to **environmental stressors**. This also helps to account for the fact that people do not develop alcohol problems in environments where alcohol does not exist--such as in the pre-Columbus Inuit culture.

Choice theory is also essential in understanding why people overdrink and in helping them to overcome their bad habits. Talking about choice is something of a heresy in scientific circles where people try to reduce everything to a deterministic cause and effect model[2]. However, scientific studies have shown that self-efficacy is a major factor in successful behavioral change. Believing that you have the power of choice and the power to change your actions is an important quality in people who succeed in changing their behaviors.

People choose to use alcohol as a tool to achieve certain results--to wit:

- To alleviate pain
- To have fun/to enhance a good time
- To improve performance/overcome anxiety and shyness

---

[2] Some people like Jeffrey Schaler prefer to talk about voluntary vs. involuntary behaviors in order to avoid the philosophical problem of free will vs. determinism.

Edward Khantzian's **self-medication hypothesis** tells us that people choose to use mood altering substances like alcohol in order to medicate problems like depression or insomnia or to overcome problems like anxiety or shyness and thus improve performance. People also choose to use alcohol to have fun or enhance fun. These reasons sum up **choice theory**.

Volitionality is an important dimension to consider when talking about mental health. Things like schizophrenia are not very much under volitional control. Things like drinking alcohol are very much under volitional control and subject to choice--it is totally possible to learn strategies to reduce drinking, to quit drinking, or to drink safely. Things like depression and anxiety are in the middle--many people can learn cognitive behavioral techniques to help control their thoughts and their depression and anxiety. These strategies involve choosing which thoughts to keep and which to discard. **Volitionality** is of course just another word for **choice**.

Finally, **conditioned response theory** plays a major role in explaining why it can be so hard to change maladaptive coping behaviors like drinking too much. Withdrawal syndrome may help to explain why it is difficult for a person who is actively drinking or using drugs to stop. But withdrawal syndrome does not explain why a person who has successfully withdrawn from alcohol or drugs has a craving to go back to them. This is, however, adequately explained by **conditioned response theory**. Every time a person drinks alcohol chemicals are released in the brain which reward the act of drinking. These chemicals form a very strong conditioned response which makes it very difficult to change one's drinking habits. In short--addiction is conditioned learning. Fortunately, conditioned responses can be dealt with via deconditioning, which can be either behavioral or chemical. We discuss chemical extinction in Appendix Three.

The most reasonable theory of why people overdrink is one that combines **choice theory** with **vulnerability-protective-factors-stress theory** and with **conditioned response theory**. We call this the **integrated theory of alcohol misuse**. Let's look at some concrete examples of how the theory works:

John is born with a system which responds strongly to alcohol. John finds drinking pleasurable. This constitutes a **genetic vulnerability**. One day John's fiancée jilts him. This is an **environmental stressor**. John feels miserable and chooses to drink a lot to deal with the pain. John's heavy drinking becomes an ingrained, daily habit. The rewarding effects of alcohol in the brain turn the drinking into a conditioned response which is hard to change. John has adopted a maladaptive coping mechanism. Alcohol begins to cause many problems in John's life but he finds it hard to quit or cut back because of the conditioning effect.

Let us look at another example. Jim is also jilted by his girlfriend but Jim was born with Asian Flush Syndrome--a condition similar to an allergy which makes Jim feel sick rather than euphoric when he drinks alcohol. This is an example of a **genetic protective factor**. Since Jim does not like alcohol he chooses to drown his sorrows in gambling instead and winds up developing a gambling problem. Although the genetic protective factor of Asian Flush Syndrome protected Jim from an alcohol problem it did not protect him from a behavioral addiction like excessive gambling.

Let us look at one more example. Bill is born into a traditional Jewish family which has a strong disapproval of excessive alcohol consumption. Bill considers it shameful to be "shiker vi a goy"-

-"drunk like a non-Jew." This functions as an **environmental protective factor** stemming from Bill's upbringing. However, Bill's culture has no disapproval of prescription medications. When Bill sprains his back he gets a prescription for painkillers. Even after his back gets better he chooses to ask his doctor to keep renewing the prescription because he likes the effect of the pills.

Sherri is a high school student who has been painfully shy ever since she can remember. This is her **vulnerability**. Sherri found last year at a party that a few drinks of alcohol can cure her shyness. Now Sherri is having a few drinks of booze for breakfast each morning on her way to school. Sherri is choosing a maladaptive coping strategy which is working for the present but which will very likely become a big problem farther down the road.

Joe was the chess club nerd until he found the joy of alcohol. Now he is Mr. Fun--the life of the party. In fact he doesn't even need a party--the joy of booze is enough fun in itself whether he is with others or alone. The fact that Joe did not know how to have fun was a **vulnerability**. Now he is choosing to have alcoholic fun to the exclusion of all else--this is his **maladaptive coping strategy**.

These few examples give some picture of how vulnerabilities, stressors, and protective factors interact. A propensity towards depression or anxiety or panic or insomnia, etc. can also function as a **vulnerability** which is susceptible to treatment with alcohol or some other drug or other form of addictive behavior. Alcohol starts off being a good solution to a problem but then when it is overused turns into a problem in and of itself.

We start off choosing to use alcohol to cope or to have fun because it works for us at the time. As we get into the habit of using too much it starts to become a problem in and of itself. It becomes a maladaptive coping mechanism. Sometimes this happens so gradually that we do not even notice it till it has been going on for years.

When a behavior switches over from being positive to being maladaptive might be the ideal time to change it, but the simple fact is that many people do not realize that the line has been crossed until long, long after the fact. And even then, inertia can lead us to continue a habit long after we have realized that it is counterproductive. With booze the habit gets additional chemical reinforcement which leads to a strongly conditioned reflex that can be quite hard to break. It isn't withdrawal that makes addiction hard to deal with--if withdrawal was the only factor then once people get over their withdrawal symptoms they would never think of going back. It is the chemically conditioned response that keeps people going back to addictions that they have kicked in spite of the fact that those addictions have had major negative consequences attached to them.

The good news is that the chemically reinforced conditioning called addiction can be beaten and people can lead happy and fulfilled lives as a result of cutting back, safer drinking, or quitting.

When we realize that alcohol has become a problem then it is time for us to find strategies to change our drinking habits as well as finding new ways to cope and to have fun without the booze. HAMS is here to give you strategies which will work for you.

1.6) Do You Need A Higher Power To Change Your Drinking?

The answer to this is an unqualified "No". The key research on the effectiveness of various types of treatment to promote abstinence from alcohol was done by Dr. Jeffrey Brandsma and we discuss his book in detail in Appendix Four. The upshot of his research was that people who had a purely secular treatment program based on either a cognitive behavioral approach or a psychodynamic approach were more successful at changing their drinking than those who underwent a 12 step spiritual approach which required a belief in a "Higher Power".

Here at HAMS we are pragmatists and we believe in using whatever works. If going to church is a good alternative to drinking for you then by all means do it. If joining the atheist society is a good alternative to drinking for you then by all means do that.

Getting out and doing alcohol-free social activities is a great aid to achieving your drinking goal. So is following your own personal values and beliefs.

1.7) A Note on Terminology

HAMS avoids a lot of technical jargon, but the following abbreviations are in such common use that you might as well pick them up now:

- **Hamster** - A HAMS member
- **Abs** - Abstinence from alcohol - People often call their alcohol-free days "abs days"
- **Mods** - Moderate drinking, i.e. not drinking to intoxication - People often refer to a day then they engage in **moderate drinking** or **no-risk drinking**[3] but do not drink to intoxication as a "mods day". Generally this means less than three standard drinks for a woman and less than four for a man.
- **HR** - Harm Reduction. Intoxication which avoids negative consequences. "HR days" are days which people have planned carefully so that they can get intoxicated safely without bad consequences. HR can refer to either safer drinking strategies or to reduced drinking levels to avoid withdrawals. HR levels generally exceed the **"no-risk drinking"** limit.

1.8) Why I Created HAMS - Ken's Story

Quite simply put, during my short stay in AA I nearly drank myself to death. What started as a medium sized drinking problem became severe and life-threatening after I checked myself into a 12 step treatment program and started going to AA. I later learned that I was not alone and that there are many other people like me who react badly to AA's spiritual program and whose drinking and/or mental health deteriorate severely after they are exposed to AA.

As I sat there one day in county detox chock full of medication so that I would not die from the DTs and shaking from withdrawal I resolved to find a better way. I learned about Harm Reduction and Cognitive Behavioral Therapy and I started volunteering at the Minneapolis needle exchange in order to become firmly ground in Harm Reduction principles which I resolved to bring to other drinkers like myself. The more that I began to practice Harm Reduction principles in my own life, the better my life got. I went from being a homeless guy shaking with alcohol withdrawal in the county detox to leading online harm reduction groups and

---

[3] See Chapter 5 for definitions of moderate drinking and no-risk drinking.

entering The New School University in New York City to take a masters degree in psychology and substance abuse counseling.

I wish to express my most profound gratitude to the early pioneers of harm reduction who braved the odds and worked out the kinks and taught me the basic principle of harm reduction. To The New School for Social Research for being visionary enough to teach the principles of harm reduction in their classrooms and to support students in following their own paths. And last and perhaps most important of all I wish to express my gratitude to the people who have participated in our HAMS support groups and who, directly or indirectly, have contributed such a wealth of harm reduction ideas and strategies to the HAMS harm reduction program. Without the contributions of these--our members--the book which you hold in your hands could not exist today.

REFERENCES:

Bennett, ME & Gjonbalaj-Morovic, S. (2007). The Problem of Dual Diagnosis. In <u>Adult Psychopathology and Diagnosis</u>, 5th Edition

Brandsma JM, Maultsby MC, Welsh RJ. (1980). <u>Outpatient treatment of alcoholism: A review and comparative study</u>. Baltimore. University Park Press.

Eskapa, R (2008). <u>The Cure for Alcoholism: Drink Your Way Sober Without Willpower, Abstinence or Discomfort</u>. Benbella Books. Dallas, TX.

Khantzian EJ (1989). Addiction: self-destruction or self-repair? <u>Journal of Substance Abuse Treatment</u>. 6(2), 75.
PubMed Info:
http://www.ncbi.nlm.nih.gov/pubmed/2746713

Khantzian EJ (1990) Self-regulation and self-medication factors in alcoholism and the addictions. Similarities and differences. <u>Recent Developments in Alcoholism</u>. 8, 255-271.
PubMed Abstract:
http://www.ncbi.nlm.nih.gov/pubmed/2185521

Khantzian EJ (1997). The self-medication hypothesis of substance use disorders: a reconsideration and recent applications. <u>Harvard Review of Psychiatry</u>. 4(5), 231-244.
PubMed Abstract:
http://www.ncbi.nlm.nih.gov/pubmed/9385000

Liberman, RP, Kopelowicz, A, Silverstein, SM. Psychiatric rehabilitation. In Sadock, BJ and Sadock, VΛ (Eds.). <u>Comprehensive Textbook of Psychiatry</u> 2005. Baltimore, Md: Lippincott Williams & Wilkins pp. 3884–3930.

Schaler, JA. (2000). <u>Addiction is a choice</u>. Chicago, Illinois. Open Court Publishers

Zubin J, Spring B. (1977). "Vulnerability--a new view of schizophrenia". <u>J Abnorm Psychol</u>. 86(2), 103–26.
PubMed Info:
http://www.ncbi.nlm.nih.gov/pubmed/858828

CHAPTER TWO: How the HAMS Approach Works

"Can we fix it? YES! WE! CAN!" --Bob the Builder

2.1   The 17 Elements of HAMS
2.2   Getting Started With HAMS
2.3   How Long Does It Take to Change a Habit

2.1) The 17 Elements of HAMS

HAMS does not have steps--HAMS has elements. What is the difference? First: the HAMS elements can be done in any order. Second: all of the HAMS elements are optional--you get to pick and choose the ones which work for you--nothing is required. You can start at element one if you want or you can start elsewhere. Read **Section 2.2) Getting Started with HAMS** for more information about this.

HAMS is not like 12 step programs where every time that you finish step twelve you are expected to go back and start over from step one for the rest of your life. You can leave HAMS when you are done or you can choose to stick around to help others--a free choice. Here are the elements:

****

1. **Do a Cost Benefit Analysis (CBA) of your drinking**
2. **Choose a drinking goal--safer drinking, reduced drinking, or quitting**
3. **Learn about risk ranking and rank your risks**
4. **Learn about the HAMS tools and strategies for changing your drinking**
5. **Make a plan to achieve your drinking goal**
6. **Use alcohol-free time to reset your drinking habits**
7. **Learn to cope without booze**
8. **Address outside issues that affect drinking**
9. **Learn to have fun without booze**
10. **Learn to believe in yourself**
11. **Use a chart to plan and track your drinks and drinking behaviors day by day**
12. **Evaluate your progress - honestly report struggles - revise plans or goals as needed**
13. **Practice damage control as needed**
14. **Get back on the horse**
15. **Graduate from HAMS, stick around, or come back**
16. **Praise yourself for every success!!**
17. **Move at your own pace--you don't have to do it all at once**

****

A Quick Summary of the Elements

Here we present a very brief summary of what each element is. Later on we devote a full chapter to each element.

Element One: Do a Cost Benefit Analysis (CBA) of your drinking

When you do a Cost Benefit Analysis (CBA) you weigh the pros and cons of continuing to engage in a certain behavior and you weigh the pros and cons of changing that behavior. We strongly suggest that you write out your CBA using the worksheets we provide in Chapter Three. If you do not wish to write out your CBA then we suggest that you at least tell someone like a therapist or your HAMS support group about it. Doing the CBA in your head generally does not work very well--it is best to write it out or at least talk it out.

The CBA is useful not only in helping you to choose your drinking goal, but also in helping to strengthen your motivation and commitment to attaining your drinking goal. You can do the CBA many times for the same goal. Any time that you feel like you want to strengthen your commitment to change you can do the CBA again.

Element Two: Choose a drinking goal--safer drinking, reduced drinking, or quitting

This is where you choose your goal: safer drinking, reduced drinking, or quitting. If you are uncertain about your drinking goal then we suggest that you go to Chapter Four and fill out the **Drinking Goal Choice Worksheet**. If you are fairly certain of your choice of a goal you may want to go to Chapter Three to fill out a CBA to strengthen your motivation.

You may feel free to mix and match your drinking goals. You might choose to work on both safer drinking and reduced drinking at the same time. You might choose to quit for now but leave open the option of drinking again in the future. Or you might choose to quit for good.

In HAMS you are always free to switch your drinking goal at any time in the future--people tend to find out what works best for them as they go along and work at making changes.

Element Three: Learn about risk ranking and rank your risks

HAMS recognizes that harm is hierarchical--some harms are worse than others. HAMS also recognizes that there are two types of risks associated with drinking alcohol--risks associated with the quantity consumed and risks associated with situations and behaviors while drinking.

Chapter Five discusses the **Harm Reduction Pyramid, Harmful Consumption Levels**, and has a **Risk Ranking Worksheet** to help you in constructing a safe drinking plan. Always plan ahead to ensure that you will avoid the worst risks before you take the first drink.

Element Four: Learn about the HAMS tools and strategies

Chapter Six gives you tools and strategies that you can use to make you drinking safer, to cut back, or to quit. Pick and choose the tools and strategies that will work for you to construct a plan which will allow you to attain your drinking goal.

Element Five: Make a plan to achieve your drinking goal

HAMS recommends that you write out your drinking plan to in detail. Use the tools you pick from Chapter Six to put together a plan for safer drinking, reduced drinking, or quitting. Chapter Seven gives more information and a **Plan Making Worksheet** to use to make your individualized drinking plan. You may also wish to write out daily or weekly plans on your **Drinking Charts** from Chapter Thirteen.

Element Six: Use alcohol-free time to reset your drinking habits

Adding alcohol free days is a good strategy to help you reduce total alcohol consumption and it can also help you to avoid alcohol interfering in your life. Having several alcohol-free days each week can help prevent you from developing alcohol withdrawal syndrome. Doing an alcohol free period can help you to reset your drinking habits and lower tolerance. WARNING: If you have been a daily drinker and think that you might have withdrawals if you quit drinking suddenly, please be sure to taper off as described in the toolbox in Chapter Six.

Element Seven: Learn to cope without booze

Lots of times we use booze to cope with day to day stresses, depression, anxiety, boredom, etc, etc. Chapter Nine introduces some self-help techniques that we can use to cope with these issues without resorting to booze.

Element Eight: Address outside issues that affect drinking

Many outside issues impact drinking: ranging from mental health to financial health to social problems to housing to sexual health and more. Research shows that the most effective approach is to work on these outside issues and alcohol issues together. Requiring that people become totally abstinent from alcohol before dealing with issues like mental health or housing is not merely inhumane, it is also ineffective. Although HAMS cannot solve these issues for you since they are beyond our scope--you are welcome to discuss outside issues at HAMS any time you wish.

Element Nine: Learn to have fun without booze

Learning to have fun when you are alcohol-free makes it a lot easier to have alcohol-free days. It is good if you can be joyful both when you drink and when you do not.

Element Ten: Learn to believe in yourself

The more that you believe that you can change your drinking, the easier it becomes. Chapter 12 focuses on helping you to increase your belief in yourself.

Element Eleven: Use a chart to plan and track your drinks and drinking behaviors day by day

Chapter 13 defines what a standard drink is and offers **Drinking Charts** to help you track and plan your drinking. This chapter also offers **Risk Charts** to help you track your risks. Tracking your drinks and risks is a highly effective tool for behavioral change. These charts are also an aid in evaluating your behavioral change.

Element Twelve: Evaluate your progress - honestly report struggles - revise plans or goals as needed

A HAMS group is a safe place to honestly talk about your drinking--we encourage every positive change and we encourage everyone to choose goals for themselves. Sometimes you just need to make several tries to succeed with your plan. However, if your actual consumption and drinking behavior deviates a lot from your plan then you may want to consider revising the plan or the goal. Don't beat yourself up for being less than perfect, though! Research shows that beating yourself up for being less than perfect is likely to make you drink more. Instead, forgive yourself and start over. Studies show that multiple attempts at changing a habit are the rule, not the exception. Be gentle with yourself and practice damage control while you are getting set to start over. If you decide to change your plan or goal you may wish to go back and do a new **CBA** or a new **Drinking Plan Worksheet**.

Element Thirteen: Practice damage control as needed

If you slip up and fail to follow your plan perfectly then the worst possible things you can do are the following:

- Beat yourself up and tell yourself that you are weak and worthless for failing to stick to your plan
- Tell yourself that you might as well be hung for a sheep as a lamb
- Tell yourself that one drink means one drunk because you are powerless and diseased

All of these things can lead to something which we call the **Ricochet Effect**. When you have a **ricochet** your behavior is actually worse than it was before you tried to change it. People who never drank and drove in their lives may drink and drive after attempting to quit alcohol as a result of the **Ricochet Effect**. **No one *has to*** suffer from the **Ricochet Effect**. Research by Alan Marlatt proves that people who are prepared to accept the fact that change might take some time and that there may be some setbacks on the way are prepared for those setbacks. These people are far less likely to beat themselves up for their imperfections and are far less likely to have **ricochets**.

Element Fourteen: Get back on the horse

If at first you don't succeed, try, try again. Patience, persistence and practice are key to successful behavioral change.

Element Fifteen: Graduate from HAMS, stick around, or come back

Research by Prochaska and others shows us that once a person has broken a bad habit, the grip of that habit gets weaker and weaker the longer the person practices their new and healthy behaviors. Some people benefit by sticking around for continued support indefinitely. Others do best by moving on with life and graduating from their support group--too much drinking talk is no longer helpful for them. Still others like to stick around HAMS to help new people because they want to give something back or because they find that helping others helps them to consolidate their own progress.

Sometimes people who have graduated HAMS and who have been successfully following their plan decide that they want to trade in their old goal for a new one. People who have been abstaining for a few years may decide that they now want to try moderate social drinking. People who have been practicing a safer drinking plan may decide that it is now time to quit drinking. And so on and so forth. Some people may find that they are slipping a bit on their plans after a while and decide to come back for a tune-up. Whatever the reason you are always welcome back at HAMS to tune-up your old plan or to work on a new one. Or you may come back to work on a new issue--tobacco or marijuana or diet instead of alcohol.

We also love it when successful graduates of HAMS come back for a visit and tell us about what worked for them in changing their bad habits and replacing them with good habits. And we love it even more when they tell us that they now have a great life and the thought of going back to the bad old days never crosses their minds any more.

Element Sixteen: Praise yourself for every success!!

Don't feel embarrassed about breaking your arm by patting yourself on the back--you deserve to praise yourself for every positive change!

Element Seventeen: Move at your own pace--you don't have to do it all at once

Don't feel overwhelmed when you see a lot of worksheets and exercises in the following chapters--everything is optional. Some people like to jump in and do everything at once, but many people feel overwhelmed if they try and do this. Move at a pace that is comfortable for you and keep things doable.

2.2) Getting Started With HAMS

It isn't necessary to do the elements of HAMS in any particular order; different people decide to start the process of changing their drinking in different ways. The following are some common ways that people get started:

The Drinking Goal Worksheet - Some people decide to start here with the choice of a drinking goal.

The Cost Benefit Analysis (CBA) - Some people start here if they already know their drinking goal.

Drink charting - Some people start by charting their drinks and get a baseline of what their drinking is like

Damage control - If alcohol is causing a lot of immediate harm in your life then damage control may be your first step. Rank your risks and eliminate the biggest risks first.

Tapering - If you think that you might have alcohol withdrawal symptoms then it is important to taper before doing any abstinence days--alcohol withdrawal can hurt or even kill you if you stop cold turkey. See Chapter 6 for information on **How to Taper off Alcohol**.

Abstinence day - If you have been drinking every day for a long time sometimes one abstinence day is the way to get started. Be sure to taper first if necessary.

Abstinence period - An abstinence period can help to totally reset your drinking habits whether you choose a week, a month or even more. Again, taper if needed.

Baby stepping - Even if you do not have to taper for withdrawal, some people find it most effective to change a little bit each day or each week or each month instead of all at once.

The big change - Some people decide exactly what they want their drinking to be like and make the change overnight. Different strokes for different folks.

Planning - Some people already know what their goal is and want to jump right into making the plan. Making a plan before doing a CBA works fine--but we do urge you to do a written CBA eventually

Medication - Some people start out with a medication like naltrexone or Topamax to help them change their drinking.

Just hang out - If you still don't know how you want to get started just hang out with a live or online group for a while.

Anything else - If you think of some other way that you want to start then that is good, too. We find people do the best when they follow their own hearts.

2.3) How Long Does It Take to Change a Habit

You might have heard that it takes 21 days to change a habit. This myth was started by a man selling a 21 day program. Other people who were selling a 28 day program said it took 28 days-- and so on. The actual truth is that different people take different amounts if time to change different habits. Dr. James Prochaska has done research on change and found that tough habits like drinking or smoking cigarettes tend to have milestones at three months, six months, a year, and five years. People don't develop bad habits overnight and they don't change them overnight either. Don't be hard on yourself if you have some slips and don't become perfect overnight--or even in the mythical 21 days.

REFERENCES:

Marlatt A, Gordon J. (1985). <u>Relapse Prevention: Maintenance strategies in the treatment of addictive behaviors</u>. New York, Guilford.

Prochaska JO, Norcross JC, DiClemente CC. (1994). <u>Changing for good</u>. New York, Morrow.

PART II: HOW TO BUILD YOUR OWN ALCOHOL HARM REDUCTION PROGRAM - THE HAMS ELEMENTS

"Make everything as simple as possible, but not simpler" --Albert Einstein

CHAPTER THREE: *Weighing the Pros and Cons of Your Drinking*

"I hate to advocate drugs, alcohol, violence, or insanity to anyone,
but they've always worked for me." --Hunter S. Thompson

- **HAMS Element One: Do a Cost Benefit Analysis (CBA) of your drinking**

3.1 What Is a Cost Benefit Analysis (CBA)?
3.2 My Drinking CBA
3.3 Sample Drinking CBA
3.4 My Generalized CBA
3.5 Sample Generalized CBA

3.1)   What Is a Cost Benefit Analysis (CBA)?

A Cost Benefit Analysis (CBA) is a tool for behavioral change. Some researchers refer to the Cost Benefit Analysis as a Decisional Balance Sheet. These two words just refer to the same thing. CBAs have been studied by psychological researchers for over 30 years now and there is ample evidence that they are useful tools for helping people to make decisions and to change their habits. Patt Denning has shown how the CBA can be used as a harm reduction tool.

When you do a Cost Benefit Analysis (CBA), you weigh the pros and cons of continuing to engage in a certain behavior and compare these to the pros and cons of changing that behavior. Usually when we talk about a CBA we are referring to a written worksheet like that in Section 3.2, although it is also possible to do a Cost Benefit Analysis orally with a HAMS group or a therapist. Trying to do the CBA in your head, however, does not work very well.

You might think it strange that you are being asked to list both the pros and the cons of the bad habit that you are trying to change. Wouldn't it be better to just list all the bad things about the habit that you want to change and none of the good things? The answer is that this has been tried and for most people it just doesn't work. When you list the bad things about your habit you make yourself conscious of them. If you don't list the good things about the habit you leave them festering in your subconscious where they just get stronger and stronger until they burst forth and lead you right back to your old bad habit again. If you make them conscious by listing them then you actually take away their power. Once you look at them in the clear light of day you see that they are not very good reasons after all.

Miller and Rollnick (2002) say, "Often individuals considering changing a problem behavior will concentrate on all the negative aspects of the behavior. 'I know how bad my drinking is for me,' they say. In fact, they can often produce a litany of reasons why what they are doing is bad for them. Clinician and client are often baffled by the fact that even with all these negatives, change does not occur. The reality is that if the behavior were not in some way beneficial to the client, he or she would not be doing it. Until the client acknowledges the 'good things' about the behavior, they cannot prepare to combat temptation once they make an attempt to change. The decisional balance [in other words the Cost Benefit Analysis] helps facilitate this process. Once the client has evaluated the benefits of the behavior, they move to focusing on the 'not so good things.'"

In The Enlightened Smoker's Guide to Quitting, Bear Jack Gebhardt tells people to learn to enjoy smoking so that they can learn to enjoy quitting. If you hate yourself each time you smoke you only make it harder to quit. If you can learn to consciously enjoy each cigarette, you can learn to enjoy quitting smoking, too.

If you have already decided on a drinking goal--safer drinking, reduced drinking, quitting, or both safer and reduced drinking, then go ahead and fill out the CBA in this chapter. If you have not yet decided on your drinking goal, then we have a special form of **CBA** called a **Drinking Goal Worksheet** in Chapter Four. We suggest that you fill out this worksheet to help you to decide what the best drinking goal is for you right now. Don't be afraid to commit to a drinking goal, remember that this is HAMS and you are allowed to switch to a different goal any time that the change seems right to you.

We also suggest that you do a CBA periodically in order to keep building motivation as you continue down the path of change. You may find that as time goes by the items on your CBA change considerably. This is good because it means that you are evolving and growing as a person.

What you see next is a **Blank CBA** for you to fill out and a **Sample CBA** to give you some ideas of how to fill it out.

3.2) My Drinking CBA - Cost Benefit Analysis

free download at http://hamsnetwork.org/worksheets

Continue my drinking the same as always.

Pros	Cons

Opt for (circle one)

Safer Drinking ♦ Reduced Drinking ♦ Quitting ♦ Safer & Reduced Drinking

Pros	Cons

Continue my drinking the same as always.

Pros	Cons
Change is hard Drinking is fun Drinking helps me socialize	I hate blackouts I got yelled at for missing too much work

Opt for (circle one)

Safer Drinking ♦ **(Reduced Drinking)** ♦ **Quitting** ♦ **Safer & Reduced Drinking**

Pros	Cons
I won't wake up all shaky My wife will be happier I will have more time to look for a better job I will save money	I will be bored The guys will think I am weird I won't know what to do for fun I get all antsy when I don't drink

You can also do a **CBA** for any aspects of your plan or any change at all. We call this a **Generalized CBA**. Just a few possibilities of things that you can do a CBA for are: adding abstinence days, stopping sooner, starting later, not drinking at home, sticking to moderate drinking limits, etc, etc. **Chapter Six: The HAMS Toolbox** gives you a host of possibilities for a **CBA**. If you wish you can do a **CBA** for every tool you choose. Below we give a sample **CBA** for adding abstinence days.

3.4) My Generalized CBA - Cost Benefit Analysis

free download at http://hamsnetwork.org/worksheets

Continue my drinking the same as always.

Pros	Cons

Change my drinking by _____ *.

Pros	Cons

---

* Some options for filling in this blank are: a) quitting, b) adding alcohol-free days, c) safer drinking, d) sticking to moderate limits, e) stopping earlier, f) not drinking on work nights, etc. etc.

3.5) Sample Generalized CBA - Cost Benefit Analysis

free download at http://hamsnetwork.org/worksheets

Continue my drinking the same as always.

Pros	Cons
I can relax after class	It interferes with doing my schoolwork
It helps me enjoy music	It is hard to pay attention in class when I am hungover
I like the taste	I am always tired
It helps me sleep	

Change my drinking by ___adding alcohol-free days___.

Pros	Cons
Clearer mornings	It will be hard to relax after school
More productive days	It will be hard to sleep
More time to do homework	
Don't have to go to class hungover	

REFERENCES:

Colten ME, Janis IL. (1982). Effects of moderate self-disclosure and the balance sheet procedure. In: Janis, I.L., ed. <u>Counseling on Personal Decisions: Theory and Research on Short-Term Help Relationships</u>. New Haven, CT: Yale University Press,. pp. 159-171.

Denning P. (2000). <u>Practicing Harm Reduction Psychotherapy</u>. Guilford Press.

Gebhardt J. (1998, 2008). <u>The Enlightened Smoker's Guide to Quitting</u>. Benbella Books

Janis IL, Mann L. (1977). <u>Decision Making: A Psychological Analysis of Conflict, Choice, and Commitment</u>. London: Cassel and Collier Macmillan.

Mann L. (1972). Use of a 'balance-sheet' procedure to improve the quality of personal decision making: A field experiment with college applicants. <u>Journal of Vocational Behavior</u>. 2, 291–300.

Miller WR. (1999). <u>SAMHSA TIP 35. Enhancing motivation for change in substance abuse treatment</u>. Rockville, MD: US Department of Health and Human Services.
Free Full Text:
http://www.ncbi.nlm.nih.gov/bookshelf/br.fcgi?book=hssamhsatip&part=A61302

Miller WR, Rollnick S. (1991, 2002). <u>Motivational Interviewing: Preparing People to Change Addictive Behavior</u>. New York: Guilford Press.

Prochaska JO, Velicer WF, Rossi JS, Goldstein MG, Marcus BH, Rakowski W, et al. (1994). Stages of change and decisional balance for 12 problem behaviors. <u>Health Psychology</u>. 13, 39–46.
PubMed Abstract:
http://www.ncbi.nlm.nih.gov/pubmed/8168470

CHAPTER FOUR: Choosing Your Drinking Goal

"No price is too high to pay for the privilege of owning yourself" --Friedrich Nietzsche

- **HAMS Element Two: Choose a drinking goal--safer drinking, reduced drinking, or quitting**

4.1 What Are the HAMS Drinking Goals?
4.2 My Drinking Goal Worksheet
4.3 Sample Drinking Goal Worksheet

4.1) What Are the HAMS Drinking Goals?

HAMS encourages goals of safer drinking, reduced drinking, or quitting. When you choose a goal for changing your drinking, this is your immediate goal for changing your drinking. You might find that you want to switch your goal later on down the line. This is fine. Or you might find that your immediate goal suits you well. Great! Remember, at HAMS you can always decide to change your drinking goal later on down the line. The following are the possible goals that you can choose from.

Safer drinking

At HAMS we try to encourage all our members to engage in safe drinking practices--the life you save may be your own. We say that people who are working on safer drinking are doing **Harm Reduction** or **HR** for short.

Reduced drinking

Reduced drinking falls into two categories: no-risk drinking and reduced-risk drinking

No-risk drinking

According to the NIAAA people who stay within the following limits given in **Table 4.1** are at no more risk for alcohol related problems than are people who do not drink.

Table 4.1) No-Risk Drinking Limits		
	Daily	**Weekly**
Men	**4 standard drinks**	**14 standard drinks**
Women	**3 standard drinks**	**7 standard drinks**

At HAMS we usually refer to people who stay within these limits as **drinking moderately** or **doing mods**.

Reduced risk drinking

No-risk drinking does not appeal to everyone--some people like to drink because they like to get intoxicated. Many people who come to HAMS want to reserve the right to get intoxicated sometimes--they just don't want to do it so frequently that it interferes with other things in their lives. At HAMS this goal is just fine. We usually say that these people are working a Harm Reduction program--or "doing HR" for short. It is quite reasonable to choose to have some **abs days** (i.e. alcohol abstinence days), some **mods days** and some **HR days**. Mix and match in the way that suits you the best. It is also totally reasonable to work on both **Reduced Drinking** and **Safer Drinking** at the same time.

Quitting drinking

Quitting is the simplest and most clear cut of the goals--that is its greatest advantage--no gray areas. If you don't want to commit to quitting forever then you can choose to quit indefinitely. At HAMS there is no stigma or shame if you decide that later you wish to try a **Safer Drinking** plan or a **Reduced Drinking** plan.

Choosing Your Goal

The following worksheet can help you to choose your drinking goal if you are uncertain which goal is best for you. If you have already decided what your goal is, then that is fine too. We suggest that you do the CBA in Chapter Three to help to increase your drinking goal motivation

You can find the tools you need for achieving your drinking goal in Chapter Six. Chapter Seven will help you put these tools together into a plan to help you to achieve the goal that you have chosen. We discuss **risk** and **risk ranking** in Chapter Five.

4.2) My Drinking Goal Worksheet

free download at http://hamsnetwork.org/worksheets

Page 1 of 2

The advantages of continuing to drink the same as always:	The disadvantages of continuing to drink the same as always

Advantages of safer drinking	Disadvantages of safer drinking:

28

Advantages of reduced drinking:	**Disadvantages of reduced drinking:**

Advantages of quitting:	**Disadvantages of quitting:**

Always be sure to write down both positives and negatives. If you do not acknowledge the positives of your bad habits they will get stuck in your unconscious and they will sneak up and blindside you. If you bring them forth into the light of day you often see that they have little to recommend them after all.

Don't be afraid to write down anything even if it sounds silly. This is a chance to work things out of your system safely without harming yourself or others.

4.3) Sample Drinking Goal Worksheet

free download at http://hamsnetwork.org/worksheets

The advantages of continuing to drink the same as always:	The disadvantages of continuing to drink the same as always
<ul><li>Change is hard</li><li>Change takes effort</li><li>Staying where I am at is easy</li><li>I love to get loaded</li><li>I am a romantic--live fast and die young</li></ul>	<ul><li>I have a DUI that will cost me a fortune</li><li>If I kill someone driving drunk I could go to prison</li><li>I am afraid the boss will smell alcohol on my breath if I come in hungover</li><li>I have no time to do anything but drink</li></ul>
Advantages of safer drinking	**Disadvantages of safer drinking:**
<ul><li>I will not get another DUI</li><li>I will not go to prison for killing someone driving drunk</li><li>I won't get my pocket picked in a bar when I am drunk</li><li>I won't get beaten up drunk in a bar</li></ul>	<ul><li>I will always have to plan ahead</li><li>If I am drunk I might forget to be safe</li><li>It is a lot of work to plan to avert all bad things</li><li>I can't be a romantic risk-taker rock star if I think ahead</li><li>It is really hard to walk to the bar or take a taxi instead of driving</li><li>Drinking at home instead of going out is no fun</li></ul>

Advantages of reduced drinking:	Disadvantages of reduced drinking:
• I will save money • I won't have to worry about the boss smelling alcohol on my breath when I am hungover • I will have more time to do my homework • I will get better grades in school • I will have more time for friends and family	• I won't know what else to do with my time • Moderate drinking isn't real drinking • Getting intoxicated one day a week is not enough
Advantages of quitting:	**Disadvantages of quitting:**
• Quitting is simple and clear cut • I won't have to worry about doing stupid things when I am drunk • I won't have to worry about going over my limit • I will save a lot of money • I will have more time to do my homework • I will get better grades in school • I will have more time for friends and family • My wife says she wants me to quit for good	• I can't have fun with alcohol anymore • My friends will think I am a weirdo • I won't be able to blow off stress with alcohol • I will be afraid to talk to new people if I am not drinking

Always be sure to write down both positives and negatives. If you do not acknowledge the positives of your bad habits they will get stuck in your unconscious and they will sneak up and blindside you. If you bring them forth into the light of day you often see that they have little to recommend them after all.

Don't be afraid to write down anything even if it sounds silly. This is a chance to work things out of your system safely without harming yourself or others.

REFERENCES:

CDC. Alcohol and Public Health - FAQs
http://www.cdc.gov/alcohol/faqs.htm
Accessed November 10, 2009

NIAAA (2005). Helping. Patients Who. Drink Too Much. A CLINICIAN'S GUIDE. Updated 2005 Edition.
http://pubs.niaaa.nih.gov/publications/Practitioner/CliniciansGuide2005/clinicians_guide.htm
Accessed November 10, 2009

SAMHSA Alcohol abuse, long-term effects of alcohol at SAMHSA's NCADI
http://ncadi.samhsa.gov/govpubs/ph326X
Accessed November 10, 2009

USDA. (1997). DOES ALCOHOL HAVE A PLACE IN A HEALTHY DIET?
http://www.cnpp.usda.gov/Publications/NutritionInsights/insight4.pdf
Accessed November 10, 2009

CHAPTER FIVE: Risk Ranking

"If you can't be good, be careful"

- **HAMS Element Three: Learn About Risk Ranking and Rank Your Risks**

5.1 Risk Ranking
5.2 My Risk Ranking Worksheet
5.3 Sample Risk Ranking Worksheet

5.1) Risk Ranking

The forbidden fruit always tastes the sweetest. HAMS does not limit you to a certain number of drinks per week and tell you that you are forbidden to go over that limit. Such an approach is almost a challenge to people to cross the line and go over the limit. Likewise we do not have a rule like "drinking and driving is absolutely forbidden" because the minute that you set up a rule like that, you are tempting people to break it. Such is human nature. Mark Twain once said, "The more things are forbidden, the more popular they become."

Rather than set up rules and limits, a harm reduction approach asks you to decide which sorts of alcohol related harms you think that it is best to try to avoid. We ask you to rank which harms you think are the worst and which you personally feel are acceptable risks. It is certainly much easier to avoid something which one believes to entail many negative consequences and few positive pay-offs than it is to avoid the forbidden fruit.

Most people will agree that they do not wish to drink such large quantities of alcohol that they risk withdrawal seizures, hallucinations, and death from a heart attack when they stop drinking. Most people can also agree that the risk of killing someone and going to prison for it because they drove drunk is just not worth it. That is why HAMS encourages people to think before they drink and to have their transportation plans in place before taking the first drink. It is really preferable not to drive after even one drink. Even though you may not be legally intoxicated you could be held legally responsible for an accident if you are declared to be impaired by alcohol.

Harm is hierarchical--some harms are worse than others. Figure 5.1 places alcohol-related harms in a Harm Reduction Pyramid.

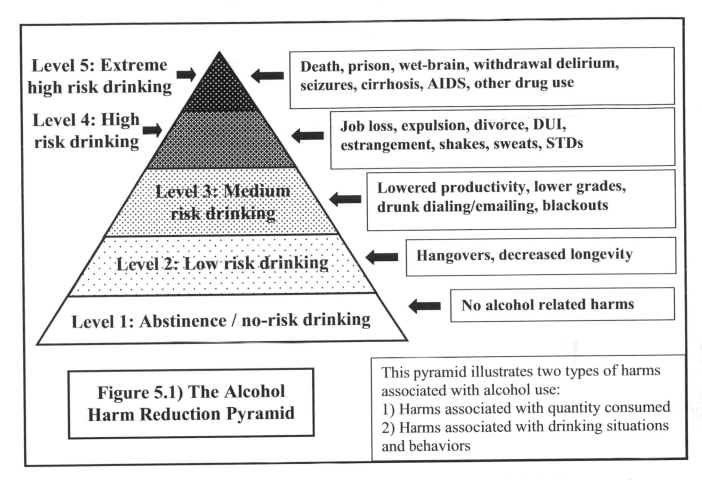

Level 5: Extreme high risk drinking → ← Death, prison, wet-brain, withdrawal delirium, seizures, cirrhosis, AIDS, other drug use

Level 4: High risk drinking → ← Job loss, expulsion, divorce, DUI, estrangement, shakes, sweats, STDs

Level 3: Medium risk drinking ← Lowered productivity, lower grades, drunk dialing/emailing, blackouts

Level 2: Low risk drinking ← Hangovers, decreased longevity

Level 1: Abstinence / no-risk drinking ← No alcohol related harms

Figure 5.1) The Alcohol Harm Reduction Pyramid

This pyramid illustrates two types of harms associated with alcohol use:
1) Harms associated with quantity consumed
2) Harms associated with drinking situations and behaviors

We can also talk about alcohol-related risk purely in terms of the quantity of alcohol consumed. According to the USDA, men who have two standard drinks per day and women who have one standard drink per day are actually healthier then people who abstain from alcohol or people who drink more than this amount. This is how the USDA and other US government agencies define **Moderate Drinking**.

The NIAAA also has a category of **No-Risk Drinking**. No-Risk drinking for men is no more than four standard drinks per day and no more than fourteen per week. For women it is no more than three per day and no more than seven per week. No-Risk Drinkers are no more likely to have alcohol related problems than are those who do not drink at all.

As drinking levels increase above the No-Risk category so does alcohol related risk. However, there is still a world of difference between the guy who has five beers on a Saturday night and doesn't drink the rest of the week, and the guy who has quart of vodka every day, seven days a week. We illustrate this in Figure 5.2.

Alcohol Drinking Level and Risk				
	Men Daily	Women Daily	Men Weekly	Women Weekly
Very High Risk	20+ drinks	15+ drinks	80+ drinks	60+ drinks
High Risk Drinking	13 - 19 drinks	9 - 14 drinks	50 - 79 drinks	40 - 59 drinks
Medium Risk	8 - 12 drinks	6 - 8 drinks	30 - 49 drinks	25 - 39 drinks
Low Risk Drinking	5 - 7 drinks	4 - 5 drinks	15 - 29 drinks	8 - 24 drinks
No-Risk Drinking	3 - 4 drinks	2 - 3 drinks	14 or fewer	7 or fewer
Healthy Drinking	1 - 2 drinks	1 drinks	1 - 14 drinks	1 - 7 drinks
Alcohol Abstinence	0 drinks	0 drinks	0 drinks	0 drinks

When using Figure 5.2 you will need to look at both your daily and your weekly risk levels to determine how risky your drinking habits are. If either your daily or your weekly drinking level falls into a high risk category then we suggest that you take steps to reduce the harmful impact which your drinking may have on you. We realize that some people like to engage in recreational intoxication so we recommend that these people take steps to practice **safe drinking** on their intoxication days. People who fall into the weekly high risk categories are at risk of organ damage and we urge them to take some steps to **reduce overall alcohol consumption**.

Since alcohol related harms are hierarchical, we offer the following risk ranking worksheets as tool which you can use to help you rank the risks associated with your drinking, remember that it is best to work on eliminating the most harmful aspects of your drinking first.

REMEMBER

THINK BEFORE YOU DRINK!

5.2) My Risk Ranking Worksheet

free download at http://hamsnetwork.org/worksheets

Write down any risky behaviors you have engaged in while drinking and rank them.

Problem Behavior	Very High Risk	High Risk	Moderate Risk	Low Risk
	4	3	2	1
	4	3	2	1
	4	3	2	1
	4	3	2	1
	4	3	2	1
	4	3	2	1
	4	3	2	1

Write down a plan to avoid each of these risks in the future.

Behavior	My Plan

5.3) Sample Risk Ranking Worksheet

free download at http://hamsnetwork.org/worksheets

Write down any risky behaviors you have engaged in while drinking and rank them.

Risks Associated With My Drinking	Very High Risk	High Risk	Moderate Risk	Low Risk
Drunk driving	(4)	3	2	1
Unsafe sex with strangers	(4)	3	2	1
Drunk dialing	4	3	(2)	1
	4	3	2	1
	4	3	2	1
	4	3	2	1
	4	3	2	1

Write down a plan to avoid each of these risks in the future.

Behavior	My Plan
Drunk driving	Leave car keys at home and take taxi to and from bar
Unsafe sex with strangers	Always carry condoms
Drunk dialing	Turn my cell phone off and put it in a drawer when I drink at home

CHAPTER SIX: The Alcohol Harm Reduction Toolbox

"When the going gets weird, the weird turn pro" --Hunter S. Thompson

- **HAMS Element Four: Learn about the HAMS tools and strategies for changing your drinking**

All of the following tools and strategies are optional elements which you may choose to use as a part of you drinking plan. We don't expect anyone to use all of them--some are even mutually contradictory. For example, people who want to reduce their drinking may choose to quit drinking at home and only drink when they go out to bars. Whereas people who want to work on safer drinking may choose to quit drinking in bars and to only drink at home. What is important is that you pick and choose the strategies and tools which are useful to you for your individual plan.

6.1) Having Alcohol-Free Time / Quitting Drinking

In Chapter 8 we will talk about why alcohol-free time is useful. Here we discuss some ways to achieve it.

6.1.1) AVRT for Alcohol-Free Days

Jack Trimpey is the founder of Rational Recovery and has created a technique called AVRT (pronounced "avert") which the Rational Recovery program teaches to people who are seeking permanent abstinence from alcohol. In this section we will adapt some of the Rational Recovery ideas for people who wish to add abstinence days into their alcohol harm reduction plans. For more information on using AVRT for permanent abstinence please visit the Rational Recovery web page http://rational.org.

The letters AVRT stand for Addictive Voice Recognition Technique. AVRT recognizes that the human brain can be divided into two parts: There is the primitive animal brain which consists of the limbic system, the brain stem and so forth which is essential for basic survival, and there are frontal lobes which are responsible for abstract thought, planning, and the other things which make us uniquely human.

The animal brain is responsible for essential things like breathing and sex, but it is also responsible for the formation of conditioned reflexes including that special subset of conditioned responses which we refer to as addiction. It is the limbic system which is responsible for the voice of craving--for the idea that one must pursue alcohol or drugs or other potentially destructive behaviors for the sake of short term reward at all costs--sometimes even at the cost of one's life. AVRT calls this the Beast Brain. In contrast to the Beast Brain, it is the frontal lobes-- the uniquely human part of the brain--which tell us that we sometimes need to put aside immediate gratification for the sake of more important long term gains. The frontal lobes are the rational part of the brain and the real "you".

AVRT teaches people to clearly distinguish the voice of the beast brain from the voice of their real self. AVRT teaches us to talk back to the voice of the craving. When the Beast Brain starts telling you that you "have to have a drink or a drug because you are stressed or anxious or depressed or feeling social phobia", then you need to talk back to the Beast Brain.

Telling the voice of craving to "shut the F-- up" or if you say to it "I am not gonna drink today and you can't make me! So there!! Nyah nyah nyah nyah nyah!!" can be an excellent tool to help you to abstain from alcohol.

Trimpey also talks about Enemy Voice Recognition. If you have chosen to have an abstinence day then ANY thoughts you have in your head that tell you that you need to drink are the ENEMY. No one ever puts a gun to your head and forces you to drink. Bottles of booze never jump off the shelf at the liquor store and come rolling up to your house and knock on your door and say "Drink me!" You are NEVER powerless over alcohol. It is always YOU who chooses to drink or not to drink. You either choose to listen to that mental voice or you reject it. AVRT is a tool to help you succeed at rejecting it. So recognize that voice which tells you to drink on an abstinence day as the ENEMY and CHOOSE to reject it.

The ENEMY voice will put forth irrational ideas and beliefs to try and make you drink, but you can defeat the voice of the ENEMY by disputing these irrational ideas.

Here are some examples of the voice of the ENEMY:

- I am so depressed/anxious/stressed that I have to drink right now!
- I can't stand one single day without alcohol!
- My husband/wife is driving me to drink by being IMPOSSIBLE!
- I can't do a whole abstinence day--it is too HARD!
- It isn't FAIR that I have to do an abstinence day!

Here are some examples of how you can use your rational voice to dispute these irrational ideas:

- Being depressed/anxious/stressed really sucks but I can deal with it for one day. Think of how proud I will feel tomorrow after I accomplish my abstinence day!

40

- I didn't need to drink alcohol when I was a baby--I surely don't HAVE to drink it now that I am an adult.
- My spouse's bad actions cannot force me to drink. I may really dislike my spouse's bad actions but I can still choose to abstain for MY benefit!
- Can't do one day? Shut up Beast Brain! Of course I am strong enough to do one day!
- Fair? Beast Brain--you are really clutching at straws now! False imprisonment might be unfair but an abstinence day is just a way to flex my muscles.

AVRT can be a very helpful technique to help you to abstain on your designated abstinence days and to reserve the drinking for the designated drinking days where it can be an enjoyment instead of a BEAST!

6.1.2) CBT for Alcohol-Free Days

Cognitive Behavioral Techniques (CBT) and Rational Emotive Techniques (RET) are ways of using your rational mind to combat various forms of irrational negativity--including cravings for alcohol. We refer you to Chapter 9 where we discuss these techniques in detail.

6.1.3) Wallop Your Cravings with Psychic Jiu-Jitsu

Next time you get a craving to drink don't just sit there with your fists clenched saying "I won't drink, I won't drink" over and over. This just keeps the thought of drinking in your head. Instead, get out a piece of paper and start writing about your craving. Go into every detail of the good and the bad and the ugly of the thing. Pull no punches--say why you like booze and why you hate it both. Exhaust the craving completely by writing till you are blue in the face. Facing up to it will take the wind out of its sails. This is how you use psychic jiu-jitsu. Stop being afraid and face it down.

Get silly with your craving--write a Dr. Seuss rhyme about it

> Would you drink me with a mouse?
> Would you drink me in a house?
> I would not drink you with a mouse
> I would not drink you in a house
> I would not drink you here or there
> I would not drink you anywhere
> I will not drink you booze-I-am
> I do not like you boozy man

If you manage to get totally silly about your craving and laugh at it you will find that it is greatly weakened.

Rate your craving on a scale from one to ten

How bad is your craving? Could it be worse? If you rank it you might find that it is not so bad after all. Surf the urge and watch it fluctuate. Cravings only last about five minutes then go away. Just watch it rise and fade and rate it again.

6.1.4) Smack Down The Witching Hour With A Club Sandwich

Lots of people find that they have a craving for a drink after they get home from work and before they eat dinner. Some people call this time "The Witching Hour." An empty stomach and lowered blood sugar are a large part of this craving. Having a snack when you get home can make this craving go away completely for some people. Sweets are not usually as good as a nice sandwich or a salad if you prefer that.

6.1.5) Drink Refusal Strategies

How do you turn down drinks at a party of from your friends if you are doing some alcohol-free time? Here are some suggestions for refusing drinks:

- I'm taking a vacation from booze
- My liver is on vacation this month
- I can't drink on my new medications
- My stomach feels queasy--I better give it a pass
- I don't want to go off my diet

Feel free to think up some more of your own and make a list of them to use the next time that you need them. You might want to rehearse your drink refusals in front of a mirror if you aren't used to doing this.

6.1.6) Marijuana Maintenance for Quitting Drinking: Cannabis as a Substitute for Alcohol

A growing body of evidence suggests that Medical Marijuana is the single most effective cure for severe and otherwise intractable cases of Alcohol Dependence. Many late-stage heavy drinkers undergo major, life-threatening withdrawal symptoms such as seizures and withdrawal delirium after drinking even relatively small amounts of alcohol because they have undergone kindling and reverse tolerance (defined later in this book). Others who suffer from severe Alcohol Dependence feel compelled to continue drink the morning after and may go on benders which can last anywhere from days to weeks to months. These people also often go through life-threatening withdrawals when they stop drinking, not to mention the health ravages and accidents and loss of employment or marriages which can occur during these benders.

 For people with late-stage Alcohol Dependence, quitting alcohol completely is often the only viable solution; however, statistics show that abstinence-only programs such as AA or twelve step treatment programs fail to help the majority of these late stage chronic drinkers. The good news is that there has been an extremely high success rate when these late stage chronic drinkers are treated with medical marijuana.

> **When late-stage heavy drinkers are allowed to get high by smoking marijuana they no longer have a need to get high by drinking alcohol.**

Using cannabis as a substitute for alcohol is referred to as **Marijuana Maintenance**. The late Dr. Tod Mikuriya, MD was one of the first pioneers in the use of Medical Marijuana to treat Alcohol Dependence. Mikuriya prescribed Medical Marijuana to ninety two patients who were suffering from severe Alcohol Dependence (Mikuriya, 2004). All ninety two patients reported major reduction in alcohol consumption and major reductions in alcohol related harm. All reported that using Medical Marijuana caused far fewer life problems than did using alcohol.

In 2009, Dr Amanda Reiman, PhD published the results of a survey of 350 users of Medical Marijuana. Forty percent of those surveyed reported that they used Medical Marijuana as a substitute for alcohol. The main reasons were that Medical Marijuana led to fewer negative outcomes and had less potential for withdrawal syndrome. Use of Medical Marijuana did not increase the likelihood that people would drink alcohol--on the contrary it helped to greatly reduce alcohol consumption among people who had previously had problems with Alcohol Abuse or Dependence.

As of the time of this writing, Medical Marijuana is available legally in fourteen states: Alaska, California, Colorado, Hawaii, Maine, Michigan, Montana, Nevada, New Jersey, New Mexico, Oregon, Rhode Island, Vermont and Washington.

If you are suffering from severe Alcohol Dependence and nothing else seems to help, a Marijuana Maintenance program just may be a life saver for you.

6.1.7) More about Quitting Drinking

At HAMS our main focus is on safer drinking and reduced drinking because there are already some fine books and programs out there which concentrate on quitting drinking. We do have an Alcohol-Free Hamsters group online for people who quit drinking using a harm reduction approach, though. However, if you would like additional support for staying off alcohol we recommend the following support groups:

- **SMART Recovery** - SMART teaches cognitive behavioral strategies for dealing with urges to drink.
- **SOS - Seculars On Sobriety** - SOS offers religion-free support groups for those who do not like the "spiritual" approach of AA.
- **WFS - Women For Sobriety** - WFS is a support group for women which concentrates on empowerment rather than the AA approach of indoctrinating powerlessness

We also recommend the following books as helpful:

- The Small Book (Rational Recovery Systems) by Jack Trimpey; introduction by Albert Ellis.
- Goodbye Hangovers, Hello Life: Self Help for Women by Jean Kirkpatrick
- How to Quit Drinking Without AA, Revised 2nd Edition: A Complete Self-Help Guide by Jerry Dorsman
- When AA Doesn't Work For You: Rational Steps to Quitting Alcohol by Albert Ellis And Emmett Velten
- Alcohol: How to Give It Up and Be Glad You Did by Philip Tate
- The Easy Way to Stop Drinking by Allen Carr
- Sex, Drugs, Gambling & Chocolate: A Workbook for Overcoming Addictions by A. Thomas Horvath.

6.2) Double-Barreled Harm Reduction Strategies

Some harm reduction strategies can help you to both drink less and to drink in a safer manner. We call these "Double-Barreled Harm Reduction Strategies". You can kill two birds with one stone.

6.2.1) Eat first and hydrate

Quantity: this helps you to drink more slowly so that you will drink less alcohol overall

Safety: this helps to keep your BAC from spiking so you can avoid blackouts and other forms of drunken craziness

Eat first and be well hydrated before you start drinking alcohol. Your stomach has only a few square feet of surface area to use to absorb liquids, but your small intestine has many thousands of square feet available to absorb liquids. The stomach is built to mash food and mix it with digestive juices, whereas the small intestine is built to be an extremely efficient liquid extraction device. This is because the inside of the small intestine is covered with tiny hair-like extensions called villi which exist for the sole purpose of increasing the surface area to make the small intestine more efficient at the absorption of liquids.

When you eat food, a valve closes between the stomach and the small intestine to hold the food in the stomach so that the stomach can mash it up and mix it with digestive juices. So long as this valve is closed, only small trickles of liquid can pass from the stomach into the small intestine. Therefore, if you eat before drinking, the alcohol will pass into your bloodstream much more slowly than if you do not. The larger the meal the longer it is held in the stomach. Additionally, fats are held in the stomach longer than proteins, and proteins are held there longer than carbohydrates. This is why bluesman Charlie Patton would say "Eat a lot of fat meat when you play a dance so you don't get too drunk." A large meal with plenty of fat can remain in the stomach up to six hours.

Drinking plenty of water before you drink any alcohol prevents you from being thirsty. You will drink more slowly if you are not dehydrated and don't feel thirsty. Remember, alcohol causes dehydration--this is why alcoholic beverages do not quench your thirst and why the more beer or booze that you drink the thirstier you actually feel. People often feel sated after drinking a single non-alcoholic beer, but are still ready to keep going after drinking half a dozen real beers.

Therefore, eat well and be well hydrated before you start drinking alcohol.

6.2.2) Choose your drink

Quantity: drinking more slowly helps to reduce the overall quantity one drinks. Once your BAC spikes you may stop caring how much you drink.

Safety: preventing BAC spikes helps prevent blackouts and alcohol poisoning.

What you choose to drink can have a lot to do with how quickly you drink. Sometimes "alcoholism experts" can be heard to declare, "It does not matter what you drink--alcohol is alcohol and the effect is always the same." The reality is that nothing could be further from the truth. While it may be true that alcohol is still alcohol regardless of what drink it is in, your choice of drink can have a tremendous impact on how quickly you consume it. Moreover, factors other than alcohol itself can determine how quickly the drink is absorbed into your bloodstream. Spikes in your BAC (Blood Alcohol Concentration) are what lead to problems like blackouts. And the speed with which the alcohol gets into your bloodstream is a major determinant of your BAC. The more slowly the alcohol enters the bloodstream, the lower the BAC. Since your choice of drink can have a significant impact on both how you choose to drink it and how it is absorbed, it is of great importance to choose your drink.

Some people have had considerable success by deciding that they will only drink the good stuff-- no more cheap booze. For some people deciding to cut out the rot gut whiskey and only drink expensive Irish or Scotch whiskey leads them to savor each drink, drink more slowly, and reserve the drinking for special occasions since it is too pricey to drink every day.

Some people have success with a strategy which is almost the opposite of this--they decide to forgo their drink of choice and switch to a drink that they don't really like. Because they are drinking something which they don't like very much they find themselves drinking less per session and/or fewer days per week.

Alcohol content can be a major factor in how quickly people drink their drinks. Generally speaking, the lower the alcohol content of a beverage the more slowly the drink is ingested. Most people can toss back six shots of whiskey a lot more quickly than they can down six 12 oz beers,

Taste can also be an important factor. Generally the more tasteless a beverage is the more quickly a person will drink it. Many people report that they drink vodka more quickly than gin, and gin more quickly than whiskey, because of the respective flavors of the beverages.

The alcohol in some beverages is also absorbed more quickly than the alcohol in other beverages. The alcohol in carbonated beverages is absorbed more quickly than the alcohol in non-carbonated beverages. This means that a sparkling wine will give you a higher BAC than a non-sparkling wine with the same alcohol content even if you drink them both at the same rate. If you find that champagne makes you drunk, now you know the reason why.

However, if there is a great disparity in alcohol content then it may still be safer to go with the carbonated beverage than the non-carbonated. This is clearly the case with whiskey and beer-- everyone gets drunk more quickly on straight whiskey even though it is not carbonated.

Artificial sweeteners also affect the rate of absorption of alcohol. Researchers in Australia found that the alcohol in drinks made with diet soda is absorbed into the bloodstream significantly more quickly than the alcohol in drinks made with regular soda.

So choose your drink wisely--not all alcoholic beverages are created equal.

6.2.3) Be Cautious of Drinking Games

Quantity: the sole purpose of drinking games is to make you drink more, not less

Safety: drinking too quickly can lead to blackouts or even alcohol poisoning and death

We are not saying that you must never engage in a drinking game--HAMS has no such absolute rules. If you choose to play a drinking game be careful and use your head. When you know that you have had enough stop. Or choose not to start if you don't want to--do your own thing and don't get peer pressured. More than one person has died of alcohol poisoning by trying to drink 21 shots on their 21st birthday. Take it slow and easy; you don't have to drink faster than you really want to and you don't ever have to play a drinking game if you don't want to. You always have the right to say "no".

6.2.4) Plan and schedule!

Quantity: restricting your drinking to scheduled drinking days can greatly reduce your total alcohol consumption

Safety: drinking on impulse without planning in advance can lead you to engage in every high risk behavior imaginable

It is amazing how much we can mess up our lives sometimes by just deciding to drink on impulse. Maybe we have a big final exam in calculus tomorrow and our buddy comes over and says "Let's get wasted" and we do it and blow the exam the next day and even wind up flunking out of school because of it. Getting into the habit of always planning and scheduling our drinking days and no longer drinking on impulse can be one of our most valuable harm reduction skills. It can save jobs, marriages, and even lives. That is why lots of Hamsters decide to cut out drinking on school nights or work nights or at least limit it to moderate levels on those nights. Planning and scheduling your boozing can help you to avoid having that big client walk out the door and go elsewhere because you reeked of booze from the night before.

6.3) Safer Drinking Strategies

6.3.1) Chart Your Behaviors!

Charting is one of the best tools we know of to accomplish behavioral change. Chapter 13 has **Risk Charts** which you can use to chart and reduce your high risk behaviors. We recommend them strongly.

6.3.2) Travel in Pairs

It is always a good idea to have a good friend at your side when you participate in a drinking event. Friends can help keep each other safe when they are in bars or walking or taking public transport together home. If one falls asleep on the subway, the other is there to safeguard him/her. Pickpockets, muggers, and sexual predators all target the intoxicated. Merely being male does not safeguard one either. Having another person at your side is the best way to discourage these people from taking advantage of you.

6.3.3) Control Your Glass

Don't let strangers pour your drinks. There are a lot of creeps out there with date rape drugs in their pockets just waiting to slip them into your drink. Males are not immune from this either. Let the bartender pour your drink or pour it yourself.

6.3.4) Drink Only at Home

Some people choose to drink only at home and always abstain when they go out. Others may have a one drink limit when they go out and choose to get intoxicated only at home--or some variation on this theme. The advantage is that there is much less worry about transportation or other dangers which can befall an intoxicated person when out and about. Some people don't care to use this strategy because their purpose in drinking is to increase social conviviality. Different strokes for different folks.

6.3.5) Plan Your Transportation

It is a good idea to never drive to a drinking event. The most sensible thing is to leave your car keys at home. Walking or using public transportation is the most sensible thing. Try to avoid drinking on impulse when your only means of getting home is driving. If you plan to use public transportation it is a good idea to travel with a friend for added safety.

Drinking and driving is definitely one of the highest of high risk behaviors. The average cost of a DUI in the US is well over $10,000. According to the 2010 Illinois DUI Fact Book, the average cost of a DUI conviction in Illinois where no one is injured is $16,100. If an injury or death results this skyrockets into hundreds of thousands of dollars and prison time as well. Isn't springing for a taxi fare of 10 or 15 bucks one hell of a lot cheaper?

If you really cannot stop yourself from driving after you drink, you may be better off selling your car and buying a bus pass instead.

6.3.6) Sleep On Your Friend's Floor

Establish an understanding between yourself and your friends that you can sleep on each other's floors when you are too intoxicated to make it home for the night.

6.3.7) Always Carry Condoms

Gay or straight, male or female, it is a good idea to always carry condoms when you go drinking--and use them! You might feel that you are not the type for a one night stand--but alcohol has a way of loosening inhibitions--and soon one thing leads to another. Unplanned pregnancy or HIV are not worth the risk--carry condoms and use them!

6.3.8) Take Vitamins / Milk Thistle

Alcohol depletes vitamin B1, and a lack of vitamin B1 can cause brain damage! Alcohol induced brain damage could be eliminated entirely in the US if our government would add vitamin B1 to all alcoholic beverages--however our government has steadfastly refused to do so. So it is up to you to always take vitamin B1 to prevent alcohol induced brain damage. HAMS also encourages people who drink alcohol to take a multivitamin because alcohol tends to deplete other vitamins and minerals as well. Milk thistle appears to have a protective effect on the liver and drinkers may wish to choose to take milk thistle as well.

6.3.9) Lock up Your Car Keys

If you can't resist the urge to drive once you start drinking, you may want to lock your car keys in a safe to make them less accessible before you down your first drink. Or you may give them to a spouse or a friend or a roommate to hold while you are drinking. You might even buy a time lock safe to make sure that you cannot get at them. Some people even choose to install a breath-alcohol ignition lock on their car to insure that they will not drink and drive.

6.3.10) Turn off Cell Phones and Computers

If your problem is drunk dialing or drunk emailing--then you may want to turn off your computer or cell phone before taking the first drink. If you need a stronger deterrent, lock them in a closet or a safe. Even your subconscious will realize that it might be a bad idea to drunk dial then.

6.3.11) Be Careful Of Mixing Alcohol with Prescription or Non-Prescription Drugs and Medications

Aspirin nullifies the effect of the enzyme which breaks down alcohol--taking aspirin before you drink alcohol can lead to blackouts and it may also cause bleeding in the stomach. Mixing alcohol and Tylenol greatly increases the chance of liver damage. Mixing alcohol with Benadryl increases the sedating effect although it is not otherwise harmful. Alcohol mixed with valium can lead to death from respiratory suppression. Wellbutrin can increase the odds of withdrawal seizures and maybe blackouts, too. Etc. Appendix One: Alcohol and Drug Interactions lists many more.

6.4) Strategies for Cutting Back on Alcohol

Some people want to cut back on their weekly totals without cutting back how much they consume per session. Some people want to cut back on how much they consume per session. Some people want to change both. Whatever your goal--you will be supported at HAMS.

6.4.1) Chart Your Drinks!

Charting is one of the most effective behavioral change strategies that we know of. We discuss charting in detail in Chapter 13.

6.4.2) Baby Stepping or Gradualism

Some people decide to add on abstinence day a week for the first month, two for the second month, three for the third, and so on until they reach their desired drinking plan. Some people decide to cut back on the amount they drink per session by eliminating one drink per session for the first week--two for the second week and so on. We call these approaches which involve changing a little bit at a time "baby stepping" or "gradualism". Some people find that this is the best way to achieve their drinking goal whether the goal is cutting back on alcohol or even quitting entirely.

6.4.3) Set Limits

Many people find that rather than having a vague goal of drinking less it works better to set specific limits for how much they plan to drink per session and per week. It is okay to be flexible enough to make allowance for special occasions and there is no reason to beat yourself up for not being perfect all the time. Just keep your limits in mind as goals to shoot for. You can use the drinking charts in Chapter 13 for writing down your goals each week if you wish.

6.4.4) Add Abstinence Days

Choosing to have a certain number of abstinence days each week is a good way to cut back on your alcohol consumption. Some people add them in gradually using the baby-stepping method. Others add them in all at once. Some people decide that no alcohol on work nights or school nights is a good rule. Find what works best for you.

6.4.5) Buy Only What You Plan To Drink - Don't Keep Booze in the House

Some people find that if they have booze in the house they will drink it so they choose not to keep booze in the house and buy only what they will drink on their drinking day or else drink only in bars. Other people are not bothered by having alcohol in the house and like to keep a well stocked home bar for when friends come over. We are all different.

6.4.6) Drink Only in Bars

Some people decide to cut out drinking at home entirely and drink only in bars or restaurants as a strategy for limiting their drinking. This works very well for some people. We strongly urge you to remember to plan your transportation safely when you drink when you are out.

6.4.7) Limit Cash

Some people choose to limit the amount which they drink in bars by only bringing a set amount of cash with them to the bar and leaving their debit and credit cards at home.

6.4.8) Alternate NA Drinks

Alternating non-alcoholic beers with real beers is a good way to slow your pace down and keep yourself from drinking too fast and too much. Some people alternate with water instead. You can also alternate wine with water or plain coke with rum and coke--etc etc etc. Use your imagination and experiment with what works the best for you personally.

6.4.9) Start Later / Delay

Some people choose to schedule their drinking time and start later in the day. For some people this works fine. Others may just find themselves drinking later into the night and consuming the same number of drinks. Use it if it works for you--trash it if it doesn't.

6.4.10) Stop Sooner

Some people schedule their drinking time and choose to stop at a certain time in the evening. It works for some but not for all--try it if it seems that it will work for you.

6.4.11) Use Your Toothbrush

Lots of people who like to drink wine report that it tastes really bad after they brush their teeth. So some people go and brush their teeth when they reach their drink limit in order to put a period to the night's wine drinking.

6.4.12) Decant

Some people decide to buy a liter of whiskey and split it up into five 200 ml bottles. That way if they decide that 200 ml is their limit, they will know that it is time to stop after one bottle. Measuring your nightly dose ahead of time helps many people to stay within their limit-- whatever the size of the dose is.

6.4.13) Buy a Breathalyzer

Some people buy a personal breathalyzer and set a goal of not exceeding a certain BAC when they are drinking.

6.4.14) Beer on Weekdays

Some people find that it is helpful to avoid hard alcohol on weekdays and only drink beer instead.

6.4.15) Use a Sleep Aid Instead Of Alcohol for Sleep

Some people drink themselves to sleep every night because they have bad insomnia. However, alcohol has many negative side effects which make it a poor choice as a sleep aid. For some people the best way to abstain from alcohol is to get a sleep aid for their insomnia so that they do not have to drink to get to sleep. We discuss prescription and non-prescription sleep aids in detail in Chapter 10.

6.4.16) Ice

Some people add ice to beer or whiskey or white wine to help them slow down. In Socrates' time it was standard operating procedure to add water to wine to slow down the pace. If it was good enough for Socrates...

6.4.17) Use Blue Laws

Some states have blue laws which outlaw the sale of hard alcohol on Sundays. Some people choose to only buy alcohol and drink it on Saturday night to prevent themselves from continuing to drink on the Sunday morning.

6.4.18) Get the Right Amount

If you only buy what you will drink when you drink, it can be important to get the right amount. If 750 ml is too much and 375 ml is too little then maybe you want to buy one 375 ml bottle and one 200 ml bottle to make a total of 575 ml. While it is true that it is more expensive to buy your alcohol this way, in the long run it may actually be cheaper because of the grief that you save yourself from.

6.4.19) Get Medications

The next section goes into detail about medications to help you reduce your drinking.

6.5) Medications to Change Your Drinking

6.5.1 Naltrexone

Naltrexone is an opioid antagonist which is helpful in changing people's drinking habits because of alcohol's effects on the naturally occurring opioids in the brain. Dr David Sinclair has been doing research for the government of Finland on the use of naltrexone to treat alcohol problems for decades. The Sinclair Method of using naltrexone involves taking 50 mg of naltrexone one hour before drinking alcohol and not taking naltrexone at any other time. Research by the Finnish government shows that the Sinclair Method is 70 to 80 % successful in turning even the heaviest of drinkers into moderate drinkers or abstainers. The Sinclair Method works by extinguishing the conditioned response to alcohol--it takes about three or four months to complete, although some individuals may require six months or even a year for the naltrexone to fully take effect.

Instead of using the highly successful Sinclair Method, most American addiction experts recommend that patients be told to take naltrexone daily and to abstain from alcohol. When prescribed in this manner, naltrexone is hardly more effective than a placebo. This method of using naltrexone appears to be far inferior to the Sinclair method in terms of positive results. For more information about naltrexone and the Sinclair Method please see **Appendix Three: Naltrexone and the Magic of Pharmacological Extinction**.

6.5.2) Antabuse

Antabuse (generic name disulfiram) is the drug that makes you sick when you drink alcohol. Antabuse works by blocking the breakdown of a poisonous byproduct of alcohol metabolism called acetaldehyde. This leads to symptoms of nausea, vomiting, sweating, flushing, rapid heartbeat, and in extreme cases, death. Mixing alcohol and antabuse is nothing to fool around with. Medication compliance with antabuse is extremely low--so low in fact that several studies found that antabuse was no more effective than a placebo in helping people to achieve abstinence from alcohol (Hughs and Cook, 1997). A drug will not work if people hate it and refuse to take it because of its effects.

However, some people who are highly motivated to abstain have found antabuse an effective aid to abstinence. Others who have requested that their spouse administer the antabuse each morning have also found it effective. At least one HAMS member has found a way to use antabuse as an aid to harm reduction. She takes antabuse when she wishes to have alcohol-free days. When she decides that she wishes to have a drinking day she stops taking the antabuse four days in advance of the drinking day. This is because it takes about four days for antabuse to clear the system. Then she drinks and after she sobers back up goes back on the antabuse until she chooses to have another drinking day.

6.5.3 Topamax

Topamax is a drug which was created for the treatment of epilepsy, but which has also been found effective in helping people to reduce their consumption of alcohol or to abstain. The generic name for Topamax is topiramate.

A large scale randomized, placebo controlled, double blind study of Topamax for the treatment of heavy drinking was published in JAMA (The Journal of the American Medical Association) in 2007. 371 subjects took part in this study. Topamax was significantly better than a placebo in reducing the percentage of heavy drinking days (p = 0.002). Statistically significant improvements were also seen in the number of abstinence days, the number of drinks per day, and in liver enzyme tests.

The biggest drawback to Topamax are side effects which can include confusion, psychomotor slowing, difficulty with concentration/attention, difficulty with memory, speech or language problems, particularly word-finding difficulties, depression or mood problems, and somnolence or fatigue. These side effects have led some people to discontinue Topamax treatment. About 15% of the subjects in the JAMA study reported cognitive side effects.

6.5.4 Campral

Campral (generic name acamprosate) is an anti-craving medication. Researchers believe that Campral may reduce cravings by interacting with the GABA or the glutamate system in the brain. The evidence suggests that Campral increases the success rate of people who are highly motivated to abstain from alcohol. Campral does not appear to be effective for people with little motivation. There is no evidence that Campral is helpful in helping people to moderate their drinking.

6.6) Dietary Supplements to Change Your Drinking

6.6.1) Glutamine

Glutamine has been found to reduce alcohol consumption in rats by 35% (Rogers et al, 1955). A number of people have also reported that glutamine has helped them to reduce their drinking. Glutamine is available as an over the counter dietary supplement. In a preliminary study with human subjects, Rogers et al (1957) administered 1,000 mg of glutamine to subjects who had reported alcohol problems. Subjects were instructed to take 400 mg of glutamine with breakfast, 400 with lunch, and 200 with dinner. Subjects in this study reported much improvement after taking the glutamine; however, the sample was not large enough to allow for statistical analysis.

6.6.2) Kudzu

Kudzu root has been found to significantly reduce alcohol consumption in both rat studies and human clinical trials (Benlhabib et al, 2004, Lukas et al 2005). The dosage of kudzu root for humans is two 500 mg capsules of kudzu root extract taken three times daily--a total of 3,000 mg per day. Kudzu root is not to be confused with kudzu flower which is not effective in reducing drinking.

6.7) Other Tools

6.7.1) How to Taper Off Alcohol

Why Taper?

Some people can just quit drinking alcohol cold turkey without having significant withdrawal symptoms. Other people, however, may suffer significant withdrawal symptoms when they suddenly stop drinking. Alcohol withdrawal is potentially fatal, so if you find yourself starting to experience significant alcohol withdrawal symptoms when you stop drinking then it is important to gradually detoxify from alcohol rather than quitting all at once "cold turkey". You can gradually detoxify from alcohol by tapering off. You can taper off either by using alcohol itself or by using medications.

Who Is Likely To Have Significant Alcohol Withdrawal Symptoms?

- People who have stayed drunk several days in a row
- People who have gotten drunk every night for a month or more
- People who have drank small amounts throughout the day for a month or more
- People with a history of alcohol withdrawal symptoms

What Are Withdrawal Symptoms?

Doctors classify withdrawal symptoms into three categories: mild, moderate, and severe.

- Mild or minor alcohol withdrawal usually occurs within 24 hours of the last drink and is characterized by tremulousness (shakes), insomnia, anxiety, panic, twitching, sweating, raised blood pressure and pulse, and stomach upset.
- Moderate or intermediate alcohol withdrawal usually occurs 24-36 hours after the cessation of alcohol intake. Its manifestations include intense anxiety, tremors, insomnia, seizures, hallucinations, high blood pressure, racing pulse.
- Severe or major alcohol withdrawal aka Delirium Tremens (D.T.s). This usually occurs more than 48 hours after a cessation or decrease in alcohol consumption. It is characterized by disorientation, agitation, hallucinations, tremulousness, racing heart, rapid breathing, fever, irregular heartbeat, blood pressure spikes, and intense sweating. When untreated about one person in five will die of D.T.s (some sources say one in three). Some people refer to shakes as D.T.s but this is inaccurate.

Even mild or moderate withdrawal can be dangerous for people with high blood pressure or bad hearts. Because withdrawal raises blood pressure there can be a danger of heart attack or stroke. The longer and harder a person has drunk alcohol--the more severe the withdrawal will be.

Can People Successfully Use Alcohol To Taper Off?

An unqualified YES. People have been using alcohol to taper off from alcohol since the dawn of history. Withdrawal medications are a recent invention. The idea that tapering cannot be done is a myth created by the alcohol treatment industry.

How do I know if I need to taper off?

If, when you stop drinking, your hands are visibly shaky, you begin to sweat a lot, you have a rapid or irregular pulse, or your blood pressure is very high then it is advisable to taper off alcohol and not quit cold turkey. You can taper off by using alcohol or by getting prescription meds from your doctor. A pulse of over 100 beats per minute is a definite danger sign.

How Do I Use Alcohol To Taper Off?

Beer is the best form of alcohol to use when tapering off. If you attempt to taper off using wine or hard liquor you might just wind up getting drunk again because these have higher alcohol content than beer. Try to limit yourself to drinking no more alcohol than necessary when you start tapering. Drink just enough to keep the sweats and shakes at bay. Gradually reduce the consumption of beer as you continue to taper. If the withdrawal is not too extreme you should be tapered off in a day or so. Some people may, however, take longer--three days or even a week. If you start to feel withdrawal symptoms it is a sign that your taper is not done yet.

It is also very important when tapering off to fight dehydration and to replenish lost vitamins. If you go through a medical detox the people there may rehydrate you with an IV and may also give you vitamin shots. If you are doing a self detox be sure to drink lots and lots of fluids and to take vitamin pills. We recommend Gatorade because it has balanced electrolytes. If you choose to drink water make sure that you get enough salt for electrolyte balance so that you avoid water intoxication.

How Much Alcohol Should I Drink When Tapering Off?

The average person takes around an hour and a half to metabolize a single standard drink--for example one 12 oz beer (see Chapter 13 for the definition of a standard drink). People who have a very high tolerance to alcohol can metabolize up to two standard drinks (28 g of alcohol) per hour. People who have a very low tolerance to alcohol might require two or three hours to metabolize a standard drink. Males metabolize alcohol faster than females. The more you weigh the higher your tolerance. Heavy drinkers who have increased tolerance also metabolize alcohol more rapidly than average. On the other hand people who have liver damage and reverse tolerance metabolize alcohol more slowly than others.

Our general rule of thumb is for people to taper off by drinking one beer per hour. However, you may have to adjust this number up if your tolerance is very high, or you may have to adjust this number down to one beer per two or three hours if your tolerance is low. If you start with one beer an hour we recommend that you gradually cut this down to half a beer an hour over the course of the taper.

How Do I Taper Off With Other Meds?

If you tell your doctor that you are having a problem with alcohol withdrawal s/he will help you taper off with a benzodiazepine such as Valium or Librium. In some states such as Minnesota the doctor is required by law to commit anyone suffering from alcohol withdrawal to an inpatient detox facility for at least 72 hours. In other states the patient may be allowed to attend an outpatient detox program or the patient may be given a prescription for a benzodiazepine for use for self detox. Typical detox regimens using these medications are as follows:

- Diazepam (Valium); 10 mg 3 or 4 times in first 24 hours, then 3 or 4 times daily as needed.
- Chlordiazepoxide (Librium); 50 mg every 6 hours for four doses, then 25 mg every 6 hours for eight doses.

If you do go to a doctor for alcohol withdrawal you may have a diagnosis of alcoholism on your medical records for the rest of your life. This can make it difficult to get medical insurance and sometimes even employment. If you want to avoid this you may choose to do the self-detox using beer as described above.

Does an Instance Of Alcohol Withdrawal Mean That I Can Never Safely Drink Again?

Not necessarily. Every individual must decide for him/herself whether their best option is to pursue a goal of alcohol abstinence, moderate drinking, or harm reduction. If you choose to drink again the best way to avoid another instance of withdrawal is to avoid drinking two days in a row. If you can't do this, then at least try to get in three abstinence days during the week. Try to avoid drinking day and night. The more abstinence time you have each week the lower the chance of having another instance of withdrawal. If it is just too damn much work to pursue a goal of harm reduction or moderation with too little payoff, then you may just decide that quitting is simplest. HAMS is wholeheartedly opposed to programs which try to use fear to motivate permanent abstinence from alcohol. We see these programs as usually backfiring and leading people to ever worse binges and ever worse withdrawals. We have found that people are most successful at quitting when they choose that goal for themselves.

What Causes Alcohol Withdrawal?

Alcohol withdrawal is caused by neurotransmitter rebound. The main neurotransmitter system involved in alcohol withdrawal is the GABA (gamma-aminobutyric acid) system. Simply put, GABA receptors cause a person to feel calm, relaxed or sleepy. Alcohol enhances the functioning of these GABA receptors. This is why when people drink alcohol they will feel calm, relaxed, or sleepy. However, when the GABA receptors are exposed to alcohol over a long period of time they struggle to overcome the effect of the alcohol and to return to normal functioning. This is one reason why drinking alcohol has less and less of a payoff when consumed constantly over a long period of time. One is not nearly so relaxed by alcohol the third day into a bender as one was on the first day. After being exposed to alcohol over a long period of time the GABA receptors stop responding as efficiently to the presence of GABA. When the alcohol is suddenly no longer there, these GABA receptors now respond only very weakly to the presence of GABA. The result is anxiety, panic, and insomnia.

Another thing which happens when the function of the GABA receptor is enhanced by alcohol is that the brain tries to overcome this calming effect by producing more adrenaline and other similar neurotransmitters. When the alcohol is completely taken away then this adrenaline and its cousins are left to run rampant in the brain. This leads to raised blood pressure, raised pulse rate, rapid breathing, fever, hallucinations, seizures and D.T.s.

Alcohol also inhibits the glutamate receptor--which is the cause of staggering, slurring, and general interference with muscular coordination. Glutamate receptor rebound also appears to contribute to the withdrawal symptoms described above.

What Is "Kindling"?

Some people who have repeatedly gone through cold turkey withdrawal without tapering off become more and more likely to have bad withdrawals form even small amounts of alcohol. This phenomenon is referred to as "kindling". People who have undergone kindling can suffer withdrawal seizures from drinking as little as a six pack of beer. Some decades ago some detox facilities forced clients to undergo cold turkey withdrawal to "teach them a lesson". Not only did this fail to stop people from drinking, it resulted in many people suffering from kindling. Fortunately this barbaric practice has been discontinued. The way to avoid kindling is to taper off.

6.7.2 The Geographical Cure

When you are struggling with an alcohol problem it only makes it more difficult to struggle with additional obstacles at the same time. Some geographical areas of the US are right wing, some are left wing, some have high unemployment, some have low unemployment, some discriminate a lot against certain minority groups, others do not, etc., etc. Sometimes moving to a more suitable geographical area can spell the difference between success and failure at achieving your drinking goal. So if you feel the need for the geographical cure, go for it!

6.7.3 Journaling

Many people find that writing about the thoughts and feelings associated with the events in their lives is therapeutic--much as it can be therapeutic to tell them to a counselor. Journaling is most helpful if one writes in detail about feelings and cognitions related to life events, as one would discuss topics in therapy.

Journaling not only allows people to clarify their thoughts and feelings and gain insights into themselves, journaling can also work as a problem solving tool by letting people hash things out on paper until they come up with a solution. Journaling also allows people to process traumatic events by fully exploring and releasing the emotions surrounding them.

Research shows that if you journal then it is important to focus on both cognitions and emotions (Ullrich and Lutgendorf, 2002). Focusing solely on negative emotions can backfire and leave you feeling worse than before. So use the journaling to help you gain insight and understanding and journal about both the positive and the negative to get the best effect from this tool.

6.7.4 AA Deprogramming

First off we want to say that it is a fact many people who have alcohol problems find that AA is helpful to them personally. If you are one of them then we congratulate you. You may stop reading this chapter right now because we have no desire to convert you.

However, it is also a fact that many people with alcohol problems are not helped by AA. Many people have reported being damaged by their involvement with AA. Some people report that attending AA meetings makes them crave alcohol. Some people report that their drinking increased greatly in quantity or turned extremely dangerous after they began attending AA. Still others report that attending AA meetings makes them depressed or suicidal. If you suffer from any of these problems it may well be in your best interest to leave AA immediately. If a patient is allergic to penicillin, the answer is not to give the patient more penicillin. Likewise, if a person is allergic to AA, the answer is not more AA.

Because AA uses a number of elementary brainwashing techniques, many people find that the damage which they have suffered as a result of attending AA continues to persist long after they have left AA. The primary brainwashing techniques which AA uses involve undermining your self efficacy by forcing you to admit that you are powerless (step one) and insane (step two). People are led to believe that alcohol is more powerful than they are--but that AA itself is a "Higher Power" which can rescue them. This leads to a total dependence on AA and a hysterical fear of anything which is not AA.

However, researchers such as Dr. Albert Bandura tell us that the most powerful force for positive self change is self-efficacy. AA destroys self-efficacy and replaces it with an unhealthy dependency on AA. This is why AA members are always on the verge of relapse even after 20 years of sobriety. As AA says, "Always recovering, never recovered." This destruction of self-efficacy is also why relapse in AA is so common. Dr. James Prochaska tells us that people who change their behaviors on their own will often forget about their bad habits in a year and have no desire to return to them because they no longer think about them. People who go to AA dwell on drinking at every meeting and never get it out of their heads--they are always on the verge of relapse.

AA also keeps members mentally off balance through the use of cognitive dissonance. AA forces members to hold two contradictory beliefs at the same time. The way to recover from AA brainwashing is to realize that you are powerful and sane. AA has no power over you unless you give it power over you. AA is insane--not you.

If you have a gut feeling that AA is wrong for you then it almost certainly is. Do not allow yourself to be forced into AA against your will by anyone--not even a doctor or a psychologist or a judge or an employer or a friend or a family member. Do not allow anyone to put the notion into your head that you are diseased or powerless of that you will die without AA. The majority of people who quit drinking do so on their own--regardless of how much they drink.

The research shows that AA is one of the least effective treatments for alcohol problems out there--nowhere near as effective as more traditional forms of psychotherapy (see Appendix Four for a discussion of this). It is nothing short of criminal that medical doctors refer people with alcohol problems to something which is ineffective in general and harmful to many instead of referring them to something which could actually help them. And the same is true for courts or employers who force AA on people. Fortunately many states have recognized that forced AA participation is unconstitutional because it violates the right to freedom of religion.

If you have been harmed by participation in a 12 step program you may find the following books helpful for use in AA deprogramming:

- Alcoholics Anonymous Cult or Cure. by Charles Bufe
- The Real AA: Behind the Myth of 12-Step Recovery. by Ken Ragge
- 12-Step Horror Stories: True Tales of Misery, Betrayal, and Abuse in AA, NA, and 12-Step Treatment. by Rebecca Fransway
- Addiction Is a Choice. by Jeffrey A. Schaler
- Diseasing of America: How We Allowed Recovery Zealots and the Treatment Industry to Convince Us We Are Out of Control. by Stanton Peele
- Resisting 12-Step Coercion: How to Fight Forced Participation in AA, NA, or 12-Step Treatment. by Stanton Peele and Charles Bufe with Archie Brodsky

Several of these books are available for free on Ken Ragge's web site:

http://www.morcrevealed.com

A lot of people are AA members and believe that AA has cured them of their disease. A lot of people are Christian Scientists and believe that prayer cures cancer and surgery does not. Believing something does not make it so. Research suggests that AA tends to be helpful only for people with a dependent personality type who need a paternalistic and authoritarian figure to control them (Poldrugo and Forti, 1988). AA can be a disaster for free thinkers. Sometimes getting AA out of your head is essential for successfully accomplishing your drinking goal--whether that goal is safer drinking, reduced drinking--or even quitting.

As we have said many times--all elements, tools and strategies of HAMS are optional and not all will work for everyone--you must choose what is right for you. AA works for some people and we wish them well and have no argument with them. However, some people have been significantly psychologically harmed by AA and have increased their drinking or have become depressed or suicidal as a result. If you are one of these people you may need AA deprogramming.

6.8 Add Your Own

HAMS is not all knowing or all powerful. Feel free to add any tools that you think up for yourself to your list of alcohol harm reduction tools. You may come up with something great that no one else has even thought of yet!! Think before you drink. There's more than one way to skin a cantaloupe!

REFERENCES:

2010 Illinois DUI Fact Book
http://www.cyberdriveillinois.com/publications/pdf_publications/dsd_a118.pdf
Accessed February 4, 2010.

Anderson CM. (1999). Writing and Healing: Toward an Informed Practice.

Anton RF, O'Malley SS, Ciraulo DA, Cisler RA, Couper D, Donovan DM, Gastfriend DR, Hosking JD, Johnson BA, LoCastro JS, Longabaugh R, Mason BJ, Mattson ME, Miller WR, Pettinati HM, Randall CL, Swift R, Weiss RD, Williams LD, Zweben A; COMBINE Study Research Group. (2006). Combined pharmacotherapies and behavioral interventions for alcohol dependence: the COMBINE study: a randomized controlled trial. JAMA. May 3;295(17):2003-17.
PubMed Abstract:
http://www.ncbi.nlm.nih.gov/pubmed/16670409
Free Full Text:
http://jama.ama-assn.org/cgi/reprint/295/17/2003.pdf

Bayard M, McIntyre J, Hill KR, Woodside J Jr. (2004). Alcohol Withdrawal Syndrome. American Family Physician. 69(6):1443-50.
PubMed Abstract:
http://www.ncbi.nlm.nih.gov/pubmed/15053409
Free Full Text:
http://www.aafp.org/afp/20040315/1443.html

Benlhabib E, Baker JI, Keyler DE, Singh AK (2004). Kudzu root extract suppresses voluntary alcohol intake and alcohol withdrawal symptoms in P rats receiving free access to water and alcohol. J Med Food. 7(2), 168-79.
PubMed Abstract:
http://www.ncbi.nlm.nih.gov/pubmed/15298764

Blondell RD. (2005). Ambulatory Detoxification of Patients with Alcohol Dependence. American Family Physician. 71(3):495-502.
PubMed Abstract:
http://www.ncbi.nlm.nih.gov/pubmed/15712624
Free Full Text:
http://www.aafp.org/afp/20050201/495.html

Eskapa, R (2008). The Cure for Alcoholism: Drink Your Way Sober Without Willpower, Abstinence or Discomfort. Benbella Books. Dallas, TX.

Garbutt JC (2009). The state of pharmacotherapy for the treatment of alcohol dependence. Journal of Substance Abuse Treatment. Jan;36(1):S15-23.
PubMed Abstract:
http://www.ncbi.nlm.nih.gov/pubmed/19062347

Heinälä P, Alho H, Kiianmaa K, Lönnqvist J, Kuoppasalmi K, Sinclair JD. (2001). Targeted use of naltrexone without prior detoxification in the treatment of alcohol dependence: a factorial double-blind, placebo-controlled trial. Journal of Clinical Psychopharmacology. Jun;21(3):287-92.
PubMed Abstract:
http://www.ncbi.nlm.nih.gov/pubmed/11386491

Hughes JC, Cook CC. (1997). The efficacy of disulfiram: a review of outcome studies. Addiction. 92(4), 381-95.
PubMed Abstract:
http://www.ncbi.nlm.nih.gov/pubmed/9177060

Johnson BA, Rosenthal N, Capece JA, Wiegand F, Mao L, Beyers K, McKay A, Ait-Daoud N, Anton RF, Ciraulo DA, Kranzler HR, Mann K, O'Malley SS, Swift RM; Topiramate for Alcoholism Advisory Board; Topiramate for Alcoholism Study Group. (2007). Topiramate for Treating Alcohol Dependence: A Randomized Controlled Trial. JAMA.;298(14):1641-1651.
PubMed Abstract:
http://www.ncbi.nlm.nih.gov/pubmed/17925516
Free Full Text:
http://jama.ama-assn.org/cgi/reprint/298/14/1641.pdf

Kenna GA, Lomastro TL, Schiesl A, Leggio L, Swift RM. (2009). Review of topiramate: an antiepileptic for the treatment of alcohol dependence. Curr Drug Abuse Rev. May;2(2):135-42.
PubMed Abstract:
http://www.ncbi.nlm.nih.gov/pubmed/19630744

Lukas SE, Penetar D, Berko J, Vicens L, Palmer C, Mallya G, Macklin EA, Lee DY. (2005). An extract of the Chinese herbal root kudzu reduces alcohol drinking by heavy drinkers in a naturalistic setting. Alcohol Clin Exp Res. May;29(5):756-62.
PubMed Abstract:
http://www.ncbi.nlm.nih.gov/pubmed/15897719

Mason, B. J., Goodman, A. M., Chabac, S., & Lehert, P. (2006). Effect of oral acamprosate on abstinence in patients with alcohol dependence in a double-blind, placebo-controlled trial: The role of patient motivation. Journal of Psychiatric Research, 40, 383–393.
PubMed Abstract:
http://www.ncbi.nlm.nih.gov/pubmed/16546214

Mikuriya TH. (2004) Cannabis as a Substitute for Alcohol: A Harm-Reduction Approach. Journal of Cannabis Therapeutics. Vol. 4(1)
Free Full Text:
http://www.mikuriya.com/cw_alcsub.pdf

The New York Times (2010, January 11). NJ Legislature Approves Medical Marijuana Bill
http://www.nytimes.com/2010/01/12/nyregion/12marijuana.html
Accessed September 14, 2010

O'Brien, CP., McKay, J (2002). Pharmacological treatments for substance use disorders. In Nathan, PE., Gorman, JM. (Eds.) A guide to treatments that work (2nd ed.). (pp. 125-156). New York, NY, US: Oxford University Press.

Olmsted CL, Kockler DR. (2008). Topiramate for alcohol dependence. <u>Ann Pharmacother</u>. Oct;42(10):1475-80.
PubMed Abstract:
http://www.ncbi.nlm.nih.gov/pubmed/18698008

Paille FM, Guelfi JD, Perkins AC, Royer RJ, Steru L, Parot P. (1995). Double-blind randomized multicentre trial of acamprosate in maintaining abstinence from alcohol. Alcohol and Alcoholism. Mar;30(2):239-47.
PubMed Abstract:
http://www.ncbi.nlm.nih.gov/pubmed/7662044

Poldrugo F, Forti B. (1988). Personality disorders and alcoholism treatment outcome. <u>Drug Alcohol Depend</u>. 21(3):171-6.
PubMed Info:
http://www.ncbi.nlm.nih.gov/pubmed/3168759

Reiman A. (2009). Cannabis as a Substitute for Alcohol and Other Drugs. <u>Harm Reduction Journal</u>. 6(35).
PubMed Abstract:
http://www.ncbi.nlm.nih.gov/pubmed/19958538
Free Full Text:
http://www.harmreductionjournal.com/content/6/1/35
Accessed January 18, 2010

Rogers LL, Pelton RB, Williams RJ. (1955). Voluntary alcohol consumption by rats following administration of glutamine. J Biol Chem. Jun;214(2):503-6.
PubMed Info:
http://www.ncbi.nlm.nih.gov/pubmed/14381386
Free Full Text:
http://www.jbc.org/cgi/reprint/214/2/503.pdf

Rogers LL, Pelton RB. (1957). Glutamine in the treatment of alcoholism; a preliminary report. Q J Stud Alcohol. Dec 18(4):581-7.
PubMed Info:
http://www.ncbi.nlm.nih.gov/pubmed/13506018

Sinclair JD. (2001). Evidence about the use of naltrexone and for different ways of using it in the treatment of alcoholism. Alcohol and Alcoholism.Jan-Feb;36(1):2-10.
PubMed Abstract:
http://www.ncbi.nlm.nih.gov/pubmed/11139409
Free Full Text:
http://alcalc.oxfordjournals.org/cgi/reprint/36/1/2.pdf

Ullrich PM, Lutgendorf SK. (2002). Journaling about stressful events: effects of cognitive processing and emotional expression. <u>Ann Behav Med</u>. 24(3),244-50.
PubMed Abstract:
http://www.ncbi.nlm.nih.gov/pubmed/12173682

Whitworth AB, Fischer F, Lesch OM, Nimmerrichter A, Oberbauer H, Platz T, Potgieter A, Walter H, Fleischhacker WW. (1996). Comparison of acamprosate and placebo in long-term treatment of alcohol dependence. Lancet. 347(9013), 1438-42.
PubMed Abstract:
http://www.ncbi.nlm.nih.gov/pubmed/8676626

Wu KL, Chaikomin R, Doran S, Jones KL, Horowitz M, Rayner CK. (2006). Artificially sweetened versus regular mixers increase gastric emptying and alcohol absorption. <u>The American Journal of Medicine.</u> 119(9), 802-4.
PubMed Abstract:
http://www.ncbi.nlm.nih.gov/pubmed/16945619

CHAPTER SEVEN: *Making Your Plan*

"Failing to plan is planning to fail"

- **HAMS Element Five: Make a plan to achieve your drinking goal**

7.1 About Planning
7.2 My Drinking Plan Worksheet
7.3 Sample Drinking Plan Worksheet
7.4 Sample Drinking Plans from Our Members

7.1) About Planning

HAMS does not require people to follow a certain arbitrary moderate drinking limits or else give up alcohol entirely. HAMS meets people where they are at and encourages every positive change. Some people might not choose to change the amount that the drink at all and focus solely on safer drinking. Some might choose to drink to intoxication twice a week and abstain five days. Some might choose to drink every day of the week but never more than four drinks per day. Still others might choose to only drink on Christmas and their birthday and abstain the rest of the year, while some may choose to quit altogether. Some might choose to stay within the USDA's definition of moderate drinking (two per day for men and one peer day for women). There are as many possible different plans as there are different people.

HAMS encourages you to write out your drinking plan in detail--you may share it with a HAMS live or online group if you wish. We also strongly encourage you to use the **HAMS Drinking Plan Worksheet** (Section 7.2) as an aid in making your plan. Additionally, you may use the **HAMS Drinking Charts** (Chapter 13) to make a **daily or weekly plan** each day or week. At HAMS, if you are not satisfied with your plan you can always go back and revise it at any time. Sometimes people start with a plan that is too harsh or restrictive. Other times people feel that their plan was not ambitious enough. Feel free to revamp the plan any time it seems necessary to you.

Remember, some people change all at once and some people change a little bit at a time. We call the latter process **Baby Stepping** (some other people call it Gradualism). An example of **Baby Stepping** is to do one abstinence day per week for the first month--two in the second month, three in the third month, and so forth. The HAMS Toolbox (Chapter 6) is you source for tools and strategies for building your drinking plan.

Not every drinking plan will be long and complex. For example, you may choose to quit alcohol entirely and go on Marijuana Maintenance. In this case you may just want to add a few strategies for maintaining alcohol abstinence such as drink refusal strategies and AVRT.

When you make your own drinking plan for yourself then you are personally invested in it--far more so than if you just follow someone else's plan in a book or something. You can use the following worksheet to help you make your plan:

7.2) My Drinking Plan Worksheet
free download at http://hamsnetwork.org/worksheets

This is the worksheet to help you make your overall drinking plan. You can put down your specific daily and weekly plans each week on your drinking charts. You don't have to fill in every blank--just the ones that are the most relevant to your situation.

****

My Drinking Goal (circle one)	Quitting	Safer Drinking	Reduced Drinking	Both Safer And Reduced Drinking

****

My ideal drinking limits   Daily _____   Weekly _____

My upper drinking limits   Daily _____   Weekly _____

Alcohol abstinence days per week   Ideal _____   At least _____

My current drinking level (if known)   Daily _____   Weekly _____

****

High risk behaviors to work on _____

_____

My plan for changing these high risk behaviors_____

_____

Outside issues to work on _____

_____

My plan for addressing these outside issues _____

_____

My tools and strategies _____

_____

My damage control plan _____

_____

_____

7.3) Sample Drinking Plan Worksheet
free download at http://hamsnetwork.org/worksheets

This is the worksheet to help you make your overall drinking plan. You can put down your specific daily and weekly plans each week on your drinking charts. You don't have to fill in every blank--just the ones that are the most relevant to your situation.

****

My Drinking Goal (circle one)	Quitting	Safer Drinking	Reduced Drinking	**Both Safer And Reduced Drinking**
My ideal drinking limits		Daily 4		Weekly 20
My upper drinking limits		Daily 10		Weekly 40
Alcohol abstinence days per week		Ideal 2		At least 0
My current drinking level (if known)		Daily 10		Weekly 60

****

High risk behaviors to work on DRUNK DRIVING

My plan for changing these high risk behaviors GIVE MY CAR KEYS TO MY ROOMMATE BEFORE I START DRINKING.

Outside issues to work on FINANCIAL HEALTH, RELATIONSHIPS

My plan for addressing these outside issues FIND A SECOND JOB, JOIN EHARMONY AND FIND A BOYFRIEND

My tools and strategies DRINK CHARTING, AVRT FOR ABSTINENCE DAYS

My damage control plan I WILL NOT BEAT MYSELF UP AND ENGAGE IN A BOUT OF PITY DRINKING IF I FAIL TO STICK TO MY IDEAL PLAN. I WILL ALWAYS TRY TO GIVE MY CAR KEYS TO MY ROOMMATE BEFORE I DRINK ANYTHING AT ALL.

7.4) Sample Drinking Plans from Our Members

The following are actual plans that HAMS members have posted to the online group. These will give you some idea of what your plan might incorporate.

Sample Plan One -- Female

I want to outline my plan, so that I can be accountable, especially to myself.

I abstain on work nights; I am not a morning person, and I have to get up at 5 am for work. Even the dregs of a hangover would be counterproductive. I usually feel a bit woozy and dizzy in the mornings without alcohol in my system.

My goal is harm reduction, without limiting myself to where I feel deprived of something I want to do (drink, and get a buzz). I don't want to black out. I don't want to be mean to anyone (my husband, or possibly, an online friend). I certainly don't want to get sick, puke, or piss myself, or, God forbid, drive or walk somewhere.

And I have done well! Friday I had veggie juice and vodka. I had "two" drinks. My size drinks. I don't measure the alcohol. I'd planned on measuring as part of my plan previously, but somehow, I'd rather drink to taste. I limit myself to two. I eat first. And I have a small snack (sometimes just a diet beverage) before bed, when I am finished drinking. I wake up feeling fine, I remember my evening. Did the same on Sunday night, only with Diet Pepsi. I am good with it.

Saturday, I had finished my final paper for my class. I am working on my Master's degree in nursing. I put in a full day on Saturday, my kids were out, and my husband had his Budweiser. I had intended to drink. But, the hour became late, and I just didn't get around to that first drink. I absolutely need to know, always, that my drinking is my CHOICE. Saturday showed me that it is something I am able to control.

I am just me folks. I don't drink wine or expensive booze. I feel no social pressure to drink. My children are important to me. I am struggling continually to find a path of faith that will feed my spiritual hunger. My education has a great deal of bearing on how I define myself; I will be the first in my family to graduate college (I already am, with only a bachelor's). I have chosen a path that I am not that thrilled about (my marriage), but at the same time, I see the many blessings, and the beautiful things in my life. For those things, I rejoice.

I'd like to blame my faulty choices and the negative things that have happened to me as being the reasons that I drink, but why blame anything?

Truth be told, I drink because I like to drink. I like the time before that first drink. There is a small sense of excitement knowing that soon, I will feel a buzz and be in a slightly different place. My world will be colored a bit. It won't bother me that my father abandoned me twice, that my mother thinks I am a loser, that I have never made my sisters feel loved enough, that I am living with someone I don't like or love anymore. Any kid issue (most are so minor, thank goodness!) is placed on the back burner. With my buzz, my life is on the back burner. I am there, barely there, for the moment. Sweet escape, unless I overdo...

The escape I don't want to give up. Man has fed his head since the beginning of time, and I chalk the desire up to human nature; I do not believe it to be morally wrong. A badge of sobriety isn't something I need to own.

I am still not sure if I will drink tonight or not. I have my 1.75 L of vodka, and rum. I have a pint of Jagermeister, maybe some Kahlua. It's in the cupboard. It's there if I want it; I might want it, since after tonight I have an unusually long stretch of working.

I sound pretty in control, rereading this. HAMS is here, for me, to remind me of the problems that I can get into if I don't check my consumption within a drinking episode. I am here because I have caused destruction in the past. I'm leaving it behind, folks, and thanks for the support.

Sample Plan Two-- Male

I like to get intoxicated when I drink. I will drink a fifth of hard liquor when I choose to drink. But I always drink safely at home alone when I drink. And I never drink on a work night.

I never keep alcohol in the house; I only buy it when I choose to drink.

For me it is best to abstain five to six days a week and drink just one or two. If I do not have lots of abs days I wind up getting nothing done.

I work Fridays, Saturdays and Sundays, so my designated drinking day is Sunday night and sometimes Monday.

I do sometimes have a mods day when I have just one drink in a social situation.

But this is almost the same as an abs day for me.

I am doing much better now than in the old days when I would get loaded four nights a week and go into work hungover.

Sample Plan Three-- Female

A while back, I went from drinking straight whiskey (no mixer, no glass, straight from the bottle) to drinking beer.

The reason is, I had a horrible experience after drinking way too much whiskey, way more than normal, and the next morning, my world went crazy...I couldn't hold my hands still, and my head started bobbing around uncontrollably.

I don't measure my drinks, but I know I was drinking a ton of whiskey every day, and now I'm drinking probably 3-8 small cans (12 oz) of bud light every day. It's all I need for now.

I have no idea how much alcohol content this equals to. But I think it's a success so far, because I don't get hangovers anymore, and I don't get falling down drunk, but at the same time, I do get buzzed adequately.

So far, I haven't been able to commit to any abs days, or mods days. But I am keeping it to a manageable level right now. Sometimes I start drinking about noon....depending on my 'triggers'....but most often, I wait until bedtime, which usually ends up being 3-4 beers.

At first, I was bound and determined to keep some whiskey around 'just in case' I 'needed' some, and to 'prove' that I could 'handle' having it here and not drinking it. But I've been able to avoid it for the most part.

I don't have any idea how much harm reduction is taking place, but I feel a lot better staying with the beer.

Sample Plan Four -- Male

I was not drinking until I was drunk all the time, but I was drinking every night and I wanted to change that. I thought that was a bad idea.

So I decided that for the first month I would have one night of abstinence every week.

For the second month I went for two nights of abstinence every week.

Three for the third and four for the fourth.

Once I was at four nights of abstinence every week I felt satisfied with my progress.

I am not perfect now--but most of the time I manage to keep to four days of abs a week.

Sample Plan Five -- Female

My Plan for the Coming Month:

1) No hard alcohol Sun-Thursday; no more than 3 drinks on those days.

2) Wait until 5:30 or 6 PM to drink; furthermore wait until dinner to drink.

3) Have a large glass of sparkling water with lemon before my first drink. Fill it up every time I make a drink to drink alongside the alcohol drink.

4) Buy a 375 ML of whiskey (8.5 standard drinks) on Friday, I can either drink it all on Friday or drink part of it on Friday and part on sat, either way. NO going back to get more on Saturday if I drink it all on Friday. Wait until the next Friday before you buy another bottle of whiskey.

5) Stick to one type of alcohol a day. Either drink beer OR wine OR whiskey.

6) Have at least one abs stretch a month which lasts from 3-10 consecutive days to make sure that all the alcohol is cleared out of my system at least once a month.

7) No more than 25 drinks a week.

Sample Plan Six - Female

1. One or zero drinks per day, except on days that call for more (to be determined by me).

2. Focus on not drinking out of habit, boredom or hunger.

3. Never more than 4 drinks in one day.

4. Measure and count every drink and log it on my spreadsheet.

5. Try not to fear falling asleep sober. Take a sleep aid, if needed, and don't beat myself up for it.

Sample Plan Seven

Hi all! I think my plan is this: never stop making plans.

I am constantly changing plans with drinking and in the past I thought this was a bad thing. I've decided to make it a good thing. As long as my focus is on not drinking and driving and not being a daily drunk, I think it's good.

So, December is about 3 drinks per day with once a week drunks or heavy buzzes.

In January, I will do another round of P90X (90 day intense home fitness DVDs) but with minimal alcohol consumption. So for 90 days I will try to cut down to 1 per day, just for the calories.

In March, I have a physical so I'll have all the liver tests done. I've given up meat so that should help, too.

But for now, bottoms up (with minimal guilt)!

CHAPTER EIGHT: *Alcohol-Free Time*

"I don't do drugs - I AM drugs" --Salvador Dali

- **HAMS Element Six: Use alcohol-free time to reset your drinking habits**

8.1 Why Have Alcohol-Free Time?
8.2 Members Share How They Did Alcohol-Free Days

8.1) Why Have Alcohol-Free Time?

Many people find that doing a period of abstinence from alcohol is a useful tool for changing their drinking habits. An alcohol-free period gives you a chance to practice drink refusal strategies, to identify those "automatic" drinks that you drink without thinking, and to practice not drinking in all the situations where you used to drink. It is also a good idea to have several alcohol-free days per week if you want to avoid a physical dependence on alcohol.

How long should your alcohol-free period be? It is up to you to choose how long you wish to abstain from alcohol if you choose to do an alcohol-free period. For people who have been drinking daily for a long time it can be a major triumph to do even a single day of abstinence. Some people who have developed tolerance for alcohol wish to do a period of alcohol abstinence in order to lower their tolerance. Generally it takes around thirty days to return liver enzymes and neurotransmitters back to a lower level. Abstaining longer than this won't have a lot of additional effect on liver enzymes and neurochemicals. However, some people choose to abstain for sixty days or ninety days or even longer to address the HABIT part of their drinking habit. Whatever abstinence period you choose--a day, a week, a month, or even more--you are to be applauded for the effort!

In HAMS you never lose your alcohol-free days. If you aim for thirty days and make twenty then you will still always have those twenty days of success. You don't have to beat yourself up or call yourself a failure for not doing the full thirty. Chapter 6 contains plenty of strategies and tools for getting through your alcohol-free time successfully. You may choose to do a Cost Benefit Analysis (CBA) in order to increase your motivation for doing an alcohol-free period. You might also want to make a list of the tools and strategies which you plan to use to help and get you through your alcohol-free period.

Some people choose to do an indefinite alcohol-free period rather than a set number of days. Choose whatever works best for you. Remember, you can do as many alcohol-free periods as you want to. An alcohol-free period shouldn't have to feel like a prison sentence or an act of penance. You can use this as an opportunity to learn how to have fun without alcohol. Take a look at Chapter 11 on having fun without alcohol. Enjoy your alcohol-free time! And enjoy your drinking time too!! HAMS believes that life should be a ball!

CAUTION: If you think that you may have alcohol withdrawal if you suddenly stop drinking, please be sure to taper off safely as described in Chapter 6.

8.2) Members Share How They Did Alcohol-Free Days

HAMS members share stories of how they did their first alcohol abstinence (abs) day or tips on how they do abstinence days on a regular basis.

JH writes:

I did my first abs day in a long time this Tuesday by planning ahead and getting something nice to drink as a non-alcoholic drink. I bought pomegranate/cherry juice and some sparking water to mix with it. That way when my husband was having a beer before and during dinner, I could have my "drink" on ice in a fancy glass. I had to work that day so that kept me busy during the day. Then I shopped at the grocery store for something special for dinner (in this case, shrimp and spinach salad with oranges and zucchini). It took awhile to make this which also kept me busy. It was such a healthy meal that it made me feel better due to all the vitamins in it. I read in the evening to keep my mind occupied and off alcohol.

PCT writes:

When I was living in Japan I started drinking myself to sleep every night. I drank daily for a couple of years until one day when I realized that the alcohol was making me feel normal rather than making me feel intoxicated--I felt abnormal the whole day until I drank. I decided that this was a bad sign and I decided to take a nine month vacation from drinking alcohol. I went to my best friend and drinking buddy's house and told him that I was taking nine months off from drinking and asked if I could hang out with him for the first day. He said yes. He was Japanese and a painter. We spent the day stripping paint off of old canvases. I had some minor withdrawal. My eyes were grainy and I felt shaky and sleepless. It took about 36 hours before I could go to sleep. When I went to the restaurant I ate at every night I told the owner that I was off of alcohol for 9 months. He did not believe me and mixed me a drink anyway. I refused it. Then I stayed dry for the next nine months.

One trick that I find really useful if I am having a hard time sticking to an abs day is to talk back to my cravings. I will say "I am NOT gonna drink and wild horses can't make me drink against my will once I have made up my mind!! So there!! F@#K OFF MR. CRAVING!!"

BE writes:

Me and some Mom's in our group are doing our first abs day tonight. I can't speak for the others, but I must stay busy. Mostly, my mind. I also MUST eat a big dinner. That works every time.

HJ writes:

We got home at 9pm from the water park, everyone was exhausted. I fell asleep on the couch.

That was an "unplanned" abs day.

Planned ones are hard for me. I pace, I eat, I surf the net. But the most relaxed way for me to deal with an abs day (I have a very strong, daily habit.... not excessive, just habitual) is a long bath and read in bed until I fall asleep. I do not have an easy time of it. I think I need more practice.

71

JH writes:

I didn't drink yesterday even though it wasn't a planned abs day simply because I did not feel like drinking.

Sometimes though I think I do drink even if I don't feel like it, just out of habit. Like if I have mandatory abs days then the drinking days must therefore be mandatory drinking days or something silly like that.

It's good to ask before a drink, do I even feel like drinking? Do I really even want a drink? If one doesn't even feel like drinking then why bother?

CHAPTER NINE: *Coping With Life Without Relying on Booze*

"Drinking when you feel bad is bad drinking"

- **HAMS Element Seven: Learn To Cope Without Booze**

9.1 Booze Is a Coping Mechanism
9.2 The ABCs of RET
9.3 RET Worksheet
9.4 CBT - Change Your Thoughts to Change Your Moods
9.5 DBT - Dialectical Behavior Therapy
9.6 The Roots of RET, CBT, and DBT
9.7 Social Skills Training
9.8 Should I Consult a Professional?

9.1) Booze *Is* a Coping Mechanism

People use booze as a coping mechanism because--at least at first--it works. The problem is that farther down the road booze works less well. Eventually it can even turn around and bite you in the ass and start causing more problems than it was intended to solve in the first place. When this happens it may be time to make a change in your drinking habits.

Lots of Hamsters have found that the statement "Drinking when you feel bad is bad drinking" rings true for them. HAMS does not have a rule against using alcohol to cope with bad feelings like anxiety or depression--in fact there are no absolute rules in HAMS. From the harm reduction point of view all risks and harms are relative and the goal is to avoid the worst ones first. If your only coping method is alcohol then we have no intention of taking that away from you without providing you with new coping strategies: after all, being dead drunk is better than being dead. Booze is sometimes a suicide substitute. Moreover, there can be times when it is appropriate to drink such as at your best friend's wake.

However, many Hamsters find that learning and applying new coping strategies works better than booze for dealing with bad feelings. AA has a saying "HALT - when you feel Hungry, Angry, Lonely, or Tired, this is the time to stop and not drink". To this we could add "BAD - if you are Bored, Anxious or Depressed it can be a BAD time to drink." So **HALT BAD drinking**. Try to avoid alcohol if you are **Hungry, Angry, Lonely, Tired, Bored, Anxious, or Depressed**. Many people find that the quantities which they drink spiral out of control if they drink when they are angry or depressed or having other of these sorts of bad feelings. Sometimes actions also spiral out of control and people do bad things in a blackout which they later regret if they drink in feel-bad mode. This is why many Hamsters avoid drinking when they feel bad and tend to save alcohol to enhance good times rather than to cope with bad ones.

Rational Emotive Therapy (RET), Cognitive Behavioral Therapy (CBT) and **Dialectical Behavior Therapy (DBT)** all offer many good strategies for coping with life without having to rely on booze. Moreover, **RET, CBT**, and **DBT** are rooted in philosophical traditions which many people have found useful for achieving peace of mind and for developing coping skills.

For this reason we include a brief discussion of the roots of **RET, CBT**, and **DBT**. Many people also find that they become lonely or depressed because they have poor social skills. **Social Skills Training** can help such people to learn to relate better to others and improve the social aspect of their lives. We also briefly discuss this.

Many **RET, CBT, DBT**, and **Social Skills Techniques** can be self taught with the aid of books and exercises. We offer a brief introduction to these below along with resources that you can go to for more in-depth study of **RET, CBT, DBT**, and **Social Skills Techniques**. By the way, you don't have to commit to using just one of these therapeutic modalities. You can choose to mix and match techniques from all these sources if you wish.

Some people may also find that professional help is useful in helping them to learn to cope with life without using booze. Psychiatric medications such as antidepressants can also be useful aids to some people in learning to cope with life without relying on booze all the time. If you feel that you could benefit from more help than you find in books and HAMS groups alone, then we encourage you to seek the help of a professional as an integral part of your HAMS program. We discuss professional help and psychiatric medications in more detail in Chapter 10.

9.2) The ABCs of RET

Rational Emotive Therapy (RET) was invented by Albert Ellis in the 1950s. This was one of the earliest forms of Cognitive Behavioral Therapy and it is still a very useful one and an easy one to use for self-help. Rational Emotive Therapy expands on the behaviorist concept of Stimulus Response theory by saying that between every Stimulus and every Response there lies a set of Beliefs which help to determine what the response is. The basic core of RET can be summarized as follows:

- **An individual's Beliefs help determine how an individual will Respond to a Stimulus.**
- **Different Beliefs lead to different Responses to the same Stimulus.**
- **The role of therapy is to help the individual learn to Dispute irrational Beliefs which cause misery.**
- **The irrational Beliefs are replaced by rational Beliefs which lead to Responses which benefit rather than harm the individual**

Ellis calls the Stimulus the **Activating Event = A**

Beliefs = **B**

And Ellis calls the Response the **Consequent Action/Mood = C**

This is why Rational Emotive Therapy is sometimes referred to as **ABC Theory**.

Our self-talk reflects our beliefs. Let us look at an example of a guy who is jilted by his girlfriend. He begins giving himself the following self talk:

- "It is really terrible to be jilted by my girlfriend."
- "I cannot stand it that I was jilted by my girlfriend."

- "I want to kill myself if she does not come back."
- "I will never have a new girlfriend because all women will always jilt me."
- "Anyone who was jilted like me cannot help but feel depressed."
- "I deserve to be depressed because of what I have suffered."
- "No one has suffered as much as me."
- "I am so worthless that no woman could ever love me."
- "The fact that I was jilted proves that I am worthless."

Clearly this man is talking himself into feeling depressed and suicidal. It may be natural to mourn a loss like this for a day or so, but if it continues for weeks and months it can lead to clinical depression. The ABC theory of RET says that the way to overcome the depression is to replace this man's irrational self talk with rational self talk grounded in rational beliefs. First we will identify the **irrational parts** of these statements by emphasizing them with bold type.

- "It is **really terrible** to be jilted by my girlfriend."
- "I **cannot stand** it that I was jilted by my girlfriend."
- "**I want to kill myself** if she does not come back."
- "I will **never** have a new girlfriend because **all** women will **always** jilt me."
- "Anyone who was jilted like me **cannot help but** feel depressed."
- "I **deserve** to be depressed because of what I have suffered."
- "**No one** has suffered as much as me."
- "I am **so worthless** that **no woman** could ever love me."
- "The fact that I was jilted **proves that I am worthless**."

Ellis points out that it is irrational to exaggerate how bad our situation is by using words like **really terrible, cannot stand, so worthless,** and **I want to kill myself**. Sometimes this is referred to as "Awfulizing" or "Catastrophization". It is also irrational to overgeneralize by using words like **all, always, no one,** and **never**. It is impossible to make a general rule from a single instance. Finally, it is irrational to make "should statements" like "I **deserve** to be depressed". Ellis calls these irrational statements "Shoulding" or "Musturbation". Finally there is what Ellis calls "People Rating", which judges the whole value of a person based on a single trait or event. We see an example of this in the last sentence, "The fact that I was jilted **proves that I am worthless**."

So the four kinds of irrational thought which we discuss here are:

- **Awfulizing**- for example - **really terrible**
- **Overgeneralizing**- for example - **all, always, no one, never**
- **Shoulding**- for example - **I deserve, it has to, cannot help but, must**
- **People rating** - for example - **it proves that I am worthless**

We can use these labels to tag the sentences in the above examples like so:

- "It is **really terrible** to be jilted by my girlfriend." - **Awfulizing**
- "I **cannot stand** it that I was jilted by my girlfriend." - **Awfulizing**
- "**I want to kill myself** if she does not come back." - **Awfulizing**

- "I will **never** have a new girlfriend because **all** women will **always** jilt me." - **Overgeneralizing**
- "Anyone who was jilted like me **cannot help but** feel depressed." - **Shoulding**
- "I **deserve** to be depressed because of what I have suffered." - **Shoulding**
- "**No one** has suffered as much as me." - **Overgeneralizing**
- "I am **so worthless** that **no woman** could ever love me." - **Awfulizing, Overgeneralizing**
- "The fact that I was jilted **proves that I am worthless**." - **People rating**

Ellis says that most of the irrational self-talk that leads us into feeling miserable or acting in ways that we regret contains these four categories of ideas--and that when we learn to recognize self-talk statements that contain these four categories of ideas we can recognize that they are irrational. Once we recognize that these statements are irrational we can dispute them. And when we dispute them, then we can replace them with rational beliefs.

For example:

- "It is really terrible to be jilted by my girlfriend."

Can be disputed and replaced by

- "It was unpleasant to be jilted by my girlfriend but I can survive until I find a better girlfriend for me."

- "I will never have a new girlfriend because all women will always jilt me."

Can be disputed and replaced by

- "It is too bad that this particular woman jilted me but I can find another one who is better suited to me."

- "The fact that I was jilted proves that I am worthless."

Can be disputed and replaced by

- "The fact that this woman jilted me only proves that we were not compatible."

And so forth.

9.3) RET Worksheet
free download at http://hamsnetwork.org/worksheets

Now it is time for an exercise to practice what you have learned. Bill likes to drink after work every day. This is the self-talk that goes through Bill's head every day after work. Circle the irrational words in each statement and tag each statement as Awfulizing, Overgeneralizing, Shoulding, or People Rating. You might use more than one tag for some.

- **I had a hard day and I deserve a drink.** _____

- **I can't stand it if I can't have a drink.** _____

- **I have no way to tolerate this job unless I drink.** _____

- **Everyone has a drink after a hard day at work.** _____

- **Not drinking everyday is just awful.** _____

- **I can't help it that I drink because I am a powerless alcoholic.**

  _____

Now write a new rational statement to counter each of these irrational statements:

- **I had a hard day and I deserve a drink.**

- _____

- **I can't stand it if I can't have a drink.**

- _____

- **I have no way to tolerate this job unless I drink.**

- _____

- **Everyone has a drink after a hard day at work**

- _____

- **Not drinking everyday is just awful.**

- _____

- **I can't help it that I drink because I am a powerless alcoholic.**

- _____

77

If you practice being aware of and listening to your self-talk then you can learn to start overcoming these irrational statements. If you don't think that you hear any self-talk but instead you feel like you are just simply overwhelmed by a craving or an emotion, try sitting down and writing about it and very likely the self-talk will reveal itself as you write. Then you will be able to dispute it.

To learn more about using RET we recommend that you read:

A Guide to Rational Living by Albert Ellis and Robert A. Harper
How to Refuse to Make Yourself Miserable about Anything: Yes Anything! by Albert Ellis

If you feel that you need more help than is available in a self-help manual then you might want to consult with a therapist who specializes in RET.

RET is also sometimes called REBT--Rational Emotive Behavior Therapy--it is the same thing as RET.

9.4) CBT - Change Your Thoughts to Change Your Moods

Cognitive Behavioral Therapy (CBT) is a close relative of RET. Cognitive behavioral therapy works on the premise that moods follow thoughts--if you change your thinking you can change your mood. Specifically, CBT teaches that mood disorders such as chronic depression or anxiety are--at least in part--a result of bad thinking habits and irrational thinking habits. CBT teaches people to be aware of their thinking and to replace their negative or irrational thoughts with positive and rational ones. CBT alone or in conjunction with medication has proved a very powerful tool in helping people to overcome mood disorders such as chronic depression or anxiety or PTSD.

Many people who drink too much alcohol also have issues with anxiety, depression, social phobia, PTSD, etc. People who get these issues under better control often then find that it is much easier to control their alcohol use or to quit. The following CBT tools can help:

- **Staying in the present**
- **Observing your thoughts**
- **Thought stopping**
- **Recognizing the forms of twisted thinking**

Staying in the present

One type of negative thinking which can lead to depressed mood is constantly recalling negative events in the past. A type of negative thinking which can lead to anxiety is constant worry about the future. **Thought Stopping** is a technique which can be used to battle both these types of negative thinking and bring you back to living in the present.

Learning from the past and planning for the future are both essential life skills needed by human beings. But dwelling in the past or obsessing about the future can become maladaptive coping mechanisms which lead to paralysis instead of action. If you set aside ten minutes each day where you consciously plan for the future and another ten minutes where you sit down and consciously work to learn from the past then you are using these tools wisely. Limit yourself to these times and resolve to live in the present for the rest of the 24 hours.

Observing your thoughts

You may feel that your moods run out of control and have no connection with your thinking. However, if you begin to monitor your thoughts, you will find that very often certain thoughts precede your falling into anxiety or depression. Learning to observe your thoughts from the outside as though you were a third party can be a very useful tool for practicing CBT. When you become skillful at observing your thoughts from the outside then you can practice **Thought Stopping** when problematic thoughts arise.

Thought Stopping

Thought stopping works like this: whenever you find yourself dwelling on negative, unnecessary or distorted thoughts you consciously issue the command "Stop!" Then you replace the negative and distorted thoughts with positive and realistic ones. Thought stopping can also be used when you find yourself dwelling in the past or the future in order to bring you back into the present. You might want to shout the word "Stop" out loud. Some people even wear an elastic band around their wrist and snap themselves with it as a reminder to stop the negative thoughts.

Some cognitive distortions which can lead to depression or anxiety are: over-generalization, magnification, minimization labeling and catastrophizing. When you find you find yourself telling yourself that "nothing good ever happens" or "I am worthless" or "I am an alcoholic" or "the future is black", you can use thought stopping to stop these thoughts and to replace them with positive thoughts such as "all humans are worthwhile" or "I can control my drinking". Practice makes perfect. The more you do this the better you will get at it. When you stop playing those negative tapes in your head all the time you will start feeling better.

Recognizing the forms of twisted thinking

CBT teaches that there are a number of forms of negative and irrational thinking which you can learn to recognize and avoid. The following examples are adapted from David Burns:

1. All-or-nothing-thinking:

Seeing things in black-or-white categories. If a situation falls short of perfect, you see it as a total failure.

2. Overgeneralization:

Seeing a single negative event, such as a romantic rejection or a career reversal, as a never-ending pattern of defeat by using words such as "always" or "never" when you think about it.

3. Mental filter:

Picking out a single negative detail and dwell on it exclusively, so that your vision of all of reality becomes darkened.

4. Discounting the positive:

Rejecting positive experiences by insisting that they "don't count." If you do a good job, you tell yourself that it wasn't good enough.

5. Jumping to conclusions:

You interpret things negatively when there are no facts to support your conclusion.

5.1 Mind reading: Without checking it out first, you arbitrarily conclude that someone is reacting negatively to you.

5.2 Fortune-telling: You predict that things will turn out badly. Before a test you may tell yourself, "I'm really going to blow it. What if I flunk?" If you're depressed, you may tell yourself, "I'll never get better."

6. Magnification:

You exaggerate the importance of your problems and shortcomings, or you minimize the importance of your desirable qualities. This is also called the "binocular trick."

7. Emotional reasoning:

You assume that your negative emotions necessarily reflect the way things really are. For example: "I feel terrified about going on airplanes. Therefore, it must be very dangerous to fly."

8. "Should statements"

You tell yourself that things *should* be the way you hoped or expected them to be. After playing a difficult piece on the piano, a gifted pianist told herself, "I shouldn't have made so many mistakes." This made her feel so disgusted that she quit practicing for several days. "Musts," "oughts" and "have-tos" are similar offenders. "Should statements" that are directed against yourself lead to guilt and frustration. "Should statements" that are directed against other people or the world in general lead to anger and frustration. "He shouldn't be so stubborn and argumentative." Many people try to motivate themselves with shoulds and shouldn'ts, as if they were delinquents who had to be punished before they could be expected to do anything. "I shouldn't eat that doughnut." This usually doesn't work because all these shoulds and musts make you feel rebellious and you get the urge to do just the opposite.

9. Labeling:

Labeling is an extreme form of all-or-nothing thinking. Instead of saying "I made a mistake," you attach a negative label to yourself: "I'm a loser." These labels are just useless abstractions that lead to anger, anxiety, frustration, and low self-esteem. You may also label others. This is also harmful.

10. Personalization and blame:

Personalization occurs when you hold yourself personally responsible for an event that isn't entirely under your control. Personalization leads to guilt, shame, and feelings of inadequacy. Some people blame others or their circumstances for their problems, and they overlook ways that they might be contributing to the problem: "My disease of alcoholism makes me beat my wife, I cannot help it."

Why Do We Think This Way?

Making snap judgments based on minimal information was a survival trait back in the early days of man's evolution. In those days we had to evaluate everything in terms of flight or fight--eat or be eaten. What was a survival trait in primitive man has now sometimes become a problem trait leading to unhappiness in modern civilized man.

Further Reading:

We have just given you a taste of CBT here. If you feel that these CBT exercises are helpful you might want to study CBT more in depth. If so we highly recommend the following books:

Feeling Good: The New Mood Therapy Revised and Updated by David D. Burns
The Feeling Good Handbook by David D. Burns
Mind Over Mood: Change How You Feel by Changing the Way You Think by Dennis Greenberger and Christine Padesky

9.5) DBT - The Marriage of Opposites

Dialectical Behavior Therapy (DBT) was developed by Marsha Linehan for the treatment of Borderline Personality Disorder, but DBT concepts have been found useful in many other areas as well. DBT has strong ties with CBT.

A central idea of **Dialectical Behavior Therapy (DBT)** is the **Dialectic**. When two different ideas meet each other and merge together to form a new idea--this is an example of the Dialectic. When two opposing forces meet each other and merge to create a new force--this is also an example of the Dialectic. The Dialectic is about the synthesis of opposing forces or ideas. It is about the marriage of opposites. The dialectic can be illustrated as follows:

Thesis + Antithesis => Synthesis

There are many examples of the marriage of two opposites to create a new synthesis in DBT--for example:

- **Eastern Philosophy** meets **Western Psychotherapy** to create **a new form of psychotherapy: DBT**
- **Radical Self-Acceptance** meets **Desire To Change** to produce **Change in the Client**
- **Individual** meets **Environment** to **Develop coping skills**

DBT concentrates on teaching clients the following skills:

- **Distress tolerance skills**
- **Radical acceptance**
- **Interpersonal effectiveness skills**
- **Mindfulness skills**
- **Emotion regulation skills**

Here are some ways that these skills can apply to us drinkers:

Distress tolerance skills

Many of the DBT Distress Tolerance Skills can be directly applied to helping you to achieve some alcohol-free time. When you have the urge to drink--don't just sit there and try to fight it by saying "I will not drink." This is a willpower-based method which generally tends not to be very effective. Instead, try applying some of the DBT Distress Tolerance Skills such as:

- **Distract yourself** with a movie, a novel, watching a sporting event, doing volunteer work, going out for a meal, etc.
- **Sooth your senses** by buying a beautiful flower for your room, eating ice cream, listening to a symphony, etc.
- **Improve the moment** without resorting to alcohol by taking a hot bath, getting a massage, doing muscle relaxation exercises, focusing on the moment, etc.
- Calmly consider the **pros and cons** of abstaining from alcohol or drinking
- **Count your breaths**
- **Half smile** whenever the thought of alcohol crosses your mind.
- Use **Awareness**: make a pot of tea or coffee and be aware of every movement you make, the feel of the handle, the smell--concentrate on 100% awareness. Do the same for washing dishes, sweeping a floor, etc.

Radical Acceptance

Linehan treats Radical Acceptance as a part of Distress Tolerance. This is the acceptance definition that she gives to clients:

- Freedom from suffering requires ACCEPTANCE from deep within. It is allowing yourself to go completely with whatever the situation is. Let go of fighting reality.
- ACCEPTANCE is the only way out of hell which must not be interpreted as approval of the distressful situation
- Pain creates suffering only when you refuse to ACCEPT the pain.
- Deciding to tolerate the moment is ACCEPTANCE.
- ACCEPTANCE is acknowledging what is.
- To ACCEPT something is not the same as judging it to be good.

Interpersonal Effectiveness Skills

DBT Interpersonal Effectiveness Skills can help improve your relationships with others. When your relationships with others run more smoothly, there is less reason to indulge in alcohol because you are upset over relationship problems. A way to remember DBT Interpersonal Skills is with the acronym DEAR--as in the following example:

- **Describe the current interaction** "You keep asking me over and over again even though I have already said no." Avoid blaming the other person...i.e. don't say "you just don't want to hear me"
- **Express your opinions/feelings of discomfort about the interaction** I'm not sure that you understand what I am asking" I'm starting to feel angry about this."
- **Assert your wishes** When the other person is refusing a request, suggest that you put off the conversation to another time. Give the person another chance to think about it. When the other person is pestering you, ask them to stop
- **Reinforce** When saying no to someone who keeps asking....suggest that you end the conversation because you aren't going to change your mind anyway

This is just a small taste of DBT Skills Training. For further reading on DBT we strongly recommend:

Skills Training Manual for Treating Borderline Personality Disorder, Marsha M. Linehan
Dialectical Behavior Therapy Skills Workbook, Matthew McKay, Jeffrey C. Wood, and Jeffrey Brantley
Cognitive-Behavioral Treatment of Borderline Personality Disorder, Marsha Linehan

9.6) The Roots of RET, CBT, and DBT

Therapeutic concepts from both RET and CBT can be traced back to Greco-Roman Stoic philosophy. Sometimes people today give the word "stoicism" a bad rap because they think it means repressing one's emotions. However, this is quite different from what the early Stoic Philosophers taught. Early Stoic philosophers like Epictetus taught that even though people could not always control external events--they could control their reactions to external events. People who became masters of their own minds and their own thoughts could be happy in their own minds regardless of external events. As Shakespeare said, "There is nothing good or bad, but thinking makes it so."

People who use RET, DBT, or CBT may find that reading The Handbook (Enchiridion) of Epictetus is a very useful adjunct to their therapy. This short little manual of less than 50 pages is about becoming the master of your own mind. It is pithy, so we suggest that you read just a little bit per day.

Dr. Albert Ellis, considered the "grandfather of cognitive-behavioral therapy" (CBT), has written, "Many of the principles incorporated in the theory of rational-emotive psychotherapy are not new; some of them, in fact, were originally stated several thousands of years ago, especially by the Greek and Roman Stoic philosophers (such as Epictetus and Marcus Aurelius)."

DBT has roots in CBT and also in Zen Buddhism. Those of you using DBT may be interested in reading The Miracle of Mindfulness: A Manual on Meditation by Thich Nhat Hanh and Zen Mind, Beginner's Mind by Shunryu Suzuki.

9.7) Social Skills Training

Dale Carnegie's book <u>How To Win Friends And Influence People</u> could easily have been called Social Skills 101. This is a book which can train you to use basic social skills when dealing with others. If you treat others well and with respect then it will naturally come back to you. Why don't we treat others well? Usually it is not because we have bad hearts. Usually it is because we lack the skills and training--somehow we failed to acquire these basics when we were growing up. Good social skills can be learned. Learning good social skills can enrich you in every way. DBT also concentrates on social skills and is a good source for learning them.

Carnegie's "nutshell" summaries will give you an idea of the content of the book:

In a Nutshell - Fundamental Techniques In Handling People
• Principle 1 - Don't criticize, condemn or complain.
• Principle 2 - Give honest and sincere appreciation.
• Principle 3 - Arouse in the other person an eager want.

In a Nutshell - Six Ways To Make People Like You
• Principle 1 - Become genuinely interested in other people.
• Principle 2 - Smile.
• Principle 3 - Remember that a person's name is to that person the sweetest and most important sound in any language.
• Principle 4 - Be a good listener. Encourage others to talk about themselves.
• Principle 5 - Talk in terms of the other person's interests.
• Principle 6 - Make the other person feel important-and do it sincerely.

In A Nutshell - Win People To Your Way Of Thinking
• Principle 1 - The only way to get the best of an argument is to avoid it.
• Principle 2 - Show respect for the other person's opinions. Never say, "You're wrong."
• Principle 3 - If you are wrong, admit it quickly and emphatically.
• Principle 4 - Begin in a friendly way.
• Principle 5 - Get the other person saying "yes, yes" immediately.
• Principle 6 - Let the other person do a great deal of the talking.
• Principle 7 - Let the other person feel that the idea is his or hers.
• Principle 8 - Try honestly to see things from the other person's point of view.
• Principle 9 - Be sympathetic with the other person's ideas and desires.
• Principle 10 - Appeal to the nobler motives.
• Principle 11 - Dramatize your ideas.
• Principle 12 - Throw down a challenge.

And many more.

What makes Carnegie's book so valuable is that he gives concrete example after concrete example of how to use these skills and make them work. No wonder it is still a bestseller after all these years.

People may also find that participating in a live or online HAMS group is a safe and supportive way of working on their social skills. Particularly, online groups can help people build up courage and skills to deal with live encounters.

Recommended reading for Social Skills Training:

How To Win Friends And Influence People, by Dale Carnegie
Etiquette for Dummies, by Sue Fox

9.8) Should I Consult a Professional?

For many people self-help alone may be enough to arm them with the coping skills necessary to deal with alcohol and get on with life. However, many others may find that self-help alone just isn't cutting it. If you feel the need for medication or professional help then by all means go for it! We will discuss this in more depth in the next chapter.

CHAPTER TEN: Alcohol and Outside Issues

"Work is the curse of the drinking class." --Oscar Wilde

- **HAMS Element Eight: Address outside issues that affect drinking**

10.1) Outside Issues Impact Drinking!

Heavy drinking does not occur in a vacuum. The more that researchers learn about heavy drinking and heavy drinkers, the more it seems that there may be no such thing as a "primary disease of alcoholism." Drinking is always connected with many issues in our lives. Most if not all of us will have to address not only the issue of alcohol, but also outside issues which are intimately connected with our drinking. We will look at some of these issues and some ways to address them in this chapter.

Some of the issues that have a major impact on our drinking are more than we can deal with using the simple coping skills that we talked about in the last chapter. Sometimes people need psychiatric medications or a professional psychotherapist to help them deal with their mental health issues. Getting help with mental health issues can make it much easier to deal with your drinking.

There are many other issues that can have an impact on your drinking, ranging from your financial health to your sex life to your social life to insomnia--all of these can have a major effect on your alcohol use. If you have problems in these areas then you might wish to seek the help of a professional. These issues are beyond the scope of the HAMS program, but you are more than welcome to talk about them in HAMS groups--we will cheer you on as you seek solutions for them. Sometimes the simple act of talking a problem out can help you to find a solution to it. Therefore, HAMS welcomes you to discuss whatever it is that you need to talk about whenever you need to talk about it.

10.2 Mental Health

10.2.1 Alcohol and Mental Health - The Basics

US government surveys show that over a third of people with a diagnosable alcohol problem also have a diagnosable mental health problem. 13.4% have a **Mood Disorder** such as **Major Depression** or **Manic Depressive (Bipolar) Disorder**. 19.4% have an **Anxiety Disorder** such as **Generalized Anxiety Disorder**, **PTSD**, or **Social Phobia**. 14.3% have **Antisocial Personality Disorder** and 3.8% have **Schizophrenia** or **Schizophreniform Disorders** (Reiger et al 1990). Researchers note that people with **Borderline Personality Disorder** (DSM-IV-TR) or **Eating Disorders** (CASA, 2003) also frequently have major alcohol problems, although these have not yet been investigated been investigated by US government surveys.

HAMS offers some self-help information about ways to cope with things like depression, anxiety, or social phobia in Chapter 9 of this book. Some people might find these self-help strategies adequate for dealing with their issues, but others may find that they need more than self-help alone. Both medications and psychotherapy can be great aids to many people who have issues with alcohol and mental health. We give a brief overview of some of these issues and their treatments in this section.

10.2.2 Finding a Psychotherapist

Research by harm reduction therapists like Dr. Andrew Tatarsky and Dr. Patt Denning has clearly demonstrated that when people have both mental health issues and issues with drugs or alcohol, the most productive path is to work on both the mental health issues the chemical health issues simultaneously. Research has clearly demonstrated that abstinence from alcohol is not a necessary condition for a person to benefit from psychotherapy. Showing up to a psychotherapist appointment drunk is not desirable, but most clients will work at improving their drinking habits because they are motivated by the desire for improved mental health and happier lives. As progress occurs in chemical health, a parallel progress takes place in mental health.

It is unfortunate that some psychotherapists today still subscribe to the myth that it is impossible to do psychotherapy with a client unless that client is totally abstinent from all drugs and alcohol. This myth originated in the 12 step alcoholism treatment industry; however, it has no basis in fact. Hence, therapists who refuse psychotherapy to clients who are seeking psychotherapy and who refer them to 12 step programs instead are doing their clients a great disservice. Moreover, scientific research shows that both Cognitive Behavioral Therapies and Psychodynamic Therapies are more effective in helping clients to improve their drinking habits than are 12 step programs (Brandsma et al, 1980).

You might have to shop around quite a bit to find a therapist who understands the importance of harm reduction psychotherapy and of working on alcohol issues and mental health issues in tandem. And if you absolutely cannot find a therapist who is up to date and knows the score--you may just have to keep silent on the issue of your drinking and talk to your therapist only about your mental health issues.

Good luck in your search!!

Types of Therapy

The two most common types of therapy you will find available today are Cognitive Behavioral approaches and Psychodynamic approaches. Both approaches show good effectiveness--we suggest that you choose the style of therapy which you feel fits you the best.

Cognitive Behavioral approaches tend to be focused on the present--they work on the premise that changing your thoughts will change your mood. Some popular forms of this approach are Rational Emotive Therapy (RET), Cognitive Behavioral Therapy (CBT) and Dialectical Behavior Therapy (DBT). These approaches can be done with a therapist or by using a self-help book. We discussed them in some detail in the previous chapter.

Psychodynamic approaches tend to look into the past and try to get at root causes of your problems. These approaches range from traditional Freudian psychoanalysis to the approaches of Jung, Adler and Horney. Psychodynamic approaches are generally done with a therapist rather than as self-help. There is evidence which suggests that Psychodynamic approaches which are effective with alcohol problems tend to be more directive and more active than traditional Freudian approaches (Tatarsky, 2001).

10.2.3 Alcohol and Antidepressants

Do Antidepressants Cause People To Drink More Or To Drink Less?

Studies have shown that antidepressants can significantly reduce both alcohol consumption and the symptoms of depression in heavy drinkers who suffer from Major Depressive Disorder (Cornelius et al 1997). However, studies have also shown that antidepressants might lead to an **INCREASE** in alcohol consumption in individuals who do not suffer from depression or in individuals who only suffer from minor depression. This tendency towards increased alcohol consumption appears to be particularly pronounced in women (Naranjo et al 1995, Graham et al 2007) and in very heavy drinkers (Kranzler et al 1996).

At HAMS we recommend that our members be proactive healthcare consumers. Often doctors and psychiatrists are unaware of, or badly misinformed about, issues which affect drinkers, therefore we recommend that our members arm themselves with knowledge. If you do not suffer from depression it is probably a good idea to avoid antidepressants. These are not happy pills to be handed out every time that someone stubs their toe. In particular, if you are going through a period of mourning such as results from the death of a loved one it is probably more healthy to mourn and deal with the reality of the situation than to try and take happy pills to overcome it.

However, if you really do suffer from Major Depression then antidepressants may be just the ticket to get your drinking under control. Give them a try for a month. If they work, great! If they don't, then move on and try something else. In particular, if your antidepressants seem to make you drink more, then it may be a good idea to stop taking them. Everyone is different and not every medication works for every person. You may have to taper off of your antidepressants to get off them safely if you have been taking them for some length of time.

Do You Have To Stop Drinking For Antidepressants To Be Effective?

Some people say that "Because alcohol is a depressant it blocks the effects of antidepressants." This is not scientifically correct. Alcohol is called a depressant because it slows down the central nervous system, not because it causes people to become depressed. In this case the opposite of a depressant is a stimulant, not an antidepressant. Depressed people often drink because alcohol makes them feel better as long as they are intoxicated. However, they may be even more depressed the morning after.

Although long term heavy drinking can produce symptoms of depression (Raimo and Schuckit1998, Swendsen and Merikangas 2000), this is not evidence that alcohol blocks the effects of antidepressants. The only way to know for sure whether or not alcohol actually blocks the effect of a given antidepressant is to run a clinical trial. Unfortunately, there have been very few clinical trials of the effect of alcohol on antidepressants. So we simply do not know if alcohol reduces the effectiveness of most antidepressants.

One exception is the antidepressant imipramine. Imipramine has been proven in clinical trials to be effective in reducing depression in heavy drinkers who continued to drink as always without reducing their alcohol intake (McGrath et al 1996).

Are Antidepressants Addictive?

Yes and no. Two of the major criteria for deciding whether a substance is addictive are craving and withdrawal. When people quit substance like alcohol or heroin which induce euphoria, they often have both craving and withdrawal symptoms. On the other hand, when people quit things like gambling or marijuana there is craving but no physical withdrawal. But when people quit antidepressants, there is often no craving, but there are frequently severe withdrawal symptoms.

Because of the possibility of severe and dangerous withdrawal syndrome, people are advised to taper off of antidepressants rather than quitting them cold turkey. And since people who take antidepressants are at risk of these withdrawal symptoms we advise people to think carefully and use caution before they decide to start taking antidepressants. It is not responsible medical practice to hand out antidepressants like they were candy every time someone has a stubbed toe.

Since people do not crave antidepressants after they quit using them it is probably best to say that antidepressants are atypically addictive. The same could be said of gambling and marijuana-- they are atypically addictive.

Withdrawal symptoms from quitting antidepressants cold turkey can include:

> flu-like symptoms, anxiety, dizziness, fatigue, headache, migraine-like feelings, nerves jangling when moving eyes, continuous indigestion, neck and back pain, psychotic features such as visual and/or auditory hallucinations/illusions, insomnia, nausea, restlessness, "electrical shock" like phenomena/electrical surges or shocks through the head and/or body, hyper-sensitivity of the nervous system to light, sound, colors & stressors, tremors, tinnitus and a vertiginous-like experience, depressive thoughts, suicidal thoughts, homicidal thoughts, extreme anger, severe agitation, extreme irritability, "over-reacting", ringing in ears and throbbing in head, vomiting, paranoia, aggressive behavior, rollercoaster emotions rapidly following up on each other, out of character behavior, severe malaise, general dysphoria, derealization, panic attacks.

Can Long Term Heavy Drinking Cause Depression?

Yes, research confirms that long term heavy drinking can cause depression (Raimo and Schuckit1998, Swendsen and Merikangas 2000). However, in this case, quitting drinking or reducing alcohol intake to a more reasonable level is sufficient to cure the alcohol-induced depression. Antidepressants are normally unnecessary.

10.2.4 Alcohol and Other Psych Meds

People who suffer from Anxiety Disorders, Social Phobia, or Panic Disorders frequently use alcohol for the purpose of self medication. Benzodiazepines such as Klonopin, Xanax, Valium, Librium, Ativan, etc. are frequently prescribed for these disorders. However, it is important to remember that it can be dangerous to mix benzodiazepines with alcohol--this can lead to respiratory depression and death. BuSpar is an anti-anxiety medication which does not have a negative interaction with alcohol. If you are afraid that you might take your anti-anxiety medication while you are intoxicated, then BuSpar might be a safer choice than benzodiazepines. For more information about drug and alcohol interactions please see Appendix One: Alcohol and Drug Interactions.

10.3 Financial Health

10.3.1 Financial Health Basics

Walking around with a ton of debt, not knowing how you will eat or pay rent tomorrow, and having a threat of an eviction hanging over your head is not conducive to peace of mind. HAMS is not a financial advisor and it is beyond the scope of our program to deal with these issues. What we can do is to listen while you talk them through and to cheerlead as you seek solutions. Sometimes you can make a plan to regain financial health on your own or with a book; sometimes you will find that you need the help of a credit repair agency or other professional.

10.3.2 Employment

Many employment factors can affect our drinking. Having to go to a lousy job that one hates can drive one to drink. So can being unemployed. Showing up at work reeking of booze from the night before is a definite problem for many employers.

HAMS cannot offer you professional employment counseling. However, a HAMS group is a safe place where you can talk through your issues surrounding employment. Sometimes simply talking things through can help to suggest a solution.

10.3.3 Homelessness

Studies show that there is a high rate of substance use problems among people who are homeless and there is an even greater correlation between homelessness, substance problems and mental health problems. The traditionalist view from the temperance movement is that alcohol is to blame. AA just views this as another aspect of the "alcoholic" "hitting bottom".

Yet there is no evidence of unidirectional causality between alcohol use and homelessness. Many homeless people report that their drinking increased greatly or went out of control after they hit the street, not before. This is not surprising, because the poor quality of life associated with living on the street is enough to drive anyone to drink. No one is immune from homelessness in America today--it could strike anyone who has a run of very bad luck.

All the evidence seems to point to the conclusion that the relationship between heavy drinking and homelessness is bidirectional--that each factor tends to increase the likelihood of the other. Ditto for mental health problems.

Housing issues and drinking issues are items to be worked on in tandem--telling people that they are not allowed to have shelter unless they quit drinking for good does not work. Banning people from a homeless shelter for a month for showing up intoxicated and sending them out onto the street in 20 below weather is inhumanity bordering on murder.

There are rational approaches to the problem such as the Annex Harm Reduction Program at Seaton House in Toronto, Canada where street alcoholics are given shelter, food, and alcohol--which beats drinking mouthwash and sleeping on the street. Would that America could adopt some of the rational approaches found in Canada.

Homeless people need to work on housing and alcohol issues together.

10.4 Isolation and Socialization

A lot of people who drink too much have issues with too much isolation and not enough socialization. It really does not matter which came first--the chicken or the egg. The fact is that a lot of times when people feel lonely they will turn to the bottle for solace. Some people drink to forget that they are lonely. Some people drink to loosen up and make it easier to talk to others. But for many people, drinking too much can cause them to lose their friends, strain their relations with their families, or even lead to divorce. Often the lonelier a person is the more that the person wants to drink. And the more that the person drinks, the more the person isolates, and the more friends that the person loses. Just quitting drinking often does not cure this--because often when people quit alcohol they feel miserable and don't want to socialize with anyone.

If you are the kind of a person who is happiest when alone and does not need the company of others then we do not have a desire to change you--different strokes for different folks. But if you are not, then there are things you can do to fulfill your socialization needs.

Some people are very shy or have social phobia which makes it difficult for them to talk to new people or to almost anyone at all. For some people the internet can be a way to talk with strangers that is safer than meeting people face to face. This can be a good thing because it can help people to build up courage to later on meet people face to face. Online friendships can be as important is real life friendships--sometimes they can even become real life friendships.

The following is a list of some of the possibilities of things that you can do to increase your social contact with other people:

- **Attend HAMS meetings--live or online**

- **Join Toastmasters**
- **Volunteer at a soup kitchen, needle exchange or other program that helps others**
- **Join a church**
- **Join an atheist society**
- **Find a book club**
- **Join a Yahoo or Google email group about a topic you love**
- **Get on eHarmony or match.com and find a date**
- **Get a roommate**

If you have a persistent social phobia which resists your attempts to overcome it using self-help methods, you may wish to see a professional about it. Social phobia can be successfully treated with medications, cognitive behavioral therapy (CBT), or both combined.

10.5) Legal Problems

Having legal problems hanging over your head can be a constant source of stress and a constant reason to drink. Getting a lawyer to help settle them for good can be far better than having them hang overhead like a sword of Damocles. Taking care of your legal problems can potentially take a big load off of your mind and leave you feeling a lot better, as well as leaving you better off in the long run.

10.6) Sexual Health

A World Health Organization (WHO) working group defined sexual health as "a state of physical, emotional, mental and social well-being in relation to sexuality; it is not merely the absence of disease, dysfunction or infirmity. Sexual health requires a positive and respectful approach to sexuality and sexual relationships, as well as the possibility of having pleasurable and safe sexual experiences, free of coercion, discrimination and violence. For sexual health to be attained and maintained, the sexual rights of all persons must be respected, protected and fulfilled."

There is no question that sexual problems--ranging from the inability to find a partner to erectile dysfunction to premature ejaculation to feeling uncomfortable with one's own sexuality--can drive a person to drink. A good sex therapist can help with these issues. So can some good books.

Recommended reading:

Sexual Healing: The Complete Guide to Overcoming Common Sexual Problems by Barbara Keesling Ph.D.
The Complete Idiot's Guide to Dating, 3rd Edition by Dr. Judy Kuriansky
Dating For Dummies by Joy Browne
Relationships for Dummies by Kate M. Wachs

10.7) Insomnia

A lot of people who have insomnia wind up using alcohol as a sleep aid because it is readily available. Although alcohol can work as a sleep aid for a while, in the long run it starts having a lot of negative side effects which make it a quite poor choice for a sleep aid. Alcohol decreases your dream sleep (REM sleep), which you need to be well rested. Small quantities of alcohol can lead to people waking up in the middle of the night. Large doses of alcohol can lead to major hangovers and oversleeping. Large doses can also lead to people waking up still intoxicated and going into work still intoxicated from the night before--which can lead to job loss, DUIs, and other very bad things.

Even people who did not have insomnia before they became heavy drinkers may find that they have insomnia when they attempt to quit drinking. The good news is that this insomnia generally goes away after you have been alcohol-free for a few days. Taking vitamins to restore the vitamins which were depleted by alcohol use can also help to clear up this insomnia.

People with persistent insomnia have the option of treating it with over the counter (OTC) medications, prescription medications, a non-pharmaceutical approach, or a combo of these methods.

The FDA has approved three over the counter (OTC) antihistamines for use as sleep aids

- diphenhydramine hydrochloride
- diphenhydramine citrate
- doxylamine

The FDA has not approved any other over the counter (OTC) medications for use as sleep aids.

Diphenhydramine hydrochloride is the chemical name for Benadryl. Diphenhydramine hydrochloride is not dangerous if mixed with alcohol although this combo will increase drowsiness, so be careful. Diphenhydramine hydrochloride is used as a stand-alone medication, whereas diphenhydramine citrate is used when the diphenhydramine is to be mixed with a pain reliever like in Tylenol PM or Advil PM. Other than that, diphenhydramine hydrochloride and diphenhydramine citrate are for all intents and purposes identical.

WARNING: Because of the danger of liver damage and liver failure, people who drink alcohol should AVOID products like Tylenol or Tylenol PM which contain acetaminophen (also known as Paracetamol).

Prescription sleep aids

It is unfortunate that some doctors are unwilling to prescribe prescription sleep aids because they think that they might be "addictive"--most of today's prescription sleep aids such as Ambien or Lunesta will do a hell of a lot less damage to the body than drinking a fifth of whiskey to get to sleep every night. And they are less addicting, too. If your doctor acts like a jackass when you ask him for a prescription sleep aid then it is time to find a new doctor.

Some of the more common prescription sleep aids used today are:

- Ambien

- Lunesta
- Remeron
- Trazadone

It is generally a good idea to AVOID alcohol when using prescription sleep aids. Ambien is notorious for causing blackouts and brownouts when mixed with alcohol. Alcohol can also lower the lethal half-dose of these medications making it more likely that you could overdose when taking them. As we see in Chapter 21, over 80% of deaths by alcohol poisoning are the result of mixing alcohol with medications.

Dietary supplements used as sleep aids

Melatonin

Melatonin is a neurotransmitter which occurs naturally in the human brain. Melatonin is concerned with the regulation of the sleep/wake cycle. Clinical trials have demonstrated that melatonin is effective in helping people who have difficulty falling asleep. Because of its short half life, however, regular melatonin is not useful for people who have a problem with waking up too early (Buscemi et al 2005, 2006). Controlled release melatonin may overcome this difficulty and be helpful for people who suffer from early waking or poor quality sleep (Wade et al 2007).

Valerian and hops

Herbalists have long prescribed valerian root and hops as sleep aids. Clinical trials of a valerian hops combo suggest that it is an effective sleep aid--valerian and hops taken together appear to be more effective than either taken alone (Koetter, 2007).

A number of people have also reported that valerian works well when taken together with melatonin, because the melatonin helps them to fall asleep and the valerian helps them to stay asleep. These anecdotal claims have not yet been investigated with clinical trials.

Treating insomnia without using sleeping pills

Light therapy

Exposure to bright light immediately on waking up can help to regulate the sleep wake cycle by stimulating production of melatonin in the brain. Light therapy boxes are sometimes used for this purpose.

Eleven tips for better sleep

1. Go to bed and get up at about the same time every day, even on the weekends.
2. Don't eat or drink large amounts before bedtime.
3. Avoid nicotine, caffeine and alcohol in the evening.
4. Exercise regularly during the daytime.
5. Make your bedroom cool, dark, quiet and comfortable.
6. Sleep primarily at night.
7. Choose a comfortable mattress and pillow.

8. Start a relaxing bedtime routine--this may include taking a warm bath or shower, reading a book, or listening to soothing music.
9. Go to bed when you're tired and turn out the lights.
10. Don't agonize over falling asleep--the stress will only prevent sleep.
11. Reserve your bed for sleeping.

10.8) Spousal Abuse

If you are being abused by your spouse--using alcohol to numb yourself out is not a very effective solution. Here are some things that you can do:

- Contact the National Domestic Violence Hotline 1.800.799.SAFE http://www.ndvh.org
- Call 911 if you are in immediate danger
- Go to family court and ask for referral to a battered women's shelter and a restraining order
- Leave now if you or your children are in danger

10.9) Physical Health

We recommend that anyone who chooses to drink alcohol get an annual physical check up including a liver panel. The liver has a great capacity for regeneration if problems are caught early. Once cirrhosis develops, however, it is too late. We also strongly recommend that everyone who drinks alcohol take a multivitamin and B1 supplements to replace vitamins lost because of drinking. A shortage of B1 can lead to brain damage.

People who have issues with chronic pain sometimes turn to alcohol as a painkiller. There is an effort today to make sure that doctors prescribe painkillers to those who really need them and not withhold necessary medicine based on old wives tales about addiction.

REFERENCES:

Brandsma JM, Maultsby MC, Welsh RJ. (1980). Outpatient treatment of alcoholism: A review and comparative study. Baltimore: University Park Press.

Buscemi N, Vandermeer B, Hooton N, Pandya R, Tjosvold L, Hartling L, Baker G, Klassen TP, Vohra S. (2005). The efficacy and safety of exogenous melatonin for primary sleep disorders. A meta-analysis. J Gen Intern Med. 20(12), 1151-8.
PubMed Abstract:
http://www.ncbi.nlm.nih.gov/pubmed/16423108
Free Full Text:
http://www.pubmedcentral.nih.gov/picrender.fcgi?artid=1490287&blobtype=pdf

Buscemi N, Vandermeer B, Hooton N, Pandya R, Tjosvold L, Hartling L, Vohra S, Klassen TP, Baker G. (2006). Efficacy and safety of exogenous melatonin for secondary sleep disorders and sleep disorders accompanying sleep restriction: meta-analysis. BMJ. 332(7538), 385-93.
PubMed Abstract:
http://www.ncbi.nlm.nih.gov/pubmed/16473858
Free Full Text:

http://www.bmj.com/cgi/reprint/332/7538/385.pdf

CASA. (2003). Food for Thought: Substance Abuse and Eating Disorders
http://www.casacolumbia.org/absolutenm/articlefiles/380-Food%20for%20Thought.pdf
Accessed January 7, 2010

Cornelius JR, Salloum IM, Ehler JG, Jarrett PJ, Cornelius MD, Perel JM, Thase ME, Black A.
(1997). Fluoxetine in depressed alcoholics: a double-blind, placebo-controlled trial. Archives of
General Psychiatry, 54, 700-5.
PubMed Abstract:
http://www.ncbi.nlm.nih.gov/pubmed/9283504

Denning, Patt, (2000). Practicing harm reduction psychotherapy: an alternative approach to
addictions. New York. Guilford Press.

Diagnostic and Statistical Manual of Mental Disorders (DSM-IV-TR). (2000). Arlington
Virginia. American Psychiatric Association.

Folsom DP, Hawthorne W, Lindamer L, Gilmer T, Bailey A, Golshan S, Garcia P, Unützer J,
Hough R, Jeste DV. (2005). Prevalence and risk factors for homelessness and utilization of
mental health services among 10,340 patients with serious mental illness in a large public mental
health system. Am J Psychiatry. 162(2), 370-6.
PubMed Abstract:
http://www.ncbi.nlm.nih.gov/pubmed/15677603
Free Full Text:
http://ajp.psychiatryonline.org/cgi/reprint/162/2/370.pdf

Graham, K, Massak, A. (2007). Alcohol consumption and the use of antidepressants. CMAJ.
176(5), 633-7.
PubMed Abstract:
http://www.ncbi.nlm.nih.gov/pubmed/17325328
Free Full Text:
http://www.cmaj.ca/cgi/reprint/176/5/633.pdf

Koetter U, Schrader E, Käufeler R, Brattström A. (2007). A randomized, double blind, placebo-
controlled, prospective clinical study to demonstrate clinical efficacy of a fixed valerian hops
extract combination (Ze 91019) in patients suffering from non-organic sleep disorder. Phytother
Res. 21(9):847-51.
PubMed Abstract:
http://www.ncbi.nlm.nih.gov/pubmed/17486686

Kranzler HR, Burleson JA, Korner P, Del Boca FK, Bohn MJ, Brown J, Liebowitz N. (1995).
Placebo-controlled trial of fluoxetine as an adjunct to relapse prevention in alcoholics. American
Journal of Psychiatry, 152, 391-397.
PubMed Abstract:
http://www.ncbi.nlm.nih.gov/pubmed/7864265

Kranzler HR, Burleson JA, Brown J, Babor TF. (1996). Fluoxetine treatment seems to reduce the beneficial effects of cognitive-behavioral therapy in type B alcoholics. Alcoholism: Clinical and Experimental Research, 20, 1534-41.
PubMed Abstract:
http://www.ncbi.nlm.nih.gov/pubmed/8986200

McGrath PJ, Nunes EV, Stewart JW, Goldman D, Agosti V, Ocepek-Welikson K, Quitkin FM. (1996). Imipramine treatment of alcoholics with primary depression: A placebo-controlled clinical trial. Arch Gen Psychiatry. 53(3), 232-40.
PubMed Abstract:
http://www.ncbi.nlm.nih.gov/pubmed/8611060

Naranjo CA, Bremner KE, Lanctot KL. (1995). Effects of Citalopram and a brief psycho-social intervention on alcohol intake, dependence and problems. Addiction, 90, 87-99.
PubMed Abstract:
http://www.ncbi.nlm.nih.gov/pubmed/7888983

Pettinati HM, Volpicelli JR, Kranzler HR, Luck G, Rukstalis MR, Cnaan A. (2000). Sertraline treatment for alcohol dependence: interactive effects of medication and alcoholic subtype. Alcoholism: Clinical and Experimental Research, 24(7), 1041-9.
PubMed Abstract:
http://www.ncbi.nlm.nih.gov/pubmed/10924008

Raimo EB, Schuckit MA. (1998). Alcohol dependence and mood disorders. Addict Behav. 23(6), 933-46.
PubMed Abstract:
http://www.ncbi.nlm.nih.gov/pubmed/9801727

Regier DA, Farmer ME, Rae DS, Locke BZ, Keith SJ, Judd LL, Goodwin FK. (1990). Comorbidity of Mental Disorders With Alcohol and Other Drug Abuse: Results From the Epidemiologic Catchment Area (ECA) Study JAMA. 264(19):2511-2518.
PubMed Abstract:
http://www.ncbi.nlm.nih.gov/pubmed/2232018
Free Full Text:
http://jama.ama-assn.org/cgi/reprint/264/19/2511.pdf

Swendsen JD, Merikangas KR. (2000). The comorbidity of depression and substance use disorders. Clin Psychol Rev. 20(2), 173-89.
PubMed Abstract:
http://www.ncbi.nlm.nih.gov/pubmed/10721496

Tatarsky, A (2001). Harm reduction psychotherapy: a new treatment for drug and alcohol problems. Northvale, NJ. Jason Aronson.

Wade AG, Ford I, Crawford G, McMahon AD, Nir T, Laudon M, Zisapel N. (2007). Efficacy of prolonged release melatonin in insomnia patients aged 55-80 years: quality of sleep and next-day alertness outcomes. Curr Med Res Opin. 23(10), 2597-605.
PubMed Abstract:

http://www.ncbi.nlm.nih.gov/pubmed/17875243

WHO Defining sexual health Report of a technical consultation on sexual health 28–31 January 2002, Geneva
Free Full Text:
http://www.who.int/reproductivehealth/topics/gender_rights/defining_sexual_health.pdf

CHAPTER ELEVEN: *Having Fun Without Booze*

"Goofing off is serious therapy"

- **HAMS Element Nine: Learn to have fun without booze**

11.1) Balance Is the Key

Drinking can be fun. Drinking is a great social lubricant that can break down inhibitions and help people to socialize. Many pleasures can be enhanced by drinking including watching movies and listening to music. And drinking can also be a great antidote to boredom. There is nothing in the world wrong with recreational intoxication if you keep it in its place.

But if drinking starts to be the only way that you can have fun and if alcohol is always a necessary accompaniment to any pleasurable activity that you engage in, you may wind up drinking a lot more than you feel comfortable with. If this is the case then it is a good idea to start working at learning how to have fun without alcohol.

It is still fine to have fun with alcohol sometimes. Balance is the key. Use alcohol in a way that you are comfortable with and that makes you feel good without letting alcohol take over your whole life.

This is a very important chapter. If you are always miserable when you are not drinking then you will not be very successful at having alcohol-free time. In the best of all possible worlds we will always be joyful with our drinking when we are drinking, and we will always be joyfully alcohol-free when we are not drinking.

Demanding that a person be always joyous is a bit too much to ask in the real world. But if we are willing to work at it we can succeed in increase our joyous time both while drinking and while alcohol-free. As that great philosopher Roger Miller once said, "You can't roller-skate in a buffalo herd, but you can have fun if you've a mind to."

11.2) A List of Fun things

The following is a list of some things which our HAMS members said that they liked to do with their alcohol-free time:

- Bike riding
- Weightlifting
- Hiking
- Cooking
- Sewing

- Candle making
- NY Times crossword
- Going to libraries
- Going to live theater
- Doing research
- Reading
- Watching old movies and TV shows on DVD
- Playing guitar or bass
- Looking at decorating magazines/decorating
- Antique shopping
- Organizing family photos
- Trying new recipes
- Dogs/Cats
- Volunteer work
- Scrapbooking
- Going to movies
- Cooking
- Working out

Use this tool to make a list of all the fun things that you can do when you are not drinking. Later when you are choosing to do some alcohol abstinence time you can refer back to this sheet when you feel bored and can't think of anything to do other than to drink.

Alcohol-Free Fun Worksheet

List all the ways that you can think of to have fun without alcohol

_____

_____

_____

_____

_____

_____

_____

_____

_____

_____

_____

_____

_____

_____

_____

_____

_____

_____

_____

_____

_____

_____

CHAPTER TWELVE: *You Are What You Believe*

"Nothing succeeds like success"

- **HAMS Element Ten: Learn to believe in yourself**

12.1   **What Is Self-Efficacy?**
12.2   **How to Increase Your Belief in Yourself**
12.3   **A Self-Confidence Enhancement Exercise**

12.1) What Is Self-Efficacy?

An experiment performed by Dr. Alan Marlatt in the 1970s helps us to understand just how overwhelmingly important belief is and what a gigantic effect it can have on behavior. Dr. Marlatt took a group of individuals who had been diagnosed with severe, chronic alcoholism and put them into 4 different experimental conditions.

- The first group got a vodka and tonic mixture and were told the truth, that it contained vodka and tonic.
- The second group got a vodka and tonic mixture and were lied to and told that it contained tonic only.
- The third group got tonic only and were told the truth, that it contained tonic only.
- The fourth group got tonic only and were lied to and told that it contained vodka and tonic.

The vodka tonic mixture contained five parts tonic to one part vodka and a pretest determined that this and pure tonic were indistinguishable.

The result was that the people who believed that they were drinking alcohol drank significantly more than those who believed that they were drinking only tonic, regardless of the beverage which they actually received. Those who got tonic only and thought it was a vodka and tonic mixture drank just as much as those who believed they were getting alcohol and really got alcohol. Those who got alcohol but thought that it was only tonic drank just as little as those who got tonic and thought it was tonic.

This proved that the idea that a single drink of alcohol causes loss of control is false. Belief is stronger than alcohol!

Dr. Albert Bandura is a research scientist at Stanford University who has studied addiction and the change process. Dr. Bandura has found that a very important predictor of successful change and of successfully overcoming addiction is a person's self-efficacy beliefs. People who believe that they can overcome addictions are successful at doing so. People who do not believe that they can overcome addictions tend to fail.

Dr. Bandura tells us:

"A strong sense of efficacy enhances human accomplishment and personal well-being in many ways. People with high assurance in their capabilities approach difficult tasks as challenges to be mastered rather than as threats to be avoided. Such an efficacious outlook fosters intrinsic interest and deep engrossment in activities. They set themselves challenging goals and maintain strong commitment to them. They heighten and sustain their efforts in the face of failure. They quickly recover their sense of efficacy after failures or setbacks. They attribute failure to insufficient effort or deficient knowledge and skills which are acquirable. They approach threatening situations with assurance that they can exercise control over them. Such an efficacious outlook produces personal accomplishments, reduces stress and lowers vulnerability to depression."

Learning to believe in yourself can spell the difference between succeeding and failing at your drinking goal, whether that goal is safer drinking, reduced drinking, or quitting. Note that learning to believe in yourself does not take the place of doing a CBA to choose your drinking goal. Ultimately you have to decide based on costs and benefits whether it is better to be a drinker or to be alcohol-free. However, if you believe that it is impossible to change your drinking for the better, then this will become a self-fulfilling prophecy. If you believe that it is impossible to quit drinking then you will find that it is impossible to quit. If you believe that it is easy to quit without AA then that will be true, and if you believe that it is impossible to quit without AA then you will find that to be true as well.

12.2) How to Increase Your Belief in Yourself

Research shows that successes build up your belief in yourself. Failures undermine your belief in yourself. Setting attainable goals is a great way to build up your self-confidence. Conversely, setting up impossible goals is a sure way to sabotage yourself.

For some people who have been drinking every single day for years, a single day of abstinence from alcohol might be a good goal to shoot for. For other people a 30 day alcohol-free period or a 60 day might be just the ticket. The important thing is that you choose a goal which you believe is in your power to attain and shoot for it. Always remember that every alcohol-free day is a success!

Another way to build up your belief in yourself is through social modeling. This is where belonging to a HAMS group can be helpful. In your HAMS group you will see people successfully having alcohol-free days and successfully controlling their drinking or successfully quitting. This will serve as a proof to your subconscious that it can be done. And once your subconscious starts to believe, your conscious mind will more readily follow.

12.3) A Self-Confidence Enhancement Exercise

free download at http://hamsnetwork.org/worksheets

Make a list of the qualities you have that will help you to achieve your drinking goal

REFERENCES:

Bandura, A. (1994). Self-efficacy. In V. S. Ramachaudran (Ed.), Encyclopedia of human behavior (Vol. 4, pp. 71-81). New York: Academic Press. (Reprinted in H. Friedman [Ed.], Encyclopedia of mental health. San Diego: Academic Press, 1998).
Free Full Text:
http://www.des.emory.edu/mfp/BanEncy.html

Marlatt GA, Demming B, Reid JB. (1973). Loss of control drinking in alcoholics: an experimental analogue. J Abnorm Psychol. 81(3), 233-41.
PubMed Info:
http://www.ncbi.nlm.nih.gov/pubmed/4710045
Abstract:
http://psycnet.apa.org/journals/abn/81/3/233/

Miller WR, Rollnick S. (1991, 2002). Motivational Interviewing: Preparing People To Change Addictive Behavior. New York: Guilford Press.

CHAPTER THIRTEEN: Charting and Measuring

"Pyrex is your friend"

- **HAMS Element Eleven: Use a chart to plan and track your drinks and drinking behaviors day by day**

13.1) Charting

Tracking your behavior in some manner is really essential to changing your behaviors. If your goal is safer drinking then you will definitely want to keep a record of when you drank safely and when you didn't. If your goal is reduced drinking then you will definitely want to track your drink numbers. Even if your goal is quitting you may want to track how many days you successfully stayed off the booze.

Tracking only in your head tends not to work very well. Therefore, we very strongly urge all Hamsters to track their drinking behaviors in some sort of a more concrete manner. One way to do this is to use the formal drinking behavior charts that we supply you with in this chapter. Another way is to post your number daily to the HAMS email group. Or you can write your numbers and behaviors down on a calendar. You may choose to count your empties for the week. Or even find some new and more creative way to track your drink numbers and drinking behaviors.

Many people report that the act of charting in and of itself leads them to cut back drinking without even specifically trying to. This is because charting makes you aware of each single drink. Many times when we have a habit of drinking we just drink automatically without noticing it. Researchers like Drs. Mark and Linda Sobell, Dr. Nick Heather, Dr. Ian Robertson and Dr. Stuart Linke have all found drink charting to be an important part of their drink reduction programs.

You can also use our drink charts to plan your drinks for each week--like all elements of HAMS this is optional.

13.2) How big is a standard drink?

When we speak of Standard Drinks we are referring to the standard drink as currently defined in the United States. Other countries have standardized units which can vary quite widely from this.

A US standard drink contains 0.6 oz of pure ethyl alcohol. This is the amount of alcohol contained in a twelve oz beer at 5% alcohol, a 5 oz glass of wine at 12% alcohol, or a one and one half oz shot of booze at 40% (80 proof) alcohol. Proof in the US is always twice percentage. All of the above are Standard Drinks.

- A Standard Drink in the United States is defined as 14 g alcohol = 17.7 ml = 0.6 oz.
- A British Alcohol Unit is 7.9 g = 10 ml = 0.56 US Standard Drinks.
- An Australian Alcohol unit is 10 g = 12.7 ml = 0.71 US Standard Drinks.

It takes around an hour and a half for the average person to metabolize one standard drink--not an hour. And it is always better to err on the side of caution so be sure to always allow yourself an adequate amount of time to sober up before doing anything of possible risk such as driving. Better yet carry a portable home breathalyzer if you think there may be any possible chance that you might not be sober yet.

Use the following formulas to calculate the number of standard drinks

Ounces x Alcohol Content / 60 = number of drinks

or

Milliliters x Alcohol Content / 1775 = number of drinks

13.3) What is BAC?

Blood Alcohol Content or **Blood Alcohol Concentration** (abbreviated BAC) is the concentration of alcohol in a person's blood. In the US BAC is defined as centigrams/milliliters. This is also sometimes referred to as BAL (Blood Alcohol Level). Some people may choose to record their BAC in their drinking charts as well as their drink numbers. BAC can be estimated by using the BAC tables in Appendix Two or you may choose to buy a personal breathalyzer in order to measure it directly.

13.4) Counting at home

Counting and measuring at home is fairly simple. You may want to use a Pyrex measuring cup to measure out exactly how much five ounces of wine is--you can pour it into your favorite wineglass then and see how far it actually fills the glass. You might want to acquire a standard one and a half ounce shot glass to measure the booze that you put in your mixed drinks--one standard shot of 80 proof booze is one standard drink.

Or you can choose to count bottles. A bottle of beer at five percent alcohol is one standard drink. A bottle of 12 % wine (750 ml) has five standard drinks. A 200 ml bottle of 80 proof booze has four and a half standard drinks. A "pint" (375 ml) of 80 proof booze contains eight and a half standard drinks, a fifth (750 ml) contains 17 standard drinks, and a liter contains 23 standard drinks.

You can choose to record the drinks as you drink them with hash marks on a sheet of paper. Or you can count bottles the following day if you so choose.

13.5) Counting in bars

Counting in bars is much trickier than counting at home. Bar drinks--except for beer--are usually not standard drinks--bar drinks can contain anywhere from one to six or more drinks in what is served as "one drink". So you will have to estimate how many standard drinks are in the drink that the bartender serves you.

Not everyone is comfortable taking notes on paper in a bar--it can also interfere with the conversation. So some people choose to save their swizzle sticks or bottle caps and put them in their pocket and total them up the next day.

13.6) Tracking Your Risks

If your goal is safer drinking then it might be a good idea to chart the alcohol related risks that you manage to avoid as well as the ones that you fail to avoid. Go back to your risk ranking worksheet from Chapter 5 and take the risks that you wrote down there and use them to fill in the blanks on your Risk Tracking Chart. The Sample Risk Tracking Chart (13.10) will give you an idea of what to do.

When our sample subject did his risk ranking worksheet he ranked drinking and driving as a 4, so he fills in a 4 in the **rank** cell. He also ranked unsafe sex as a 4 so he also fills in a 4 for its **rank**. He ranked drunk dialing with a 2 so he fills in a 2 for its **rank**.

Next he needs to add up the number of times he engaged in each risky behavior throughout the week and put these numbers into the column labeled **Subtotal**. He drank and drove zero times so this gets a zero. He engaged in drunken unsafe sex on Wednesday and Friday for a total of two times so this gets a 2 in the subtotal column. There were two instances of drunk dialing on Saturday so this also gets a 2.

Now multiply subtotals by the ranks to get the totals. He drank and drove zero times this week so this is $0 \times 4 = 0$. He had drunken unsafe sex twice this week so this is $2 \times 4 = 8$. He drunk dialed twice so $2 \times 2 = 4$. Add up all the totals to get the **Grand Total**. His **Grand Total** of risk for this week is 12.

This is like playing golf--you aim for a low score.

13.7) My Drinking Chart - free download at http://hamsnetwork.org/worksheets

My drinking chart

	Sunday	Monday	Tuesday	Wednesday	Thursday	Friday	Saturday	Weekly
Plan	Plan # ___	Plan # ___	Plan # ___	Plan # ___	Plan # ___	Plan # ___	Plan # ___	Plan
mods abs hr	mods abs hr	mods abs hr	mods abs hr	mods abs hr	mods abs hr	mods abs hr	mods abs hr	
Actual	Actual # ___	Actual # ___	Actual # ___	Actual # ___	Actual # ___	Actual # ___	Actual # ___	Actual
success? Y N	success? Y N	success? Y N	success? Y N	success? Y N	success? Y N	success? Y N	success? Y N	success? Y N
Mood	Mood	Mood	Mood	Mood	Mood	Mood	Mood	Satisfaction
safety? Y N	safety? Y N	safety? Y N	safety? Y N	safety? Y N	safety? Y N	safety? Y N	safety? Y N	Notes

Abbreviations: mods = moderation; abs = alcohol abstinence; hr = harm reduction

One US standard drink contains 0.6 oz (14 g, 17.7 ml) of ethanol. This is equal to one 12 oz beer at 5% alcohol or one 5 oz glass (150 ml) of wine at 12% alcohol or one and one half oz (45 ml) of 80 proof liquor. Other countries use different measures.

Weekly rating: one star each for - charting, planning, keeping within plan, avoiding risk, doing something extra. * * * * *

109

Sample drinking chart

	Sunday	Monday	Tuesday	Wednesday	Thursday	Friday	Saturday	Weekly
Plan	#17	#0	#1	#17	#0	#0	#35	Plan
	mods **abs** hr	mods **abs** hr	mods **abs** hr	mods abs **hr**	mods **abs** hr	mods **abs** hr	mods abs **hr**	
Actual	#17	#17	#1	#17	#0	#0	#0	#52
	mods abs **hr**	**mods** abs hr	mods abs hr	mods abs **hr**	mods **abs** hr	mods abs **hr**	mods **abs** hr	mods abs **hr**
success?	Y N (**Y**)	Y N (**N**)	Y N (**Y**)	Y N (**Y**)	Y N (**Y**)	Y N (**Y**)	Y N (**Y**)	success? Y N (**N**)
Mood	happy	Tired	happy	happy	happy	happy	happy	Satisfaction Plan was mostly successful
safety?	Y N (**Y**)	Y N (**Y**)	Y N (**Y**)	Y N (**Y**)	Y N (**Y**)	Y N (**Y**)	Y N (**Y**)	
notes	$14.08	$14.08	friend's birthday party $0.00	$14.08	work night	work night	work night	Notes $42.24

Abbreviations: mods = moderation; abs = alcohol abstinence; hr = harm reduction

One US standard drink contains 0.6 oz (14 g, 17.7 ml) of ethanol. This is equal to one 12 oz beer at 5% alcohol or one 5 oz glass (150 ml) of wine at 12% alcohol or one and one half oz (45 ml) of 80 proof liquor. Other countries use different measures.

Weekly rating: one star each for - charting, planning, keeping within plan, avoiding risk, doing something extra   *(*)**

13.9) My Risk Tracking Chart - free download at http://hamsnetwork.org/worksheets

My Risk Tracking Chart

Risky Behavior	Mon	Tue	Wed	Thu	Fri	Sat	Sun	Sub-total	Rank	Total
Grand Total										

Mark down a number for each time you engaged in a high risk drinking behavior for each day. If you didn't engage in the behavior give yourself a zero.

Sample Risk Tracking Chart

Risky Behavior	Mon	Tue	Wed	Thu	Fri	Sat	Sun	Sub-total	Rank	Total
Drinking and driving	0	0	0	0	0	0	0	0	4	0
Unsafe sex	0	0	1	0	1	0	0	2	4	8
Drunk dialing	0	0	0	0	0	2	0	2	2	4
Grand Total										12

Mark down a number for each time you engaged in a high risk drinking behavior for each day. If you didn't engage in the behavior give yourself a zero.

REFERENCES

Heather N, Kissoon-Singh J, Fenton GW. (1990). Assisted natural recovery from alcohol problems: effects of a self-help manual with and without supplementary telephone contact. Br J Addict. 85(9), 1177-85.
PubMed Abstract:
http://www.ncbi.nlm.nih.gov/pubmed/2224198

Heather N, Robertson I, MacPherson B, Allsop S, Fulton A. (1987). Effectiveness of a controlled drinking self-help manual: one-year follow-up results. Br J Clin Psychol. 26 (Pt 4), 279-87.
PubMed Abstract:
http://www.ncbi.nlm.nih.gov/pubmed/3427250

Heather N, Whitton B, Robertson I. (1986). Evaluation of a self-help manual for media-recruited problem drinkers: six-month follow-up results. Br J Clin Psychol. 25 (Pt 1), 19-34.
PubMed Abstract:
http://www.ncbi.nlm.nih.gov/pubmed/3955272

Linke S, Brown A, Wallace P. (2004). Down your drink: a web-based intervention for people with excessive alcohol consumption. Alcohol Alcohol. 39(1), 29-32.
PubMed Abstract:
http://www.ncbi.nlm.nih.gov/pubmed/14691071
Free Full Text:
http://alcalc.oxfordjournals.org/cgi/reprint/39/1/29.pdf

NIAAA - What's a standard drink?
http://rethinkingdrinking.niaaa.nih.gov/WhatCountsDrink/WhatsAstandardDrink.asp
Accessed January 25, 2010

Sobell M, Sobell, L. (1993, 1996). Problem Drinkers: Guided Self-Change Treatment. Guilford.

CHAPTER FOURTEEN: Tweaking the Plan

"2 is not equal to 3, not even for large values of 2" --Grabel's Law

- **HAMS Element Twelve: Evaluate your progress - honestly report struggles - revise plans or goals as needed**

14.1   **Evaluating progress and reporting struggles**
14.2   **Updating plans and switching goals**

14.1) Evaluating progress and reporting struggles

Your drinking chart contains an area at the bottom where you can put down an evaluation of how well you did with your plans and goals for the week. Some people prefer to post to the email group rather than keeping a chart and that is okay too. HAMS is the one place where you can always honestly talk about your drinking and no one will judge you or tell you to go to AA.

Most of our members like to periodically evaluate how well they arc sticking to their plans and goals. If all is going well--great!! However, if you find yourself going over your limits a lot or engaging in lots of risky behavior then you might want to consider an abstinence period to reset your mindset about alcohol. Or you might want to relax your drinking limits if you think you have made them to strict.

If your actual consumption and drinking behavior deviates a lot from your plan then you may want to consider revising the plan or the goal. Don't beat yourself up for being less than perfect, though! Research shows that beating yourself up for being less than perfect is likely to make you drink more. Instead, forgive yourself and start over. Studies of smokers found that only one in twenty quit on the first try--multiple attempts at changing a habit are the rule, not the exception.

Some people find that their best course is to switch their drinking goal. Some want to keep the same goal but find that they need to revamp their plans. Be gentle with yourself and practice damage control while you are getting set to start over. Chapter 15 talks about how to practice damage control.

It is nice to do a new CBA several times a year even if you are happy with your progress. Doing a fresh CBA lets you see how your attitudes have changed and how you have mentally progressed, as well as strengthening, consolidating and clarifying your new attitudes.

How Do You Evaluate Whether Or Not Your Goals And Plans Are Working?

If you are charting your numbers or risks the charts have some built in evaluation procedures to help you track your progress.

If your goal is reduced drinking you can look at your charts to see if you numbers are going down and if they are approaching the projected limits in your drinking plan.

If your goal is safer drinking, then you can look to see if your risk totals are dropping to acceptable levels on your risk charts.

If your goal is alcohol abstinence then you can look to see if the number of drinking days which you have each week is dropping.

If you are not formally charting, you can still track your progress with some sort of informal recording procedure such as counting the amount of booze that you buy each week.

Not everyone needs a formal evaluation tool to know whether or not they are satisfied with the progress which they are making in changing their drinking. They can tell from the negative consequences or the lack or negative consequences. They can also tell from the good things that start happening to them when they are on the right track.

Progress checklist

You may wish to ask yourself the following questions:

For A Reduced Drinking Goal:

- Do my drinking numbers coincide with the numbers on my plan?

- Are my drinking numbers approaching the numbers in my plan?

- Are my drinking numbers the same as baseline?

- Are my drinking numbers increasing over baseline?

For A Safer Drinking Goal:

- Am I avoiding the risks that I listed in my plan?

- Have I succeeded in reducing the risks I listed in my plan?

- Am I acting as riskily as before?

- Am I acting more riskily than before?

For A Goal Of Quitting Drinking:

- Have I quit drinking?

- Have I increased the number of abstinence days or reduced drink and risk numbers?

- Has my drinking stayed the same or have I started drinking more overall or more per session?

- Have I gone on dangerous benders when I did drink?

If you are staying within your plan then WOOO HOOOOOO!! Kudos to you! Give yourself many well-deserved pats on the back.

If you are making improvements then be sure to pat yourself on the back for this as well. Maybe you need to incorporate "Baby Steps" into your plan and move towards your goal little by little. Or maybe you want to tweak some aspects of your plan. Look the situation over and do what feels right for YOU.

If you are staying the same as before, this may mean that you are in the stage of **Contemplation** or **Preparation**. (See Chapter 29 on the Stages of Change for more details about these stages.) There is nothing wrong with this. You may need to do more reading or hang out longer with your HAMS group before you are ready to change. You may want to do another CBA or Drinking Goal Worksheet to ramp up your motivation.

If your attempts to change have backfired and your drinking has gotten worse instead of better, this means that you are suffering from the **Ricochet Effect**. The trick is to practice **Damage Control**--which we discuss in detail in the next chapter.

14.2) Updating plans and switching goals

Everyone is different. Every drinking plan is unique to the individual. No two of us are exactly alike in our progress towards our goals.

Some people set their drinking goals, make their drinking plans, and accomplish them on the first try. This is great! However, the majority of people are likely to suffer some setbacks on the way. Prochaska tells us that only one person in twenty quits smoking on the first try. It is likely that most people who want to change their drinking will require more than one try as well.

The good news is that HAMS is flexible enough to allow you many attempts. HAMS is also flexible enough to allow you switch your goals or to tweak and revise your plans until you find something which is workable for you. The important thing is that you keep on trucking. "If at first you don't succeed, try, try again."

Some people need several attempts to achieve the goal that they have chosen. Some people may choose to switch to a different drinking goal if the initial goal is not working out. Some people may choose to switch goals several times.

Let's look at a few examples:

MARY:

Mary has decided to quit drinking. Mary has tried going to AA, but instead of helping the meetings make her want to drink. Then when she drinks she beats herself up and becomes miserable and drinks even more. Last time this happened she went out and totaled her car.

Mary decides to switch from a goal of abstinence to one of safer drinking. Mary's number one priority now is damage control. Mary can work at practicing damage control while she is working at overcoming her self-destructive habit of beating herself up for being human. Mary can work at quitting drinking later after she has addressed her issue of beating herself up.

GEORGE:

George has two DUIs hanging over his head and the next one will be a felony. George comes to HAMS with a goal of safer drinking. George does great with his goal of safer drinking--he drinks only at home and never endangers himself anymore. However, George came into work very hungover and his supervisor smelled booze and his breath and told him to knock it off. George has decided that safer drinking alone is not enough and has added a goal of reduced drinking by not drinking on work nights to his plan.

GRACE:

Grace's plan is for reduced drinking. Grace saw her numbers drop for the first few weeks that she started charting but soon they were right back up to the original amounts. Grace has decided to do a 30 days alcohol-free period to get her numbers back on track.

MARTHA:

Martha's plan was to always stay within the No-Risk drinking limits from Chapter 5 and thus always be a moderate drinker. Then Martha's best friend had a birthday party and they both got tipsy together. A month later she went to a New Year's Eve party and got tipsy again and drove home intoxicated. Martha has decided to revise her drinking plan to allow her to get tipsy on special occasions. She is also adding a safe drinking component to make certain that she never has to drink and drive again.

How Do You Know Whether To Switch The Goal, Tweak The Plan, Or Just Keep On Trying?

If you are not satisfied with your progress, we suggest that you go back to the Drinking Goal Worksheet (Chapter 4) and fill it out again and use it as a tool to help you decide whether or not you wish to change your drinking goal. You can also use the Cost Benefit Analysis (Chapter 3) for this purpose. These tools will help you in choosing the best goal for you.

You can go back and do the Plan Making Worksheet (Chapter 7) again and use these as a means of tweaking your plan or building a new plan.

These two tools will help you to find the goals and plans that are right for you.

You can also go back and read through The HAMS Toolbox (Chapter 6) again and see if there are additional tools which you wish to incorporate into your plan.

"Be not ashamed of mistakes and thus make them crimes" --Confucius

CHAPTER FIFTEEN: Damage Control: Dealing With Slips, Setbacks, and Ricochets

"To be prepared is half the victory"-- Miguel De Cervantes

- **HAMS Element Thirteen: Practice damage control as needed**

What Is Regression?

A **Regression** is any instance of a deviation from your change plan which makes you unhappy. It does not matter whether your plan is abstinence from alcohol, moderate drinking, or harm reduction; any return to an old pattern of behavior which you do not like and which you want to change is a **Regression**.

The HAMS Harm Reduction concept of **Regression** differs in some important respects from the 12 step disease model notion of a **"Relapse"**. We view people as responsible adults who have a right to choose what they put into their mouths. Disease theory tells people that their brains are their own worst enemy and that they must ignore what their brains tell them and follow the 12 step program no matter what. Harm reduction says that it is your right to change your mind about abstinence from alcohol and choose to attempt moderation or harm reduction instead. We feel that it is safer for a person to make such an attempt in a safe and supportive environment than to do so on one's own or even worse in secret. It is always possible to make a rational choice to return to abstinence from alcohol if moderation or harm reduction does not work out. Hence, although disease theory calls a reasoned decision to return to drinking a "relapse", harm reduction calls this an individual choice. We find that denial is rare unless people are forced into denial by unreasonable circumstances or unreasonable people around them.

HAMS classifies regressions into three categories: **slips**, **setbacks**, and **ricochets**. A **slip** is a minor and temporary lapse. A **setback** is defined by Dr. James Prochaska as a return to a previous stage of change (see Chapter 29 for a discussion of the Stages of Change). In a **ricochet** the behavior actually becomes worse than it was before an attempt was made to change it. Foreknowledge and the right attitude can go a long way towards preventing **slips** from becoming **setbacks** or **ricochets**.

One of the most important things to know is that most people don't change their habits perfectly on the first try--**regression** and multiple attempts at change are the norm. When the Prochaska group studied people who were quitting smoking they found that only one out of every twenty persons in their sample quit smoking on the first try. Most people who successfully quit smoking required several attempts. Scientists who study the way in which people change agree that each instance of a **setback** to a previous stage can potentially function as a learning experience and that when the person has learned enough through trial and error they then successfully change their behavior. What is true of quitting cigarettes--which many researchers believe to be the most difficult habit to change--is also true of changing other habits--including drinking.

Slips are minor violations of the plan. One can sometimes deal with **slips** quickly and move on. If one does not deal with them quickly they can sometimes turn into **setbacks** or **ricochets**.

Setbacks can occur when a person temporarily returns to a former stage of change--they can also occur when a person gives up on change indefinitely.

Ricochets tend to occur when the person falls into a deep state of self-loathing over their failure to change. Catastrophizing over a **slip** can help turn it into a **ricochet**. Certain 12 step disease model slogans and concepts can also tend to lead slips to become ricochets--particularly slogans like "one drunk means one drunk" and the concept that one cannot stop drinking unless one first "hits bottom" or the concept that you are "powerless" over alcohol. The fact is that alcohol is an inanimate object and it is powerless over you.

It does not matter if your goal is abstinence, moderation, or harm reduction--if you beat yourself up over a slip you can wind up drinking as badly or worse than before because you are making yourself miserable over your failure. This is what we refer to as the **Ricochet Effect**[4]. The **Ricochet Effect** has been studied in detail by Alan Marlatt and others. The best way to avoid falling victim to the **Ricochet Effect** is to forgive yourself and move on. Other things to do to avoid the **Ricochet Effect** include:

- Forgetting those twelve step mantras which set you up to go on a bender
- Giving up the habit of catastrophizing.

One reason why **regression** is common is that habits like drinking become highly **automated** and **unconscious.** Some **slips** may occur in response to an urge or a craving. Others **slips** may be a conscious choice to drink when we encounter negative situations or emotions and we think that a drink will make us feel better. According to Dr. Stephen Tiffany (1990), some **slips** are essentially unconscious in nature simply because drinking has become such an automated and ingrained habit--often a habit which responds to a certain accustomed environment.

It is important to realize that sometimes a **regression**--whether a **slip** or a **setback** or a **ricochet**--results from a **conscious decision** to deal with a **craving**, an **urge** or a **bad feeling**, and that at other times it result in an essentially **unconscious manner** as a result of **conditioned responses** which alcohol has set up in our brains.

In other words--sometimes we clearly choose to drink again--but sometimes it can seem like it happens without our even knowing it. Realizing that our drinking is a **learned habit** goes a long way towards helping people to not beat themselves up over and catastrophize **slips**. Another important thing which learning theory teaches us is the fact that the longer you are away from bad habits the less pull they have.

An excellent way to prevent a **regression** from turning into a **ricochet** is to have a **damage control plan--a plan B**--in place. Practicing the harm reduction strategies outlined in Chapter 6

---

[4] Marlatt's original term for what we call the **Ricochet Effect** is the **Abstinence Violation Effect (AVE).** Soon after Marlatt invented the term **Abstinence Violation Effect** it was discovered that this kind of overshooting or Ricochet effect can occur as a response to a failure to meet any goal--whether the goal is abstinence, moderation, or harm reduction. A good deal more information about the **Abstinence Violation Effect** and **Damage Control** can be found in Marlatt's book: Marlatt, G. A. & Gordon, J.R. (Ed.). (1985). <u>Relapse Prevention: Maintenance strategies in the treatment of addictive behaviors</u>. New York: Guilford Press.

can go a long way towards preventing you from harming yourself or someone else if you **regress**.

Besides having a **damage control plan** in place, one other good technique is to have **coping strategies** in place to deal with difficult emotions and situations. These **coping strategies** can help prevent **slips**, **setbacks**, and **ricochets** from happening at all. We discuss **coping strategies** in the Chapters 9 and 10.

Now let's take a look at some practical examples to see how practicing **damage control** can work in real life. We will start with a harm reduction example.

CASE 1 - Bob:

Bob had been in the habit of getting drunk four or five nights out of the week and coming into work hungover several times a week. After being reprimanded by his supervisor for smelling boozy in the mornings, Bob decided with the help of HAMS to adopt a harm reduction plan which involves getting drunk only two nights a week and no more drinking on work nights. Bob does fine with this new harm reduction plan for two months, then one day Bob has a **slip** and gets drunk on a work night. Bob has a **damage control plan** in place that involves calling in sick rather than going to work smelling all boozy in the morning so he does so. What does Bob do next?

Bob might start beating himself up over his failure and telling himself that he is no good. Bob might start feeling so bad about himself that he thinks the only relief from this bad feeling is to get drunk. Or Bob might decide that his **slip** proves that change is impossible and that he might as well keep drinking. Bob abandons his harm reduction plan and the **slip** turns into a **setback** or a **ricochet**.

Alternatively Bob can tell himself that change is hard and that it is difficult to get it right on the first try. But a minor slip up is no reason to give up on making a change for the better and Bob is ready to get right back on the horse today. Bob might decide to continue with his harm reduction plan, or he might take this as an opportunity to review his feelings about alcohol and do a new Cost/Benefit Analysis. Bob might decide to opt for a period of abstinence or he might even decide to change his goal from harm reduction to long term abstinence. Regardless of which route Bob chooses, he is continuing to make a change in a positive direction rather than letting his **slip** drag him down and backwards.

CASE 2 - Harry:

Now let us look at Harry. Harry has decided that the costs of drinking alcohol are not worth the benefits and has opted for indefinite abstinence from alcohol. Harry's plan has been going along swimmingly for six months. Then one night Harry is at a party where there is both spiked punch and non alcoholic punch. By mistake Harry gets a glass of spiked punch--he realizes this after drinking it and tasting the alcohol in it. What does Harry do next?

If Harry believes that "one drink means one drunk" and that he is powerless over alcohol then Harry might very well start drinking and drinking and seeking to hit some sort of bottom.

However, if Harry believes that alcohol has no power over him at all and that he is determined to quit in spite of any accident, then he will just put down the cup of spiked punch, get some non alcoholic punch, and go on as if nothing had happened.

CASE 3 - Joe:

Now let us look at the case of Joe. Joe suffers from both depression and anxiety and has used alcohol to medicate both these feelings. Joe has had a DUI and decided give up the heavy drinking and to follow a moderate drinking plan instead. Joe is successful with moderate drinking for several months and begins seeing a therapist for anxiety and depression during this time. Then Joe's anxiety and depression become overwhelming again and Joe decides to use alcohol to deal with them once again. What happens next?

If Joe has a good **damage control plan** in place then he will drink safely even though he is drinking heavily. He will plan his drinking so that he never has to drink and drive and so that it does not cause major life damage. Then when Joe is ready he will be able to pick up his moderate drinking plan once again or even decide to opt for quitting.

If Joe has no **damage control plan** in place he may cause himself some major life damage via drinking and give himself even greater reasons to be depressed or anxious.

CASE 4 - John:

John has chosen abstinence from alcohol as his goal. John's therapist is a great fan of AA--so much so in fact that he has said that he will no longer do therapy with John unless John attends AA. John has some serious issues with isolation and he hopes that AA meetings might help him with this as well as with alcohol abstinence. However, John is an atheist who suffered a severe fundamentalist upbringing--one of the reasons that John drank was that he was rebelling against his fundamentalist upbringing.

John is extremely uncomfortable at AA meetings because of their strong religious overtones and the insistence that he will die a horrible death of alcoholism unless he has a "Higher Power". John feels more alone in the AA crowd than he does when no one is around. And John feels more like drinking after an AA meeting than his does at any other time.

John has tried to explain these feelings to his therapist--but his therapist's response was that John's "addictive self" was trying to find a way to escape AA so that it could make him drink again and kill him. What will happen next?

Hopefully John will fire his therapist and get a new one. Also, hopefully John will cease going to AA and find some secular alternative which supports alcohol abstinence such as SOS or SMART Recovery. If John can find no live meetings of these organizations locally he can turn to their online support groups. John can even use the online alcohol-free HAMS group for support if he wishes.

What if John continues to attend AA? Some people are simply allergic to AA the same way that some people are allergic to penicillin. The cure for a penicillin allergy is not to give a person more penicillin--that is death. The cure is to use an alternative. The same is true with AA. Some people are simply allergic to it and the **Ricochet Effect** that results from continuing to attend AA could well kill them.

Conclusion

In conclusion what we would like you to take away from this chapter is that the best way to prevent damage from a **regression** is to have a **damage control plan** in place. As the Boy Scouts say--"Be prepared!"

REFERENCES:

Marlatt A, Gordon J. (1985). Relapse Prevention: Maintenance strategies in the treatment of addictive behaviors. New York, Guilford.

Miller W, Heather N. (1998). Treating Addictive Behaviors, (2nd Edition). New York, Plenum

Prochaska JO, Norcross JC, DiClemente CC. (1994). Changing for good. New York, Morrow.

Tiffany ST. (1990). A cognitive model of drug urges and drug use behavior: Role of automatic and nonautomatic processes. Psychological Review. 97, 147-168.
PubMed Abstract:
http://www.ncbi.nlm.nih.gov/pubmed/2186423

CHAPTER SIXTEEN: Patience, Practice, and Persistence

"Fall down seven times, get back up eight" -- Old Japanese Proverb

- **HAMS Element Fourteen: Get Back On the Horse**

If you don't succeed in achieving your drinking goal right away that doesn't mean that you should just throw in the towel and give up. Although some people manage to change a bad habit on the first try, studies show that the majority require several attempts. So if at first you don't succeed, try, try again. Slow and steady wins the race.

This doesn't mean that no one should ever switch their drinking goal. If a moderate drinking plan isn't working maybe you will want to switch to alcohol abstinence. If you picked alcohol abstinence as a goal but can't seem to stay quit--then perhaps you will have to follow a damage control plan for now.

What we mean to say is that even if it is difficult to change your drinking for the better and you may suffer some setbacks, you shouldn't get disgusted and give up.

Patience

We live in an age of instant gratification. Lots of us like alcohol because it has an immediate effect. But sometimes good things take time and are worth waiting for. You can't cook Chateaubriand in your microwave. Be prepared to have patience with yourself as you work at changing your drinking, too. Rome was not built in a day.

Persistence

There is a story about two frogs that fell into a tub of cream. One gave up and drowned. The second didn't give up; he scrambled so hard he churned the cream to butter and jumped out. Learning any new skill--from the multiplication table to riding a bike--requires that you don't give up. This is true of changing your drinking, too.

Practice

Studies show that the longer people manage to maintain a new habit the easier it gets. Like riding a bicycle or driving a car--the first time you do it, it is all you can do to maintain control. But after years of practice it is second nature. The longer you maintain your new drinking habits, the easier they get.

Some Examples of Patience, Practice, and Persistence

Edison and the Light Bulb

Thomas Edison spent over two years developing the first practical incandescent electric light bulb. During this period, he and his staff investigated every bit of published literature on the topic. They built improved vacuum pumps. They tested over six thousand different materials for the filament of the bulb. In October of 1879 they had a bulb that would last 13 hours before burning out. In late 1880 they had a bulb that would last over 600 hours. This was the result of one tiny incremental change added to another. One baby step after another. Patience added to persistence.

It is unlikely that you will need six thousand different plans to get your drinking under control. However, the people who are willing to hunker down and emulate Edison in using patience and persistence are the ones who have the most success in changing their drinking for the better.

Robert the Bruce and the Spider

Robert the Bruce, King of Scotland, had fought the British in six battles and had been defeated in all six. Badly wounded, Robert the Bruce retreated to a cave where he saw a spider attempting to spin her web. Six times the spider threw her thread to start the web and six times she failed. Robert the Bruce said to himself, "This spider is like me--she continues to try and continues to fail." But on the seventh attempt the spider threw her web and succeeded. Inspired by this, Robert the Bruce fought a seventh battle with the British and this time defeated them.

As the Tortoise told the Hare, "Slow and steady wins the race."

CHAPTER SEVENTEEN: *Graduating, Staying, or Returning*

"So you gotta let me know - Should I stay or should I go" --The Clash

- **HAMS Element Fifteen: Graduate from HAMS, stick around, or come back**

You can choose to graduate from HAMS any time that you feel that you are ready to move on with life. Or you can choose to stick around HAMS for as long as you want in order to get continuing support or to help others. You may also come back to HAMS any time that you feel a need for a tune up or any time that you want to work on a new issue or goal.

Research by people like Dr. James Prochaska shows that for many people, once they kick a bad habit like smoking or drinking too much, it is time to move on with life. In Prochaska's Stages of Change Model this is referred to as the Termination Stage of Change. Prochaska tells us that not everyone enters the Termination stage--some people stay in the Maintenance Stage of Change permanently. (See Chapter 29 for a full account of the Stages of Change Model.) People who are in the Maintenance Stage of Change may find it is helpful to stick around HAMS for continued support in order to maintain the change. They may also find that helping others at HAMS helps them to maintain and consolidate the changes they have made in themselves.

When people are in the Termination Stage of Change, however, they stop even thinking about their old bad habits. They are done with the habit for good; cravings are gone and there is no reason to even think about or talk about the old habit anymore.

One way that HAMS differs greatly from AA is that we recognize that for some people it is appropriate to graduate from HAMS and move on with life. We do not tell people that they will die if they leave HAMS, because this is not true. For many people it is not only not therapeutic, it is positively detrimental to keep dwelling on alcohol and drinking issues forever and ever after they have made their change. Some people can actually be harmed and led to return to drinking by AA's nonstop, nightly drunkalogues.

We welcome people who are doing great with their lives to come back to HAMS and visit and tell us about it--but we understand if these visits get less frequent as life goes on. Always remember that if you choose to graduate from HAMS you can still come back for a tune up any time that you need it. You don't have to wait for your problems to get bad--feel free to come back at the first sign that you are slipping back into old habits.

Some people will choose to continue with HAMS even after they have entered the Termination Stage because they enjoy helping others and like to give back what they have been given. Of course we welcome this with open arms.

As we noted above--not everyone enters the Termination Stage of Change; some people remain in Maintenance for the rest of their lives. If you are in the Maintenance Stage of Change you might find it helpful to continue to stay in touch with HAMS via live or online meetings or this book. However, you might also choose to ease up on the intensity of your HAMS contact as life gets better and you get busier with life.

- **The appropriate dosage of HAMS is "apply as needed".**

HAMS is not AA. In AA when a person leaves the group they are expected to go out and drink worse than ever before and not come back until they have hit ever more depraved new bottoms.

In HAMS we expect that many of our members will choose to get a life after they get their drinking under control. Some will choose to stick around to help others; some will choose to move on and stop participating in HAMS groups. This is fine and normal. If you have moved on but start feeling a need for a tune up you are free to come back to HAMS at anytime to fine tune your drinking. You don't have to "hit bottom" because you decided to get a life. The sooner you come back to fine tune your drinking the better.

People are also welcome to come back any time that they feel like switching to a different goal. A person may quit drinking and move on with life and then decide some years down the road to come back to HAMS to work on a goal of moderate drinking. Or a person may pursue a goal of harm reduction for several years after leaving HAMS and then come back because they want to switch to a goal of quitting drinking. Anyone is free to come back anytime that they want to switch their goal or build a different plan.

There is no shame involved in coming back. This is not like AA where you return like a whipped dog with your tail between your legs. At HAMS you return proudly with your head high because you have made a healthy decision to keep working on improving yourself.

Or maybe the alcohol is under control and now you want to use HAMS to work on tobacco or marijuana. These are also great reasons for coming back.

CHAPTER EIGHTEEN Reward, Praise, and Affirm Yourself!!

"Perfectionism is the enemy of the good"

- **HAMS Element Sixteen: Praise yourself for every success!!**

People who study behavioral change suggest that it is better to reward yourself for positive behaviors than to attempt to punish yourself for negative behaviors. Dr William Mikulas (1978) states, "As a behavior change procedure punishment has many disadvantages and possible bad side effects."

Since our society tends to look askance at boasting we can sometimes forget what a powerful motivator it can be to indulge in a little self praise. Fortunately a HAMS group is a safe place where you can talk about your successes. If you have been really struggling to get to that first alcohol-free day or that first moderate drinking day, you can come in to a HAMS group and pat yourself on the back for your success and you will have everybody join in with big kudos!

Be free with self-praise for every success you have with your drinking no matter how small, and soon the successes will start getting bigger and bigger. And feel free to reward yourself too. Treat yourself to a special piece of cake or that movie you have been dying to see as a reward for your good behavior! Research suggests that your self praise and self rewards will be most effective if you are part of a group that knows that you are working to change your behaviors for the better (Hayes, 1985).

If you set a goal of doing 30 days abstinence then be sure to praise yourself for every single day of abstinence that you achieve. Praise yourself each and every day! If you only make twenty days, don't beat yourself up! In HAMS you never lose your abstinence days. Those 20 days of abstinence are yours to keep for the rest of your life!

Every abs day is a MAJOR success!! Every time you lower your drink count you have made a GREAT achievement!! Every time you drank safely without endangering yourself or others then kudos to you!! Any step you make towards overcoming a life problem that leads to drinking is cause to pat your own back!!

Many of us have spent so much of our lives giving ourselves negative self talk that we can't even begin to imagine self-praise. Maybe we like to go to web sites like despair dot com to show how blasé we are. Beware! Because the cool persona of doom and gloom can turn around and bite you on the ass in the form of clinical depression.

Reward yourself daily with little rewards for each success

Don't be embarrassed if it is silly

Put on the hamster dance song and do a happy hamster dance

Accentuate the Positive

Eliminate the negative

Self Affirmation Statements

Studies by several researchers suggest that **Self Affirmation Statements** can increase self esteem and self efficacy and help you to accomplish positive behavioral changes (Lange et al, 1998, Peden et al, 2001 and 2005). It is important that your self affirmation statements be realistic--they should concentrate on your own abilities and qualities. Simply wishing for the external world to change to accommodate you is setting yourself up for failure. It is realistic to say "I deserve to feel happy because I am human." It is not realistic to say "I deserve to win a million dollars in the lotto today."

If you like the idea of using affirmations, we suggest that you stand in front of a mirror and repeat these affirmations to yourself daily:

- **I have the power to change my life for the better**
- **I have the power to change my drinking for the better**
- **I deserve to feel good about myself because I am human**
- **I am worthy of feeling good about myself**
- **Negativity only harms myself**
- **Happiness is a habit I will cultivate**

Many of us harm ourselves daily by repeating nullifications to ourselves instead of affirmations. Use **Thought Stopping** (Chapter 9) if you start hearing yourself repeat these nullifications.

- **I'm hopeless**
- **I'm a loser**
- **I can't change my drinking**
- **I'll never get better**
- **I am powerless**

List Successes Every Day

Try making a list of successes every day. If you have a low self esteem you might think that you have no successes. But remember, your drinking was safe enough today that you didn't kill yourself.

Here is a sample where you can start:

- **I didn't kill myself**
- **I didn't kill anyone else**
- **I didn't break a any bones**
- **Etc.**

No matter who you are you can think of at least some positive success you had with controlling your drinking each day.

Feel free to paste gold stars all over them or draw happy faces. Don't worry how silly it seems if it helps to raise your self esteem.

Make a Gratitude List

List the things that you are grateful for today. If you have trouble getting started, try the following:

- **I am thankful that I am alive**
- **I am thankful that I have food to eat**
- **I am thankful that I have a roof over one's head**

REFERENCES:

Hayes SC, Rosenfarb I, Wulfert E, Munt ED, Korn Z, Zettle RD. (1985). Self-reinforcement effects: An artifact of social standard setting? J Appl Behav Anal.18(3), 201-214.
PubMed Abstract:
http://www.ncbi.nlm.nih.gov/pubmed/16795688
Free Full Text:
http://www.ncbi.nlm.nih.gov/pmc/articles/PMC1308011/pdf/jaba00029-0017.pdf

Lange A, Richard R, Gest A, de Vries M, and Lodder L. (1998). The Effects of Positive Self-Instruction: A Controlled Trial. Cognitive Therapy and Research. 22(3), 225-236

Mikulas W. (1978). Behavior Modification. Harper & Row.
Free Full Text:
http://uwf.edu/wmikulas/Webpage/behavior/intro.htm

Peden AR, Rayens MK, Hall LA, Beebe LH. (2001). Preventing depression in high-risk college women: A report of an 18-month follow-up. Journal of American College Health. 49, 6

Peden AR, Rayens MK, Hall LA, Grant E. (2005). Testing an intervention to reduce negative thinking, depressive symptoms, and chronic stressors in low-income single mothers. J Nurs Scholarsh. 37(3), 268-74.
PubMed Abstract:
http://www.ncbi.nlm.nih.gov/pubmed/16235869

CHAPTER NINETEEN: *Moving at Your Own Pace*

"The way to eat an elephant is one bite at a time"

- **HAMS Element Seventeen: Move at your own pace--you don't have to do it all at once**

Everyone is different. Some people may do best if they jump right in and gather all their resources then make a detailed plan and change all in one fell swoop. However, many of us do better if we break things down into small and doable pieces and move along one step at a time.

Lots of times people will decide to start a new exercise routine and determine that they will go to the gym for an hour a day every day seven days a week--even though they haven't been in a gym for years. This might last for a week or two and then the person stops going to the gym at all and the very mention of the word exercise makes this person sick. Sometimes getting overly ambitious and rushing in and trying to do everything at once just gets a person totally overwhelmed and they don't want to do anything at all after a while. The person in our exercise example might have been much better off starting off with 20 minutes of exercise two days a week and gradually building up to more from there.

Don't feel overwhelmed when you see all the worksheets and exercises in this book. You don't have to do them all. Nor do you have to do them all at once. Pick the ones that seem helpful to you. Complete them at your own pace. Take a deep breath and relax. You move through HAMS at your own pace and nothing is mandatory. Slow and steady wins the race.

We cannot emphasize strongly enough that all the HAMS tools, strategies, and elements are OPTIONAL, you need to pick and choose the ones that are right for you and that fit who you are right now. Later on you might find others which you wish to add in.

If you have ever gone to AA you may have heard that the 12 steps are "merely suggestions" (Wilson 1939)--but then have been told that you "sign your own death warrant" if you fail to follow them (Wilson 1953). HAMS is not like this. When we say that something is optional we mean it is optional. Period. So use what works and leave the rest.

- **Harm reduction never forces people to change in ways which they do not choose for themselves.**
- **Harm reduction recognizes that each of us is a unique human being different from all others.**
- **Harm reduction recognizes the need for "different strokes for different folks".**
- **Harm reduction supports every positive change.**

"It does not matter how slowly you go so long as you do not stop" --Confucius

REFERENCES:

Wilson W. (1939). <u>Alcoholics anonymous; the story of how many thousands of men and women have recovered from alcoholism</u>. Works Pub., New York.

Wilson W. (1953). <u>Twelve steps and twelve traditions</u>. Alcoholics Anonymous Pub., New York.

PART III: EVERYTHING YOU ALWAYS WANTED TO KNOW ABOUT ALCOHOL* *But you got told to go to AA and not to ask

"Electricity is actually made up of extremely tiny particles called electrons that you cannot see with the naked eye unless you have been drinking" --Dave Barry

CHAPTER TWENTY: Alcohol and the Brain

"Never Trust a Man Who Doesn't Drink" --W. C. Fields

20.1   Alcohol's Effects in the Brain
20.2   Myths and Facts about Alcohol and Brain Damage
20.3   THIQs - Fact or Fantasy?

20.1) Alcohol's Effects in the Brain

Alcohol can make you laugh or it can make you cry, it can make you lively or make you sleepy, it can boost your confidence or make you act the fool. How can alcohol have all these different effects on people? If we want to know how alcohol affects our moods and behaviors we must first understand a bit about how the brain works.

The human brain is made up of about 100 billion nerve cells (also known as neurons). Everything that we think, feel or do is the result of electrical signals passing back and forth between neurons. These electrical signals require the help of chemicals called neurotransmitters in order to pass from neuron to neuron. Scientists have identified around 60 different neurotransmitters so far and tell us that there are probably many more yet to be identified.

Different neurotransmitters have different effects in the brain. For example, serotonin is connected with mood. People suffering from clinical depression tend to have a shortage of serotonin in their brains, and medications like Prozac can help to alleviate depression by increasing the availability of serotonin in the brain. Endorphins are a class of neurotransmitters which act as the brain's natural painkillers.

Electrical signals in the brain are transmitted in the following manner: The neuron which is sending the electrical signal releases a neurotransmitter, and the neuron which is receiving the electrical signal accepts the neurotransmitter at a site which is called a receptor. When the neurotransmitter from the first neuron chemically binds to the receptor of the second neuron the electrical signal is transmitted. Neurotransmitters and receptors work like locks and keys: there is at least one different receptor for each different neurotransmitter. For example, an endorphin receptor can only be triggered by an endorphin; a serotonin receptor can only be triggered by serotonin, and so on. Different neurons have different receptors. Some neurons will only be triggered by serotonin, some only by an endorphin, and so on for all the different neurotransmitters.

Okay--now what does all of this have to do with alcohol?

Every mood altering substance from heroin to coffee has an effect on the neurotransmitter system of the brain. Some psychoactive drugs affect only one specific neurotransmitter system, whereas others affect many. Morphine, for example, mimics the neurotransmitter beta-endorphin--a natural painkiller found in the brain. Morphine is shaped like beta-endorphin and binds to the beta-endorphin receptors thus acting as a painkiller and also giving rise to feelings of pleasure. Caffeine is shaped like Adenosine and acts on the adenosine receptors. Alcohol on the other hand affects many different neurotransmitters, not just one, Why is this?

Morphine and caffeine are both large molecules. Neurotransmitters are also large molecules. Morphine and caffeine have the effects which they do because of their similarity in shape to neurotransmitters which occur naturally in the brain. Alcohol on the other hand is a quite small molecule. Alcohol does not mimic a neurotransmitter. So then how does alcohol affect neurotransmitters?

Alcohol is a fat soluble molecule. Fats (called lipids) are a major component of all cell membranes, including the cell membranes of neurons. Alcohol enters the cell membranes of neurons and changes their properties. Receptors are located on cell membranes and this means that receptor properties are altered by the presence of alcohol. Cell membranes also control the release of neurotransmitters and this means that the release of neurotransmitters is also affected by the presence of alcohol.

The effects of alcohol on receptors and neurotransmitters have been well documented for several neurotransmitters and their corresponding receptors. These effects are summarized in **Table 20.1**.

Table 20.1: Alcohol's Effect on Neurotransmitters and Receptors

- Glutamate
    - Alcohol inhibits glutamate receptor function
    - This causes muscular relaxation, discoordination, slurred speech, staggering, memory disruption, and blackouts
    - Ether and chloroform have similar effects on the glutamate system

- GABA (gamma-aminobutyric acid)

    - Alcohol enhances GABA receptor function
    - This causes feelings of calm, anxiety-reduction and sleep
    - Valium has a similar effect on the GABA system

- Dopamine

    - Alcohol raises dopamine levels
    - This leads to excitement and stimulation
    - Cocaine and amphetamine have similar effects on the dopamine system

- Endorphins

    - Alcohol raises endorphin levels
    - This kills pain and leads to an endorphin "high"
    - Morphine and heroin have similar effects on the endorphin system

---

Drugs like morphine or cocaine have been referred to as "chemical scalpels" because of their very precise effects on just one neurotransmitter system. Alcohol on the other hand is much more like a chemical hand grenade in that it affects just about all parts of the brain and all neurotransmitter systems. Alcohol affects all these systems at the same time. When people drink alcohol they become lively and excited because alcohol raises dopamine levels just as cocaine does, although alcohol does not raise dopamine levels anywhere near as much as cocaine does. When people drink alcohol they feel calm and lose their anxieties because alcohol makes the GABA receptors function more efficiently just like valium does. The reason that people tend to fall asleep after drinking alcohol or taking valium is also due to this effect on the GABA receptor. And alcohol has a painkilling effect like morphine and produces a high similar to morphine because it causes a release of endorphins into the brain thus raising the endorphin levels. (Note that the effect of morphine is different from alcohol in its mechanism--morphine imitates endorphins and binds to endorphin receptors whereas alcohol increases the amounts of the naturally occurring endorphins in the brain.) Finally we come to glutamate. Alcohol greatly inhibits the functioning of the glutamate receptor. Glutamate is responsible for the formation of new memories as well as for muscular coordination. It is alcohol's effect on the glutamate receptor which leads to slurred speech, and staggering in people who have consumed alcohol, as well as the inability to remember what one did that night when the morning after comes. Perhaps the only positive effect of this effect on the glutamate receptor is a feeling of muscular relaxation. Many negative effects of alcohol such as automobile fatalities due to drunk driving are the result of the loss of coordination caused by alcohol's effect on the glutamate receptor. Even small amounts of alcohol have a major impact on coordination--so the best policy is to never, never drink and drive.

You have probably observed that alcohol seems to have different effects on different people. Some people quickly become sleepy after drinking just a little alcohol whereas others become animated and want to just go, go, go. Research on mice suggests that this difference is genetic. Scientists have been able to breed strains of mice which quickly go to sleep after ingesting alcohol. They have also been able to breed strains of mice which become very active after ingesting alcohol. This strongly suggests that genetics determines which neurotransmitter system is most strongly affected by alcohol in which individual. Individuals who become sleepy soon after drinking probably have their GABA system more strongly affected by alcohol. And individuals who become lively and excited after drink probably have their dopamine system most strongly affected.

The effects of alcohol on the brain do not end when alcohol is completely metabolized and out of the system--what happens next is something called neurotransmitter rebound. This rebound effect is most easily illustrated if we look at what happens to many people when they use a drink or two as a sleep aid. These people often tend to wake up in the middle of the night and find themselves unable to fall back asleep. What is happening is this--alcohol has enhanced the functioning of the GABA system and has made these people feel relaxed and sleepy. The entire time that alcohol is present the GABA system is struggling to overcome the effects of alcohol and return to normal functioning. When all the alcohol is finally out of the body, the GABA system overshoots the mark and leaves people feeling restless and wide awake. This is why alcohol is not a good sleep aid. Large quantities of alcohol can keep a person asleep longer, but drinking large quantities of alcohol has its own negative effects. Neurotransmitter rebound seems also to be implicated in symptoms of hangovers such as hyper-sensitivity to light and in alcohol withdrawal syndrome giving rise to feelings of anxiety and panic and other symptoms as well.

Have scientists discovered everything that there is to know about alcohol's effects on the brain? It seems that this is clearly not the case. Scientists believe that alcohol probably affects many more neurotransmitters than the four discussed in this article. There is constant and ongoing research to discover how alcohol might affect other neurotransmitters. The future is likely to bring us much new knowledge about alcohol and the brain.

20.2) Myths and Facts about Alcohol and Brain Damage

Many claims about alcoholic brain damage are exaggerated; heavy drinking does not in general cause the death of brain cells or permanent cognitive dysfunction. Although heavy drinking can cause a great deal of health damage ranging from cirrhosis of the liver to pancreatitis, horror stories of alcoholic brain damage are largely a myth. Although **wet brain** is real it can be prevented by proper nutrition and is not directly caused by alcohol itself.

Alcohol, Brain Cells, and Brain Shrinkage

It has long been an established fact that actively drinking, alcohol dependent subjects have smaller brain volumes than normal control subjects who do not drink alcohol. Early researchers assumed that this was because alcohol killed the brain cells of alcohol dependent subjects, but current research proves that this hypothesis is largely untrue. Unless there has been brain damage as a result of **liver failure** or **thiamine deficiency**, the majority of brain cells of heavy drinkers are intact even though the brain has shrunk. Researchers have also discovered that a long period of abstinence from alcohol or moderate drinking tends to restore the volume of heavy drinker's brains back to normal.

The human brain consists of white cells and gray cells. The gray cells are responsible for thinking and feeling and decisions--they correspond to the Central Processing Unit (CPU) of your computer. The white cells are like the cables of your computer which connect the keyboard and the monitor to the CPU. In 1993 Jensen and Pakkenberg did brain cell counts which compared the number of cells in the brains of heavy drinkers with those of nondrinkers. What they found was that the number of gray cells was the same in both the heavy drinkers and the nondrinkers. However, there were fewer white brain cells in the brains of the drinkers which implies that alcohol kills white brain cells.

In 2009 George Fein discovered that there was one part of the brain in the parietal lobe--which is associated with spatial processing--where alcohol kills gray cells. Fein claims that this explains why even after alcohol dependent subjects regain use of all their other cognitive functions they still seem to have difficulties with spatial processing. Studies by Pfefferbaum (1995, 1998) show that with long periods of abstinence or moderate drinking the brains of alcohol dependent subjects return to nearly the same size as their nondrinking counterparts. It is not conclusive whether shrinkage is more pronounced in males, in females, or the same in both (Hommer, 2003).

To summarize: The brains of long term, heavy drinkers shrink, but they return to almost full normal size after a long period of alcohol abstinence or moderate drinking. Long-term, heavy drinking kills some white brain cells and some of the gray cells responsible for spatial processing; however, it does not kill any other gray cells. In particular, the gray cells which are responsible for our thinking, decision making, and other cognitive processes remain intact even in long-term, heavy drinkers. Unless there is brain damage which is due to **thiamine deficiency** or **liver failure**, nearly all brain functions of alcohol dependent drinkers can be returned to normal with a long period of abstinence or moderate drinking. Cognitive functioning tends to return to normal when brain size returns to normal.

There is some evidence that both the amount of brain shrinkage and the amount of cognitive deficit are dependent on the quantity of alcohol consumed and the number of years of heavy drinking; it is not established whether this relationship is linear or not.

Amnesia and Dementia Due To Thiamine Deficiency - Wernicke-Korsakoff Syndrome Aka Wetbrain

The condition known as **wetbrain** or **Wernicke-Korsakoff Syndrome** is a form of brain damage which is characterized by severe amnesia, confabulation (false memories), and sometimes dementia (Emsley, et al. 1996). It is not caused by direct effects of alcohol on the brain. It is caused by a severe deficiency of **Thiamine** (vitamin B1) and is often precipitated by a sudden influx of glucose. A number of things have been shown to lead to a severe enough thiamine deficiency to trigger wetbrain. These include a diet consisting solely of polished rice, prolonged bouts of morning sickness, bulimia and severe alcohol dependence.

Wetbrain has a sudden onset--it is not something which happens gradually over time. The first stage of wetbrain is called Wernicke's encephalopathy. When there is a sudden influx of glucose in a brain which is deprived of thiamine the brain cells begin to die. This is because the chemical reactions which supply these brain cells with energy for life use thiamine to turn glucose into energy in a chemical process called the Krebs cycle. When there is an influx of glucose and no thiamine to help metabolize it, these brain cells burn out like a car engine running on high octane gasoline at high speed with no oil. The brain cells which die first are the ones which require the most thiamine to function. These brain cells are located around the middle of the brain and are the brain cells which are associated with memory and muscular movement. The brain cells of the cerebellum, which controls balance, are also affected.

The symptoms of Wernicke's encephalopathy are confusion, lack of coordination, and involuntary eye movements. If Wernicke's encephalopathy is immediately treated with thiamine it can be stopped and largely reversed. However, if Wernicke's encephalopathy is not immediately treated, it quickly turns into Korsakoff's psychosis, which is permanent and largely resistant to treatment. Symptoms of Korsakoff's syndrome include loss of past memories, inability to learn new things, confabulation (remembering things which never happened), lack of coordination and unsteady gait, and in severe cases dementia. In some cases physicians who should have known better have precipitated Wernicke-Korsakoff syndrome in alcohol dependent patients by putting them on a glucose drip instead of a thiamine drip.

Alcohol tends to block absorption of thiamine by the human body, so all people who drink alcohol should be careful to eat well and should also take vitamin B1 pills to make sure that they are getting enough thiamine. Very heavy drinkers who consume around a fifth or a quart of vodka per day are often too nauseous to eat well and may tend to vomit up what they do eat. Moreover, if these people are living on the streets, they may be unwilling to spend money on food which could be used to buy alcohol. These people are in the greatest danger of developing Wernicke-Korsakoff syndrome.

Breedlove et al (2007) tell us that all cases of wetbrain due to alcohol ingestion could be prevented by government regulations requiring that thiamine be added to alcoholic beverages. It is unfortunate that our puritanical US government prefers to send people to abstinence-based programs which fail rather than to eliminate much human suffering by implementing the simple harm reduction policy of adding thiamine to alcoholic beverages.

HAMS recommends that all drinkers be sure to eat nutritious meals and take vitamins--especially thiamine--to help ward off wetbrain. It is also good to try and have some abstinence days or otherwise reduce alcohol intake to help prevent this.

Wetbrain is sometimes complicated by **hepatic encephalopathy**.

Hepatic Encephalopathy

Hepatic encephalopathy is damage to the brain which is a result of liver failure, which may be caused by cirrhosis, hepatitis, etc. One job of the liver is to screen out toxins so that they can be disposed of as waste rather than circulate in the blood and damage delicate tissues like the brain. When the liver fails it is believed that toxins like ammonia and manganese cross the blood-brain barrier and cause damage to the brain--i.e. hepatic encephalopathy.

Symptoms of hepatic encephalopathy include lethargy, apathy, disorientation, inappropriate behavior, and slurred speech. In severe cases there may be coma. If alcohol causes liver failure, then hepatic encephalopathy can be one result.

Alcohol and Cognitive Dysfunction

People who drink massive quantities of alcohol suffer brain shrinkage and cognitive dysfunction as a result. However, the good news is that if these heavy drinkers do not have thiamine-related brain damage or liver-related brain damage then this cognitive dysfunction and brain shrinkage is almost entirely reversible with a change from heavy drinking to reduced drinking or alcohol abstinence.

Although most researchers emphasize alcohol abstinence, research from Sullivan et al (2000b) demonstrates that reduced drinking also restores cognitive function in formerly alcohol dependent drinkers: abstinence is not the only solution

The data in **Table 20.2** is a conflation of information contained in two papers by George Fein about recovery of cognitive function after stopping heavy drinking. One paper is a literature review published in 1990 and the other is a study published in 2006.

Table 20.2) Presence of cognitive dysfunction after cessation of heavy drinking				
	Acute detox	Early abs	Mid abs	Late abs
	Less than 2 weeks	2 weeks to 2 months	2 months to 5 years	7 years average
Distractibility	YES	NO	NO	NO
Mild confusion	YES	NO	NO	NO
Irritability	YES	NO	NO	NO
Attention and concentration	YES	YES	NO	NO
Reaction time	YES	YES	NO	NO
Verbal learning ability	YES	YES	NO	NO
Verbal abstract reasoning	YES	YES	NO	NO
Verbal short-term memory	YES	YES	NO	NO
Nonverbal abstract reasoning	YES	YES	YES	NO
Mental flexibility	YES	YES	YES	NO
Nonverbal short-term memory	YES	YES	YES	NO
Visuospatial abilities	YES	YES	YES	MAYBE

Although Fein's 1990 paper gives a spread of two months to five years for mid stage recovery of cognitive function, Fein's 2006 paper narrows this down and tells us that that these cognitive functions are generally recovered at the end of the first year after ceasing heavy drinking. Parsons (1998) states that remission of cognitive dysfunction occurs 4 to 5 years after ceasing heavy drinking.

In Fein's 2006 study, the male drinkers consumed 361.8 ± 257.2 standard drinks per month for a period of 51.0 ± 30.9 months at the peak of their drinking. The female drinkers consumed 264.0 ± 202.8 standard drinks per month for a period of 92.1 ± 81.2 months at their peak. (One standard drink = 14g ETOH.) This is around a half a liter of vodka (80 proof) per day every day for the men and around a "pint" (375 ml) of vodka per day every day for the women. Control subjects averaged less than half a drink per day. According to Parsons (1998) there is no significant difference between alcohol dependent males and females on the variable of cognitive dysfunction.

Although the dose, the frequency, and the duration of alcohol consumption all appear to have an effect on the degree of cognitive dysfunction (as well as degree of incoordination) the relationship is not entirely clear cut. Parsons (1998) proposes a nonlinear, tripartite, threshold model of the effect of alcohol dose on cognitive dysfunction as exemplified in **Table 20.3**.

Table 20.3) Alcohol Dose and Cognitive Dysfunction	
Number of standard drinks per week	**Degree of cognitive dysfunction**
17 or less	None
18 - 35	Small
36 - 50	Medium
51 or more	Large

(Note: In their original paper Parson and Nixon used the old definition of a US standard drink--12g ETOH. This has been corrected to the current 14g definition here.)

Sullivan (2000c) tells us that light relapsers performed comparably to abstinent subjects on cognitive tests at the mid stage period of recovery of cognitive function which suggests that reduced drinking may be as good a strategy as abstinence for the recovery of cognitive function in formerly dependent drinkers.

We should also note that these cognitive deficits are present statistically--when we look at actual individuals there are some alcohol dependent subjects in acute detox stage who show better cognitive function than some normal controls--it is just that they are a small minority. Parsons (1998) found 85% discrimination between the control group and the alcohol dependent group when the means of several tests were taken into account. This means that 15% of the alcohol dependent subjects were showing cognitive functioning equal to that of the controls.

In summary: Heavy drinkers who consume around a quart of booze or so every day suffer from cognitive defects and brain shrinkage. When these heavy drinkers quit drinking or reduce their consumption of alcohol to reasonable levels most of these cognitive dysfunction and much of this brain shrinkage goes away by the end of the first year. Virtually all of the cognitive dysfunction and brain shrinkage is gone at the at the end of five or so years except for some loss of white matter, a small loss of gray matter which controls spatial processing, and some minor dysfunction of spatial processing in some individuals. This is true for heavy drinkers who do not have thiamine related brain damage or brain damage related to liver failure.

Conclusion

We should have learned long ago that scare tactics based on lies not only fail, but backfire and lead to worse problems than before. When kids found that "Reefer Madness" was a lie they stopped believing warnings about heroin, too. Since we know that heavy drinkers like Hemingway, O'Neill, Faulkner and Steinbeck managed to win the Nobel Prize in Literature in spite of their drinking habits, this puts a lie to the myth that every drinker turns into a brain damaged idiot. The time to put an end to the lies is now. Drinking a fifth of liquor a day is clearly not good for your health, but if you watch your nutrition and keep a handle on things then occasionally engaging in recreational intoxication is not nearly so bad as the fear-mongers would lead us to believe.

Lying to kids by telling them that a single night of heavy drinking will turn their brain into a walnut is irresponsible. Kids observe adults engaging in occasional recreational intoxications without suffering major brain damage and they know that they are being lied to. Once you lie to kids you lose your credibility for good. Once you have cried wolf then kids will not believe you when you warn them about real dangers like drinking and driving, the addictive nature of heroin, or the fact that drinking a fifth of liquor a day can rot your liver.

Let's stop all the scare tactics and tell kids the truth for a change--okay?

20.3) THIQs - Fact or Fantasy?

In 1970 Dr. Virginia Davis et al published experimental research on alcoholic rats which found evidence of THIQs (tetrahydroisoquinolines) in their brains. Since THIQs are chemically related to opiates it was thought that this might explain the difference between alcoholic drinkers and normal drinkers. In 1983 Sjoquist et al published autopsy results on alcoholics which seemed to confirm the presence of THIQs in their brains. However, other researchers had difficulty replicating these results. THIQs were also found to be present in the brains of non-drinkers. While the academic debate raged, workers at rehab centers began to tell clients that there was proof that their "alcoholic" brains were different than normal brains because of THIQs.

A 2006 article by Quertemont and Didone notes that measuring the presence and quantities of THIQs in brain is not an easy task and that more sophisticated measures are needed. It is not a simple matter of "People with THIQs in their brains are alcoholics and those without are not". Most contemporary researchers agree that it is still an open question what effect, if any, THIQs have on the brains of heavy drinkers.

REFERENCES:

Breedlove SM, Rosenzweig MR, Watson NV. (2007). Biological Psychology: An Introduction to Behavioral, Cognitive, and Clinical Neuroscience. Fifth Edition. Sinauer Associates, Inc.

Davis VE, Walsh MJ. (1970) Alcohol, Amines, and Alkaloids: A Possible Biochemical Basis for Alcohol Addiction. Science. 167(3920), 1005-7.
PubMed Abstract:
http://www.ncbi.nlm.nih.gov/pubmed/5460776

Dlugos CA, Pentney RJ. (1997). Morphometric evidence that the total number of synapses on Purkinje neurons of old F344 rats is reduced after long-term ethanol treatment and restored to control levels after recovery. Alcohol and alcoholism (Oxford, Oxfordshire). 32(2), 161-72.
PubMed Abstract:
http://www.ncbi.nlm.nih.gov/pubmed/9105510
Free Full Text:
http://alcalc.oxfordjournals.org/cgi/reprint/32/2/161.pdf

Emsley R, Smith R, Roberts M, Kapnias S, Pieters H, Maritz S. (1996). Magnetic resonance imaging in alcoholic Korsakoff's syndrome: evidence for an association with alcoholic dementia. Alcohol and alcoholism (Oxford, Oxfordshire). 31(5), 479-86.
PubMed Abstract:
http://www.ncbi.nlm.nih.gov/pubmed/8949964
Free Full Text:
http://alcalc.oxfordjournals.org/cgi/reprint/31/5/479.pdf

Fama R, Marsh L, Sullivan EV. (2004). Dissociation of remote and anterograde memory impairment and neural correlates in alcoholic Korsakoff syndrome. <u>Journal of the International Neuropsychological Society: JINS</u>. 10(3), 427-41.
PubMed Abstract:
http://www.ncbi.nlm.nih.gov/pubmed/15147600

Fama R, Eisen JC, Rosenbloom MJ, Sassoon SA, Kemper CA, Deresinski S, Pfefferbaum A, Sullivan EV. (2007). Upper and lower limb motor impairments in alcoholism, HIV infection, and their comorbidity. <u>Alcoholism, clinical and experimental research</u>. 31(6), 1038-44.
PubMed Abstract:
http://www.ncbi.nlm.nih.gov/pubmed/17403062

Fama R, Pfefferbaum A, Sullivan EV. (2004). Perceptual learning in detoxified alcoholic men: contributions from explicit memory, executive function, and age. <u>Alcoholism, clinical and experimental research</u>. 28(11), 1657-65.
PubMed Abstract:
http://www.ncbi.nlm.nih.gov/pubmed/15547452

Fein G, Shimotsu R, Chu R, Barakos J. (2009). Parietal gray matter volume loss is related to spatial processing deficits in long-term abstinent alcoholic men. <u>Alcoholism, clinical and experimental research</u>. 33(10), 1806-14.
PubMed Abstract:
http://www.ncbi.nlm.nih.gov/pubmed/19645730

Fein G, Torres J, Price LJ, Di Sclafani V. (2006). Cognitive performance in long-term abstinent alcoholic individuals. <u>Alcoholism, clinical and experimental research</u>. 30(9), 1538-44.
PubMed Abstract:
http://www.ncbi.nlm.nih.gov/pubmed/16930216
Free Full Text:
http://www.ncbi.nlm.nih.gov/pmc/articles/PMC1868685/pdf/nihms20940.pdf

Fein G, Bachman L, Fisher S, Davenport L. (1990). Cognitive impairments in abstinent alcoholics. <u>The Western journal of medicine</u>. 152(5), 531-7.
PubMed Abstract:
http://www.ncbi.nlm.nih.gov/pubmed/2190421
Free Full Text:
http://www.ncbi.nlm.nih.gov/pmc/articles/PMC1002406/pdf/westjmed00117-0069.pdf

Harper C, Kril J. (1991). If you drink your brain will shrink. Neuropathological considerations. <u>Alcohol and alcoholism (Oxford, Oxfordshire)</u>. Supplement 1, 375-80.
PubMed Abstract:
http://www.ncbi.nlm.nih.gov/pubmed/1845566

Harper C, Kril J. (1994). An introduction to alcohol-induced brain damage and its causes. <u>Alcohol and alcoholism (Oxford, Oxfordshire)</u>. Supplement 2, 237-43.
PubMed Abstract:
http://www.ncbi.nlm.nih.gov/pubmed/8974342

Hommer DW. (2003). Male and female sensitivity to alcohol-induced brain damage. <u>Alcohol research & health</u>. 27(2), 181-5.
PubMed Abstract:
http://www.ncbi.nlm.nih.gov/pubmed/15303629
Free Full Text:
http://pubs.niaaa.nih.gov/publications/arh27-2/181-185.pdf

Jensen GB, Pakkenberg B. (1993). Do alcoholics drink their neurons away? <u>Lancet</u>. 342(8881), 1201-4.
PubMed Abstract:
http://www.ncbi.nlm.nih.gov/pubmed/7901529

Moselhy HF, Georgiou G, Kahn A. (2001). Frontal lobe changes in alcoholism: a review of the literature. <u>Alcohol and alcoholism (Oxford, Oxfordshire)</u>. 36(5), 357-68.
PubMed Abstract:
http://www.ncbi.nlm.nih.gov/pubmed/11524299
Free Full Text:
http://alcalc.oxfordjournals.org/cgi/reprint/36/5/357.pdf

Oscar-Berman M, Marinković K. (2007). Alcohol: effects on neurobehavioral functions and the brain. <u>Neuropsychology review</u>. 17(3), 239-57.
PubMed Abstract:
http://www.ncbi.nlm.nih.gov/pubmed/17874302

Oscar-Berman M, Kirkley SM, Gansler DA, Couture A. (Apr 2004). Comparisons of Korsakoff and non-Korsakoff alcoholics on neuropsychological tests of prefrontal brain functioning. <u>Alcoholism, clinical and experimental research</u>. 28(4), 667-75.
PubMed Abstract:
http://www.ncbi.nlm.nih.gov/pubmed/15100620

Parsons OA. (1998). Neurocognitive deficits in alcoholics and social drinkers: a continuum? <u>Alcoholism, clinical and experimental research</u>. 22(4), 954-61.
PubMed Abstract:
http://www.ncbi.nlm.nih.gov/pubmed/9660328

Parsons OA, Nixon SJ. (1998). Cognitive functioning in sober social drinkers: a review of the research since 1986. <u>Journal of studies on alcohol</u>. 59(2), 180-90.
PubMed Abstract:
http://www.ncbi.nlm.nih.gov/pubmed/9500305

Pfefferbaum A, Sullivan EV, Mathalon DH, Shear PK, Rosenbloom MJ, Lim KO. (1995). Longitudinal changes in magnetic resonance imaging brain volumes in abstinent and relapsed alcoholics. <u>Alcoholism, clinical and experimental research</u>. 19(5), 1177-91.
PubMed Abstract:
http://www.ncbi.nlm.nih.gov/pubmed/8561288

Pfefferbaum A, Sullivan EV, Rosenbloom MJ, Mathalon DH, Lim KO. (1998). A controlled study of cortical gray matter and ventricular changes in alcoholic men over a 5-year interval. Archives of general psychiatry. 55(10), 905-12.
PubMed Abstract:
http://www.ncbi.nlm.nih.gov/pubmed/9783561

Quertemont E, Didone V. (2006) Role of Acetaldehyde in Mediating the Pharmacological and Behavioral Effects of Alcohol. Alcohol Research & Health. 29(4), 258-65.
PubMed Abstract:
http://www.ncbi.nlm.nih.gov/pubmed/17718404
Free Full Text:
http://pubs.niaaa.nih.gov/publications/arh294/258-265.pdf

Salen PN. Wernicke Encephalopathy. eMedicine.
http://emedicine.medscape.com/article/794583-overview
Accessed October 29, 2009.

Sjoquist B, Perdahl E, Winblad B. (1983) The effect of alcoholism on salsolinol and biogenic amines in human brain. Drug and alcohol dependence. 12(1), 15-23.
PubMed Abstract:
http://www.ncbi.nlm.nih.gov/pubmed/6196169

Sullivan EV, Marsh L. (2003). Hippocampal volume deficits in alcoholic Korsakoff's syndrome. Neurology. 61(12), 1716-9.
PubMed Abstract:
http://www.ncbi.nlm.nih.gov/pubmed/14694035

Sullivan EV, Deshmukh A, Desmond JE, Lim KO, Pfefferbaum A. (2000). Cerebellar volume decline in normal aging, alcoholism, and Korsakoff's syndrome: relation to ataxia. Neuropsychology. 14(3), 341-52.
PubMed Abstract:
http://www.ncbi.nlm.nih.gov/pubmed/10928737

Sullivan EV, Rosenbloom MJ, Pfefferbaum A. (2000). Pattern of motor and cognitive deficits in detoxified alcoholic men. Alcoholism, clinical and experimental research. 24(5), 611-21.
PubMed Abstract:
http://www.ncbi.nlm.nih.gov/pubmcd/10832902

Sullivan EV, Rosenbloom MJ, Lim KO, Pfefferbaum A. (2000). Longitudinal changes in cognition, gait, and balance in abstinent and relapsed alcoholic men: relationships to changes in brain structure. Neuropsychology. 14(2), 178-88.
PubMed Abstract:
http://www.ncbi.nlm.nih.gov/pubmed/10791858

Sullivan EV, Desmond JE, Lim KO, Pfefferbaum A. (2002). Speed and efficiency but not accuracy or timing deficits of limb movements in alcoholic men and women. Alcoholism, clinical and experimental research. 26(5), 705-13.
PubMed Abstract:

http://www.ncbi.nlm.nih.gov/pubmed/12045480

Sullivan EV, Fama R, Rosenbloom MJ, Pfefferbaum A. (2002). A profile of neuropsychological deficits in alcoholic women. Neuropsychology. 16(1), 74-83.
PubMed Abstract:
http://www.ncbi.nlm.nih.gov/pubmed/11853359

Wolf, DC. Encephalopathy, Hepatic. eMedicine.
http://emedicine.medscape.com/article/186101-overview
Accessed October 29, 2009.

Xiong, GL. Wernicke-Korsakoff Syndrome. eMedicine.
http://emedicine.medscape.com/article/288379-overview
Accessed October 29, 2009.

CHAPTER TWENTY ONE: Alcohol and the Body

"When I read about the evils of drinking, I gave up reading." --Henny Youngman

21.1) How the Body Breaks Down Alcohol

Introduction

When you drink beverage alcohol around 2 to 8 percent is lost through urine, sweat, or the breath. The other 92 to 98 percent is metabolized by your body. All ethyl alcohol which is broken down in the human body is first converted to acetaldehyde, and then this acetaldehyde is converted into acetic acid radicals--also known as acetyl radicals. Acetaldehyde is a poison which is a close relative of formaldehyde and which we will discuss it in more detail later on. Acetic acid is the essential component of vinegar. The acetic acid radical is the combining form of acetic acid. This acetic acid radical combines with Coenzyme A to form acetyl-CoA. The acetyl-CoA then enters the Krebs Cycle, which is the basic powerhouse of the human body. Inside the Krebs Cycle this acetyl radical is eventually broken down into carbon dioxide and water.

There are three different enzymes which the body uses to convert alcohol to acetaldehyde. All three of these enzymes work by stripping two hydrogen atoms off from the alcohol molecule. This converts the alcohol molecule into a molecule of acetaldehyde as shown in **Figure 21.1**.

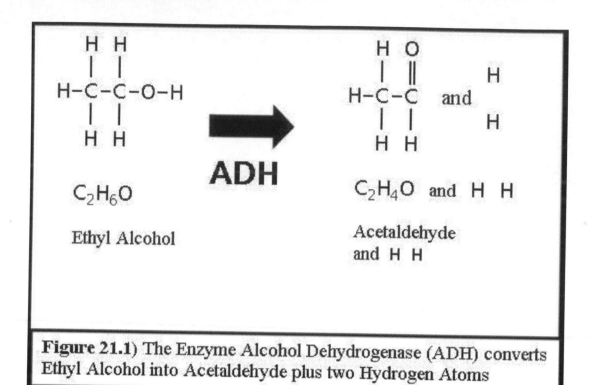

Figure 21.1) The Enzyme Alcohol Dehydrogenase (ADH) converts Ethyl Alcohol into Acetaldehyde plus two Hydrogen Atoms

The acetaldehyde is then converted by a different enzyme into the acetyl radical as shown in **Figure 21.2**.

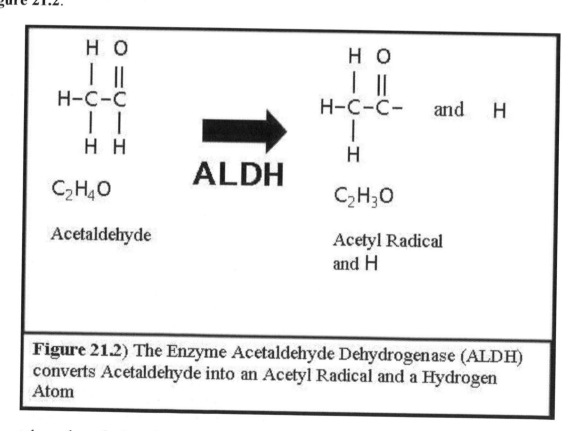

Figure 21.2) The Enzyme Acetaldehyde Dehydrogenase (ALDH) converts Acetaldehyde into an Acetyl Radical and a Hydrogen Atom

Let us take a closer look at the enzymes which convert alcohol into acetaldehyde.

147

The Three Alcohol Enzymes

The three enzymes which can convert alcohol to acetaldehyde are:

- alcohol dehydrogenase (ADH) ·
- cytochrome P450 (CYP2E1) ·
- catalase

These three enzymes are each found in different parts of the body and each of them handles the hydrogen atoms which are stripped off from the alcohol molecule in a different way. Let us first look at alcohol dehydrogenase.

Alcohol dehydrogenase: The name "alcohol dehydrogenase" sounds like quite a mouthful, but it is quite self-explanatory if we break it down into its component parts. "de-" is a prefix which means "to remove". We find it in such words as "dethrone" which means "to remove from the throne". "-ase" is a suffix which means "enzyme". Any time you see a chemical term which ends in the suffix "-ase" you know that you are dealing with an enzyme. "hydrogen" means "hydrogen" of course. So "de-hydrogen-ase" means "an enzyme which removes hydrogen atoms", and "alcohol dehydrogenase" means "an enzyme which removes hydrogen atoms from the alcohol molecule". The name alcohol dehydrogenase is sometimes abbreviated to ADH.

Alcohol dehydrogenase is the workhorse of the alcohol enzymes--it breaks down the majority of the alcohol that enters the human body. Alcohol dehydrogenase is actually the name for a family of enzymes which break down alcohol--each of which has a slightly different molecular structure. Researchers have identified as many as 10 varieties of the alcohol dehydrogenase molecule. All of them bring about the same chemical reaction--the difference is that some varieties of alcohol dehydrogenase work more efficiently than others. As we shall see below, these variations in the alcohol dehydrogenase molecule can explain why some individuals react differently to alcohol than others.

The alcohol dehydrogenase molecules do their work primarily in the stomach and the liver, although traces of them are found in other tissues as well. The hydrogen which is released when alcohol dehydrogenase turns alcohol into acetaldehyde is bound to a compound called NAD+ (Nicotinamide Adenine Dinucleotide) to form NADH (this is short for Nicotinamide Adenine Dinucleotide plus Hydrogen). Alcohol dehydrogenase does its work in the cellular fluid (cytosol) of the cell.

Cytochrome P450 2E1 (CYP2E1): In light social drinkers nearly all the alcohol consumed is taken care of by alcohol dehydrogenase as described above. However, the enzyme Cytochrome P450 2E1 (abbreviated CYP2E1) becomes quite active in metabolizing alcohol in chronic heavy drinkers. CYP2E1 does its work in the liver. The hydrogen released by this reaction is bound to oxygen and to NADPH to form water and NADP+. This reaction takes energy rather than producing it.

CYP2E1 does its work in the microsomes of the cell. This is sometimes referred to as MEOS (Microsomal Ethanol Oxidizing System). CYP2E1 is a member of the Cytochrome P450 enzyme family.

Catalase: Catalase is found in tiny organs inside of cells called peroxisomes. Catalase is found all over the human body. When catalase turns alcohol into acetaldehyde the hydrogen which is released is bound to hydrogen peroxide molecules which then become water. Although catalase is active everywhere in the body, catalase is of particular interest to researchers because it metabolizes alcohol in the brain. The acetaldehyde released into the brain by the metabolism of alcohol by catalase has the potential to combine with neurotransmitters to form new compounds known as THIQs (tetrahydroisoquinolines, also sometimes called TIQs). Some researchers believe that THIQs are the cause of alcohol addiction and that the presence of THIQs distinguishes addicted drinkers from social drinkers. Other researches strongly dispute the validity of the THIQ hypothesis of alcohol addiction.. The actual role of THIQs remains controversial and a topic for further research.

Summary: Figure 21.3 summarizes how the three enzymes interact with alcohol to produce acetaldehyde.

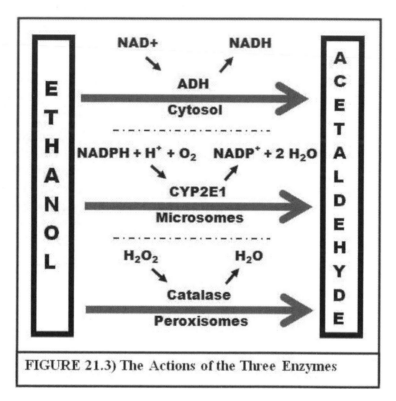

FIGURE 21.3) The Actions of the Three Enzymes

How Acetaldehyde Dehydrogenase Works

Acetaldehyde dehydrogenase does its work in the mitochondria of cells and removes a hydrogen atom from acetaldehyde to produce an acetic acid radical as is shown in **Figure 21.2** above. This hydrogen atom combines with NAD+ to form NADH.

There are several varieties of aldehyde dehydrogenase found in the human body. The one which normally breaks down acetaldehyde is called ALDH2. There is another variety aldehyde dehydrogenase found in the human body which is called ALDH2*2. ALDH2*2 is only about 8% as efficient as ALDH2 in metabolizing acetaldehyde. Some East Asian people have ALDH2*2 instead of ALDH2 in their bodies. These individuals find the effect of alcohol to be very unpleasant as we discuss below. The aldehyde dehydrogenase enzymes are found in many tissues of the body, but are at the highest concentration in the liver.

The Problem with Too Much NADH

Alcohol metabolism produces excess amounts of NADH (Nicotinamide Adenine Dinucleotide plus Hydrogen). This excess of NADH can lead to acidosis from lactic acid build-up and hypoglycemia from lack of glucose synthesis. It can also lead to weight gain, fatty liver, and heart attack. Fatty liver can progress to liver disease and cirrhosis.

Alcohol Affects Some People Differently from Others

Women: If a woman and a man of the same weight drink the same amount of alcohol under the exact same circumstances, the woman will on the average have a much higher BAC (Blood Alcohol Content) than the man. This is because women have much less of the enzyme alcohol dehydrogenase in their stomachs than men do. If the same man and woman are given an injection of alcohol instead of drinking it they will tend to have the same BAC. This is because when the alcohol is injected it bypasses the alcohol dehydrogenase in the stomach.

East Asians: Most individuals use a form of acetaldehyde dehydrogenase called ALD2 to metabolize the acetaldehyde which results from alcohol metabolism. However, many East Asians produce a form of acetaldehyde dehydrogenase called ALD2*2 which is far less efficient at breaking down acetaldehyde than ALD2. ALD2*2 is only about 8% as efficient as ALD2 at metabolizing acetaldehyde.

Additionally many East Asians have a form of alcohol dehydrogenase that is more efficient at turning alcohol into acetaldehyde than that of people from other genetic backgrounds. The end result is that these people wind up with large amounts of the poisonous compound acetaldehyde in their bodies whenever they drink alcohol. This acetaldehyde causes their faces to flush and leads to headaches, nausea, vomiting, heart palpitations and other extreme physical unpleasantness. This reaction to alcohol is sometimes referred to as the "flush syndrome". The symptoms of flush syndrome are exactly the same as the symptoms caused in people who take the anti-drinking medication antabuse. Antabuse also causes a build-up of acetaldehyde within the body. As many as 50% of people of Japanese descent are estimated to show flush syndrome. Flush syndrome is more severe in some individuals than others. It is estimated that individuals with severe flush syndrome do not develop alcohol problems because they find drinking alcohol to be extremely unpleasant.

Older Males: As men age they tend to produce less alcohol dehydrogenase. Older men are likely to become more intoxicated on smaller amounts of alcohol than younger men. Alcohol dehydrogenase in women is apparently not affected by age.

Menopausal Women: Apparently hormone changes which occur at menopause can cause menopausal women to become more intoxicated on smaller doses of alcohol.

People with Liver Damage: People with liver damage produce less alcohol dehydrogenase than do those with healthy livers and thus can become more intoxicated on smaller doses of alcohol. This phenomenon is referred to as Reverse Tolerance.

Frequent Heavy Drinkers: Frequent heavy drinkers produce more alcohol dehydrogenase than other people and thus become less intoxicated on larger quantities of alcohol. These people can metabolize up to 38 ml (over 2 standard drinks) of alcohol per hour whereas the average person metabolizes only around 13 ml (about 0.7 standard drinks) per hour.

How Antabuse Works

Antabuse is the drug that makes people sick if they drink alcohol. The drug antabuse binds to the enzyme acetaldehyde dehydrogenase and prevents it from breaking down the acetaldehyde produced by the metabolism of alcohol. Since acetaldehyde is a poison, as it builds up it produces very unpleasant symptoms including facial flushing, headaches, nausea, vomiting, heart palpitations and other extreme physical unpleasantness. Large quantities of alcohol mixed with antabuse can lead to death.

Why You Shouldn't Drink on an Empty Stomach

The surface area of the human stomach is only a couple of square feet, but because the small intestine has protrusions called villi, the surface area of the small intestine is thousands and thousands of square feet. Because of this fact the small intestine is many, many times more efficient than the stomach at absorbing alcohol. If you want the alcohol to be absorbed into the bloodstream slowly so that your BAC will only rise slowly, your best bet is to keep the alcohol in the stomach for as long as possible. This actually can be done. There is a valve between the stomach and the small intestine called the pyloric valve, and when this valve is closed the alcohol will stay in the stomach. This valve stays closed when the stomach is full of food. So this is why eating a full meal helps keep you from becoming rapidly intoxicated. Fatty foods and heavy foods tend to stay in the stomach longer than vegetables or sugars. Bluesman Charlie Patton spoke the truth when he said "If you eat a lot of fat meat you don't get so drunk." This was his formula for maintaining when he played at parties where the booze flowed all night long.

What You Drink Does Matter!!

Some people say that alcohol is alcohol and it doesn't matter what you drink. The actual fact--as I am sure that many of us know from experience--is that it makes a great deal of difference what one drinks. This is true for several reasons.

Alcohol Concentration: Many people find that they get much more intoxicated when drinking straight vodka than they do when drinking beer. This is because they get a lot more alcohol in their bodies in a lot shorter period of time when drinking the vodka. As a general rule of thumb the less concentrated the alcohol in a drink the less alcohol one will put into their body per hour.

Flavor: People also tend to drink strongly flavored drinks more slowly than tasteless drinks. So most people will get more alcohol into their system per hour when drinking vodka than they will when drinking whiskey.

Carbonation: Carbonation speeds the absorption of alcohol into the bloodstream. People drinking carbonated drinks will become intoxicated more quickly and achieve higher BACs than people dinking the same amount of alcohol per hour in the form of non-carbonated drinks. There is, however, a trade-off here because many people drink carbonated drinks more slowly than non-carbonated drinks.

Diet Soda: Diet soda interacts with alcohol too, so people who drink mixed drinks made with diet soda will become intoxicated more quickly and achieve higher BACS than people drinking identical drinks made with regular soda. Researchers in Adelaide, Australia found that the stomach emptied into the small intestine in 21.1 minutes for the people who drank mixed drinks made with diet soda. When people drank drinks made with regular soda, the stomach emptied in 36.3 minutes (P < .01). Peak blood alcohol concentration was 0.053 g% for the diet drinks and 0.034 g% with the regular drinks.

Beware Mixing Alcohol with Your Medications

Appendix One lists some of the more common alcohol-medication interactions. We recommend that you check a trusted source such as the PDR (Physician's Desk Reference) or drugs.com for information about possible interactions with alcohol any time that you begin taking a new medication.

Just for a quick reference we will note here some very common Over The Counter (OTC) and prescriptions medications and a few other substances which you should be very cautious about mixing with alcohol. Some of them may surprise you.

Aspirin: For some reason we are not quite sure of aspirin appears to block the action of alcohol dehydrogenase. What this means is that if you take aspirin before drinking you will became much more intoxicated on a much smaller dose of alcohol than usual. It is generally recommended that you do not take aspirin for around six hours before drinking alcohol. If you have taken aspirin before drinking be cautious and try to limit your alcohol intake as much as possible.

Cayenne pepper: Cayenne pepper dilates the blood vessels and apparently leads higher BACs and more exposure of the brain to alcohol. In short if you drink alcohol while ingesting a lot of cayenne pepper you will become much drunker than usual. Avoid red pepper vodka!

Tylenol (acetaminophen, paracetamol): Even by itself Tylenol can cause liver failure. Combining Tylenol with alcohol is a horrible one-two punch to the liver. If you love your liver then don't take Tylenol or Tylenol PM or anything else containing acetaminophen with alcohol or when you are hungover. Else you might as well fry up your liver with onions!!

Ambien: Mixing alcohol with ambien is just about a sure recipe for a blackout or a brownout. People who mix the two also often report sleepwalking or even sleep eating. Best to take one or the other and not mix them together.

Narcotic painkillers: Another recipe for blackout and disturbed behavior. Avoid mixing alcohol with Percocet, percodan, vicodin, oxycontin, codeine, morphine or any other narcotic pain killers.

Benadryl (diphenhydramine), Dramamine (dimenhydrinate), and Unisom Nighttime (doxylamine): Mixing alcohol with any antihistamine which causes drowsiness will definitely enhance the feeling of drowsiness many times over. All OTC sleep aids consist of one of the above named antihistamines. Mixing them with alcohol is not medically dangerous, but beware of the added drowsiness.

Wellbutrin (Zyban): Wellbutrin increases the risk of withdrawal seizures and may increase the risk of blackouts.

The Effect of Smoking Tobacco (Nicotine):

Cigarette smoking slows gastric emptying and as a consequence delays alcohol absorption.

Routes of Alcohol Ingestion

The only normal route of ingesting alcohol is drinking it--but this is not the only route possible. Other more exotic routes are used on occasion. Alcohol can be inhaled, absorbed through the skin, injected, or given as an enema. Let us take a look at each of these methods:

Inhalation: AWOL (Alcohol With Out Liquid) is an alcohol inhalation device that has been released in the US and the UK. AWOL's manufacturers claim that when alcohol is vaporized and inhaled it can lead to intoxication as much as 10 times as quickly as drinking and allows one to sober up with no hangover in an equally rapid time frame. Doctors are still debating the safety of AWOL. At least 22 states in the US have banned AWOL.

Injection: Some scientific researchers give alcohol injections to research subjects when they wish to bypass the stomach. It was the comparison of the effects of injected alcohol with orally ingested alcohol which led scientists to conclude that women have less alcohol dehydrogenase in their stomachs than men do. Self-administration of alcohol by injection is extremely dangerous and should never be attempted. The risk of death by alcohol poisoning is extremely high.

Alcohol enema: This is another rather dangerous and sometimes deadly form of alcohol administration. If the internet is to be believed then alcohol enemas are not uncommon at sex parties. A beer enema might be safe enough. However the simple fact is that alcohol is absorbed very rapidly through the large intestine and the rectum and there are no enzymes here to break it down. Thus the same dose of alcohol given by enema will produce a much higher BAC than if one drinks it. There was a famous case of death by sherry enema in Texas where the wife was acquitted of murder charges. And a vodka enema is deadly for sure.

Transdermal: Alcohol can also be absorbed through the skin although this is quite a slow and impractical method of ingesting it.

Why Alcohol Has a Steady State Metabolism Rather Than a Half Life

When a drug like valium is broken down by the human body the resultant metabolites are harmless. It is for this reason that drugs like valium are broken down as quickly as the body can process them--and hence they have a half life. The half life of valium is 35 hours on the average. This means that if you take a 10 mg dose of valium, then 35 hours later half of it will have been metabolized and only 5 mg will remain. In another 35 hours half of this will be metabolized and only 2.5 mg will remain and so on. When we plot the metabolism of valium on a graph we get an exponential curve--in other words--drugs which have a half life have an exponential rate of decay. Chemists refer to this as a First Order Reaction.

Alcohol, on the other hand, shows a steady state metabolism not an exponential metabolism. The body of the average human metabolizes around 13 ml of alcohol per hour regardless. When we plot the metabolism of alcohol on a graph we get a straight line--in other words the rate of decay of alcohol is linear. Chemists refer to this as a Zero Order Reaction. The reason why alcohol has a steady state metabolism rather than a half-life metabolism is because the primary decay product of alcohol metabolism--acetaldehyde--is poisonous. The body must eliminate the acetaldehyde produced by the breakdown of alcohol before any more alcohol can be processed in order to avoid acetaldehyde poisoning. This slows down the rate of alcohol metabolism to a Zero Order Reaction rather than a First Order Reaction.

Figure 21.4 graphically illustrates the difference between steady state metabolism and half life metabolism.

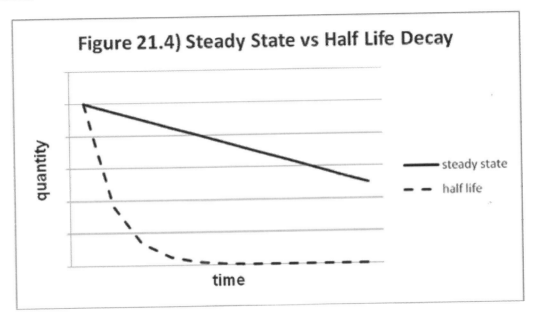

Why Do Humans Have a Way To Break Down Alcohol?

Practically every animal from the fruit fly to the elephant has a way to break down ethyl alcohol because ethyl alcohol is found everywhere in nature. Every time you eat a piece of fresh fruit, drink a glass of fresh orange juice, or have a slice of freshly baked bread then chances are that you are getting trace amounts of alcohol along with it. It is not uncommon to see intoxicated birds which have eaten fermented fruit. Monkeys are known to seek out fermented fruit for the intoxicating effect and Indian elephants have been known to break into breweries or wineries to drink up what is stored there.

Not only are we constantly ingesting alcohol along with the food we eat, our own bodies produce alcohol as a part of the digestive process. Our digestive tracts contain millions of micro-organisms which are necessary for us to properly digest our food. Among these micro-organisms are yeasts which produce alcohol from sugars within our own bodies.

With alcohol so omnipresent in nature it is necessary that animals have a way to break alcohol down, otherwise it would just accumulate in the body and no animal could function properly because the animals would always be constantly intoxicated.

Other alcohols such as methyl alcohol (wood alcohol) and isopropyl alcohol (rubbing alcohol) do not normally occur in nature. This is why we do not have a mechanism to break them down and why they are poisonous.

Poisonous Alcohols

The difference between wood alcohol--also known as methyl alcohol or methanol--and ethanol is that wood alcohol has one less carbon and two less hydrogen atoms. The chemical formula for ethanol is C_2H_6O whereas the formula for methanol is CH_4O. Alcohol dehydrogenase converts methanol into formaldehyde (CH_2O) and aldehyde dehydrogenase turns this formaldehyde into a formic acid radical (CH_2O-). Both formaldehyde and formic acid are highly poisonous and quickly lead to blindness and death.

Another highly poisonous alcohol is ethylene glycol ($C_2H_6O_2$) which is used in antifreeze. A metabolite of ethylene glycol is the highly poisonous oxalic acid.

Rubbing alcohol (C_3H_8O)--also known as isopropyl alcohol--is more poisonous than ethanol but not as poisonous as methanol. Some chronic alcoholics turn to drinking rubbing alcohol when ethanol is unavailable--and some even come to prefer it.

Alcohol and Blood Sugar

Although alcohol may cause a slight rise in blood sugar levels when initially ingested--the overall effect of alcohol is to cause a drop in blood sugar. The more you drink the more the blood sugar drops. Eating before, during or after drinking can help to alleviate this blood sugar drop somewhat. Drinks with lots of carbs like beer or mixed drinks with sugary mixers can lead to blood sugar spikes preceding the blood sugar drop.

Because of alcohol's effect on blood sugar people with diabetes are recommended to have no more than one or two standard drinks per day and to avoid drinks high in carbs. Untreated diabetes can lead to severe consequences including blindness, amputation of limbs affected by gangrene and even death--so diabetics are recommended to be especially cautious about their alcohol intake.

21.2) Alcohol and Cirrhosis

The Kamper-Jorgenson Study of 2004 - Cirrhosis and the Threshold Effect

The Kamper-Jorgenson study was a longitudinal study which followed the liver health of 6,152 heavy drinkers in Denmark from 1977 to 1992--a period of over 14 years per drinker. The age of the drinkers ranged from 15 to 83--the average age was 38. Subjects drank between 30 and 210+

standard American drinks[5] per week (i.e. 4.2 to 30+ per day). Heavy drinking careers ranged from 4 years to 20+ years. On the average the men in the study consumed 480 drinks per week (17 per day) and the women 408 per week (14.6 per day). This is around three fourths of a liter of vodka (80 proof) per day for men and two thirds of a liter per day for women.

The most surprising result of this study was the fact that those who averaged 210 drinks per week were no more likely to develop cirrhosis of the liver than those who drank 30 drinks per week. Once a certain threshold had been crossed chances of getting cirrhosis were equally good. Around 4.6% of the heavy drinkers in this study died of cirrhosis. This is around 30 times the incidence of cirrhosis in the general Danish population. The length of a person's heavy drinking career also had no significant effect on the likelihood that the person would develop cirrhosis. People who had been drinking for 4 years were just as likely to develop cirrhosis as people who had been drinking for over 20 years. It also made no difference if the drink of choice was beer, wine or hard liquor.

It is only the lighter drinkers who have been drinking less than 4 years and/or less than 30 per week who are less likely to develop cirrhosis. The only other significant factor was that people who did not drink daily were about half as likely to develop cirrhosis as daily drinkers.

Figure 21.5 illustrates the percentage of deaths from cirrhosis in heavy drinkers in relation to the amount of alcohol consumed daily. There is no significant difference in any of these categories-- people drinking an average of more than 4 standard American drinks per day are just as likely to get cirrhosis as those drinking over 30 drinks per day. The only significant difference is between the rate of cirrhosis in heavy drinkers versus the rate of cirrhosis in the general population; it is roughly 30 times as great.

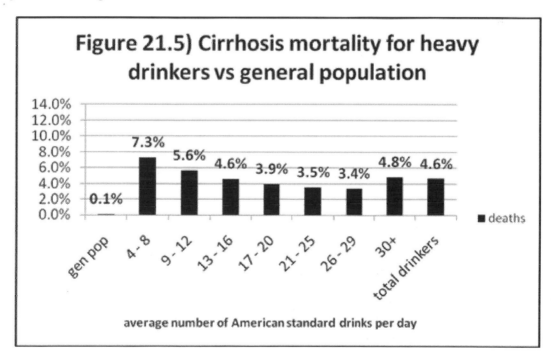

---

[5] All drink numbers have been converted from Danish standard drinks (12g ETOH) to American standard drinks (14g ETOH).

Becker et al 1996 - Cirrhosis in Light Drinkers Compared to Heavy Drinkers

The Becker study was a longitudinal study of 13,285 members of the Danish general public--ranging from teetotalers to light drinkers to heavy drinkers. The study covered 12 years from 1976 to 1988. Whereas the Kampar-Jorgenson study only recorded deaths from cirrhosis, the Becker study recorded all cases of cirrhosis whether they resulted in death or not--hence the Becker study reports about twice as many cases of cirrhosis as does Kamper-Jorgenson since about half of these did not result in death. Becker also reported on non-cirrhotic alcoholic liver disease in this paper.

Becker reports that there is a steep dose-dependent increase in risk of alcoholic liver disease with increased alcohol consumption. Women who drink two standard drinks per day (14 per week) and men who drink three standard drinks per day (21 per week) are at a significantly higher risk for liver disease than are lighter drinkers. Risk level increases with each additional daily drink until a threshold is reached at around nine standard drinks per day. Drinkers at this level have about an 8 percent chance of getting cirrhosis and a four percent chance of dying of cirrhosis. Also, about three percent of those who drank nine or more drinks per day had non-cirrhotic alcoholic liver disease--i.e. around 11 percent of the heavy drinkers suffered from some form of liver disease.

Figure 21.6 illustrates the dose-dependent relation between drinking and liver disease found by Becker.

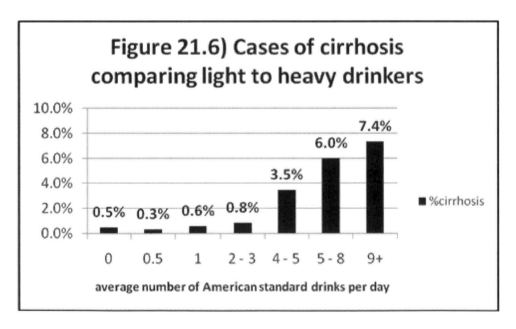

When comparing **Figure 21.5** to **Figure 21.6** it is important to note that **Figure 21.5** graphs deaths from cirrhosis whereas **Figure 21.6** graphs cases of cirrhosis. Only about half of the cases of cirrhosis in **Figure 21.6** ended in death in the Becker study.

Conclusion

HAMS strongly recommends that anyone who drinks alcohol gets an annual liver check up. If there are signs of liver damage try cutting back on your consumption and see if your liver improves. If you continue to show signs of liver damage it is safest to give up alcohol entirely. The liver has a great capacity for regeneration if not abused beyond its limits. If you still wish to engage in recreational intoxication in spite of liver disease, we recommend a move to **Marijuana Maintenance** (Chapter 6) because marijuana does not cause liver damage.

21.3) Alcohol, Gender, and Mortality

Introduction

In 1998 and 1999 Dr Jarque-Lopez and his colleagues conducted a study which recorded drinking data for every patient admitted into the University Hospital of the Canary Islands. Over this two year period 2,913 admissions were made to the hospital. Of these admissions, 224 men and 23 women met Dr Jarque-Lopez's criteria for being heavy drinkers. **Figure 21.7a** gives the average number of drinks consumed per day, **Figure 21.7b** gives the average age at admission to the hospital, **Figure 21.7c** gives the average number of years drinking, and **Figure 21.7d** gives the reasons for hospital admission.

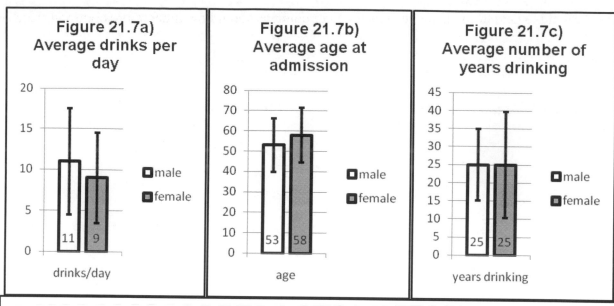

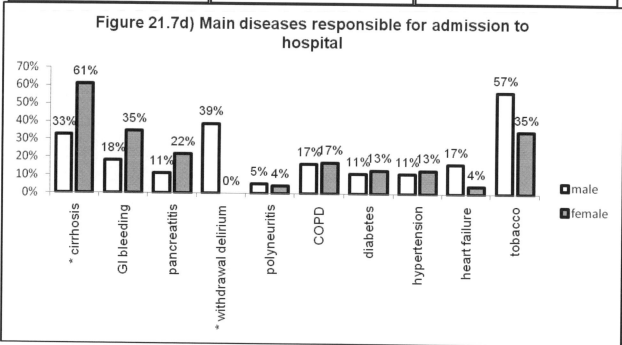

In this study the women heavy drinkers reported drinking an average of just under two bottles of wine (9 standard drinks = 129g ETOH) per day 7 days a week. The men heavy drinkers reported drinking an average of just over two bottles of wine (11 standard drinks = 153g ETOH) per day 7 days a week. The error bars on the graph show that some drank far more than this and some far less. The average age of admission was around 52 years old for men and 57 years old for women. Both men and women reported that they had been drinking for an average of around 25 years.

When we look at the reasons for hospital admission we find that only two reasons show statistically significant differences. A significantly larger number of women were admitted for **cirrhosis** than were men (p = 0.008). And a significantly larger number of men were admitted for **withdrawal delirium** than were women (p < 0.001). However, since the number of women in the sample (23) is small we can draw no conclusions about how much more common these sex related maladies are--a much larger sample is needed for this.

Next we will take a look at mortality rates. There was no significant difference between the number of heavy drinkers who died while hospitalized and the number of non-heavy drinkers who died while hospitalized--mortality rates were around 10% for both populations. This is illustrated in **Figure 21.8a**. There was also no significant difference between the percentage of male and female heavy drinkers who died while hospitalized. However, there was a significant difference in the average age of heavy drinkers who died while hospitalized when compared to non-heavy drinkers ($p < 0.0001$ for both male and female). This is illustrated in **Figure 21.8b** and **Figure 21.8c**.

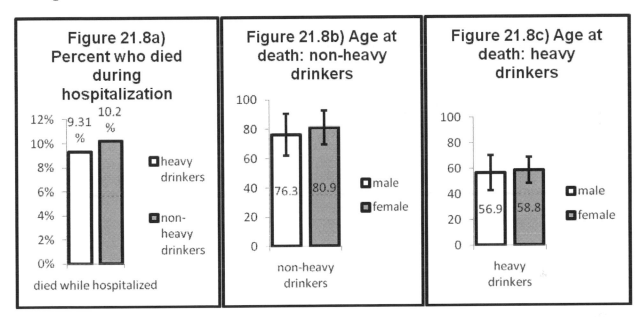

Conclusion

Although popular writers on the topic of alcohol claim that alcohol takes a far greater toll on women than men in terms of health consequences and longevity, this is not borne out by the data from Dr Jarque-Lopez. These data tell us that whereas male heavy drinkers are more likely to have problems with alcohol withdrawal, female heavy drinkers are more likely to have problems with cirrhosis.

These data show that both male and female heavy drinkers who were hospitalized died at a significantly younger age than hospitalized non-heavy drinkers. However, female heavy drinkers did not die at a younger age than male heavy drinkers. The average age of the female heavy drinkers in this study who died was actually greater than that of the males although the numbers were not significant.

Dr Jarque-Lopez and colleagues also point out that we must be cautious in drawing conclusions about what these data mean for populations who are not in the hospital. Some studies suggest that there may be less difference in age at death for these populations in other settings.

21.4) Alcohol Poisoning

The NIAAA estimates that each year 317 Americans die as a direct result of alcohol poisoning. Alcohol poisoning is a secondary contributing factor in the deaths of another 1,076 Americans annually. It is uncertain exactly how many of the 317 deaths directly due to alcohol poisoning are the result of an overdose of beverage alcohol (ethanol) and how many are the result of drinking a poisonous alcohol such as wood alcohol, isopropyl alcohol, or antifreeze since MDs specifying the cause of death frequently fail to specify which alcohol is the cause of death.

The Lethal Half Dose (LD50) of beverage alcohol (ethanol) in humans is around a BAC (Blood Alcohol Concentration) of 0.45. Lethal half dose is defined as the dose at which half the test subjects die. Some people are more sensitive to the effects of beverage alcohol than others, and deaths from alcohol poisoning have been reported at BAC levels of 0.3. The BAC tables in Appendix Two spell out how many drinks it takes a person of a given size and sex to reach these BAC levels. A 90 pound woman can reach a dangerous BAC of 0.3 by drinking 6 drinks in an hour; a 140 pound male has to drink roughly twice as much in an hour to achieve the same BAC.

Chronic heavy drinkers not only have elevated liver enzymes which process alcohol more quickly than light drinkers, they can also tolerate a much higher BAC and live than can light drinkers. It is not uncommon for a person admitted to a detox unit to have a BAC of 0.7. Since inexperienced drinkers are the ones most likely to suffer alcohol poisoning it is not a fun joke to feed inexperienced drinker large amounts of alcohol. You might be putting that person's life in danger by playing drinking games or asking him/her to drink their age.

Alcohol irritates the stomach and causes people to vomit--this fortunately prevents many cases of alcohol poisoning. However, alcohol also affects the central nervous system and suppresses the gag reflex; this sometimes prevents vomiting or can sometimes cause a person to choke to death on their own vomit. Moreover, alcohol in the bloodstream or the small intestine cannot be vomited out. The Mayo Clinic gives the following cautions concerning alcohol poisoning:

- If the person is unconscious, breathing less than eight times a minute or has repeated, uncontrolled vomiting, call 911 or your local emergency number immediately. Keep in mind that even when someone is unconscious or has stopped drinking, alcohol continues to be released into the bloodstream and the level of alcohol in the body continues to rise. Never assume that a person will "sleep off" alcohol poisoning.

- If the person is conscious, call 800-222-1222, and you'll automatically be routed to your local poison control center. The staff at the poison control center or emergency call center can instruct you as to whether you should take the person directly to a hospital. All calls to poison control centers are confidential.

- Be prepared to provide information. If you know, be sure to tell hospital or emergency personnel the kind and amount of alcohol the person ingested, and when.

- Don't leave an unconscious person alone. While waiting for help, don't try to make the person vomit. People who have alcohol poisoning have an impaired gag reflex and may choke on their own vomit or accidentally inhale (aspirate) vomit into their lungs, which could cause a fatal lung injury.

The Mayo Clinic also suggests that you watch for the following as signs of alcohol poisoning:

- Confusion, stupor
- Vomiting
- Seizures
- Slow breathing (less than eight breaths a minute)
- Irregular breathing
- Blue-tinged skin or pale skin
- Low body temperature (hypothermia)
- Unconsciousness ("passing out")

We suggest that you be kind and let unseasoned drinkers go at their own pace--no need to rush them and put them in the hospital--they will not thank you for it.

Of the 1,076 Americans for whom alcohol poisoning is a contributing factor--90% die of a combined drug and alcohol overdose. Appendix One gives a listing of drug and alcohol interactions--we suggest that everyone who likes to drink alcohol be careful of what medications they mix it with. The remaining 10% die in alcohol-related accidents.

REFERENCES:

American Diabetes Association. Alcohol.
http://www.diabetes.org/type-1-diabetes/alcohol.jsp
Accessed June 15, 2009

Anderson C, Andersson T, Molander M. (1991). Ethanol absorption across human skin measured by in vivo microdialysis technique. Acta Dermato Venereologica. 71(5), 389-93.
PubMed Abstract:
http://www.ncbi.nlm.nih.gov/pubmed/1684466

Becker U, Deis A, Sorensen TI, Grønbaek M, Borch-Johnsen K, Muller CF, Schnohr P, Jensen G. (1996). Prediction of risk of liver disease by alcohol intake, sex, and age: a prospective population study. Hepatology. 23(5), 1025-9.
PubMed Abstract:
http://www.ncbi.nlm.nih.gov/pubmed/8621128

Bellentani S, Saccoccio G, Costa G, Tiribelli C, Manenti F, Sodde M, Saveria Croce L, Sasso F, Pozzato G, Cristianini G, Brandi G. (1997). Drinking habits as cofactors of risk for alcohol induced liver damage: the Dionysos Study Group. Gut, 41, 845–850.
PubMed Abstract:
http://www.ncbi.nlm.nih.gov/pubmed/9462221
Free Full Text:
http://www.ncbi.nlm.nih.gov/pmc/articles/PMC1891602/pdf/v041p00845.pdf

Boggan B. Alcohol, Chemistry and You: Metabolism of Ethyl Alcohol in the Body
http://chemcases.com/alcohol/alc-06.htm
Accessed February 1, 2010

Braun S. (1996). Buzz: The Science and Lore of Alcohol and Caffeine. Oxford University Press.

Day CP. (1997). Alcoholic liver disease: dose and threshold--new thoughts on an old topic. Gut. 41(6), 857-8.
PubMed Abstract:
http://www.ncbi.nlm.nih.gov/pubmed/9462225
Free Full Text:
http://www.ncbi.nlm.nih.gov/pmc/articles/PMC1891615/pdf/v041p00857.pdf

Drugtext: Alcohol
http://www.drugtext.org/sub/alcohol.html
Accessed February 1, 2010

Elmhurst College: Alcohol Metabolism Effects
http://www.elmhurst.edu/~chm/vchembook/642alcoholmet.html
Accessed February 1, 2010

Frezza M, di Padova C, Pozzato G, Terpin M, Baraona E, Lieber CS. (1990). High blood alcohol levels in women. The role of decreased gastric alcohol dehydrogenase activity and first-pass metabolism. New England Journal of Medicine. 322(2), 95-9.
PubMed Abstract:
http://www.ncbi.nlm.nih.gov/pubmed/2248624

Jarque-López A, González-Reimers E, Rodríguez-Moreno F, Santolaria-Fernández F, López-Lirola A, Ros-Vilamajo R, Espinosa-Villarreal JG, Martínez-Riera A. (2001).Prevalence and mortality of heavy drinkers in a general medical hospital unit. Alcohol Alcohol. 36(4), 335-8.
PubMed Abstract:
http://www.ncbi.nlm.nih.gov/pubmed/11468135
Free Full Text:
http://alcalc.oxfordjournals.org/cgi/reprint/36/4/335.pdf

Johnson RD, Horowitz M, Maddox AF, Wishart JM, Shearman DJ. (1991). Cigarette smoking and rate of gastric emptying: effect on alcohol absorption. BMJ. 302(6767), 20-3.
PubMed Abstract:
http://www.ncbi.nlm.nih.gov/pubmed/1991182
Free Full Text:
http://www.ncbi.nlm.nih.gov/pmc/articles/PMC1668727/pdf/bmj00107-0026.pdf

Kamper-Jørgensen M, Grønbaek M, Tolstrup J, Becker U. (2004). Alcohol and cirrhosis: dose--response or threshold effect? J Hepatol. 41(1), 25-30.
PubMed Abstract:
http://www.ncbi.nlm.nih.gov/pubmed/15246203

Maher JJ. (1997). Exploring alcohol's effects on liver function. Alcohol Health Res World. 21(1), 5-12.
PubMed Abstract:
http://www.ncbi.nlm.nih.gov/pubmed/15706758
Free Full Text:

http://pubs.niaaa.nih.gov/publications/arh21-1/05.pdf

The Mayo Clinic Website - Alcohol Poisoning
http://www.mayoclinic.com/health/alcohol-poisoning/ds00861
Accessed January 27, 2010

MSNBC (2007). Elephants electrocuted in drunken rampage
http://www.msnbc.msn.com/id/21432722/?GT1=10450
Accessed February 1, 2010

The Psychology Wiki: Alcohol flush reaction
http://psychology.wikia.com/wiki/Alcohol_flush_reaction
Accessed February 1, 2010

The Psychology Wiki: Blood alcohol concentration.
http://psychology.wikia.com/wiki/Blood_alcohol_concentration
Accessed February 1, 2010

Quertemont E, Didone V. (2006) Role of Acetaldehyde in Mediating the Pharmacological and
Behavioral Effects of Alcohol. Alcohol Research & Health. 29(4), 258-65.
PubMed Abstract:
http://www.ncbi.nlm.nih.gov/pubmed/17718404
Free Full Text:
http://pubs.niaaa.nih.gov/publications/arh294/258-265.pdf

RCSB Protein Data Bank
Alcohol Dehydrogenase
January 2001 Molecule of the Month
by David S. Goodsell
http://www.rcsb.org/pdb/static.do?p=education_discussion/molecule_of_the_month/pdb13_1.html
Accessed February 1, 2010

Reuters. Charges dismissed in Texas sherry enema death - By Erwin Seba
Wed Oct 3, 2007 7:18pm EDT.
http://www.reuters.com/article/newsOne/idUSN0325982220071003
Accessed February 1, 2010

Schuppan D, Afdhal NH. (2008). Liver cirrhosis. Lancet. 371(9615), 838-51.
PubMed Abstract:
http://www.ncbi.nlm.nih.gov/pubmed/18328931
Free Full Text:
http://www.ncbi.nlm.nih.gov/pmc/articles/PMC2271178/pdf/nihms-42379.pdf

UpToDate. Patient information: Diabetes mellitus type 2: Alcohol, exercise, and medical care
http://www.uptodate.com/patients/content/topic.do?topicKey=~btiSIVAV2lvR5
Accessed June 15, 2009

Wikipedia: Acetaldehyde dehydrogenase
http://en.wikipedia.org/wiki/Acetaldehyde_dehydrogenase
Accessed February 1, 2010

Wikipedia: Alcohol dehydrogenase
http://en.wikipedia.org/wiki/Alcohol_dehydrogenase
Accessed February 1, 2010

Wikipedia: Aldehyde dehydrogenase
http://en.wikipedia.org/wiki/Aldehyde_dehydrogenase
Accessed February 1, 2010

Wikipedia: AWOL - Alcohol Without liquid
http://en.wikipedia.org/wiki/Alcohol_without_liquid
Accessed February 1, 2010

Wikipedia: Hangover
http://en.wikipedia.org/wiki/Hangover
Accessed February 1, 2010

Wu KL, Chaikomin R, Doran S, Jones KL, Horowitz M, Rayner CK. (2006). Artificially sweetened versus regular mixers increase gastric emptying and alcohol absorption. The American Journal of Medicine. 119(9), 802-4.
PubMed Abstract:
http://www.ncbi.nlm.nih.gov/pubmed/16945619

Yoon YH, Stinson FS, Yi HY, Dufour MC. (2003). Accidental alcohol poisoning mortality in the United States, 1996-1998. Alcohol Res Health. 27(1), 110-8.
PubMed Abstract:
http://www.ncbi.nlm.nih.gov/pubmed/15301405
Free Full Text:
http://pubs.niaaa.nih.gov/publications/arh27-1/110-120.pdf

Zakhari S. (2006). Overview: how is alcohol metabolized by the body? Alcohol Res Health. 29(4), 245-54.
PubMed Abstract:
http://www.ncbi.nlm.nih.gov/pubmed/17718403
Free Full Text:
http://pubs.niaaa.nih.gov/publications/arh294/245-255.htm

CHAPTER TWENTY TWO: Preventing Alcohol Withdrawal

22.1) What Is Alcohol Withdrawal?

Alcohol withdrawal is different from withdrawal from most other drugs because alcohol withdrawal can be deadly. The only drugs as likely to cause death from withdrawal as alcohol are the benzodiazepines. Heroin withdrawal rarely if ever kills anyone. But untreated major alcohol withdrawal can kill one person in three (some sources say one in five). Fortunately these fatalities are almost completely preventable if people are properly tapered off from their alcohol use. Chapter 6 contains information about how to taper off alcohol safely. Section 22.2 gives information about how to prevent alcohol withdrawal.

The Levels of Alcohol Withdrawal

Doctors generally recognize three levels of alcohol withdrawal:

- **Level 1) Minor Withdrawal:** Shaky hands. Sweating. Mild anxiety. Insomnia. Nausea. Headache. These symptoms may appear within 6 to 12 hours after quitting drinking.

- **Level 2) Mid-level Withdrawal:** Minor withdrawal symptoms at a more intense level plus visual, auditory or tactile hallucinations. The patient generally is aware that the hallucinations are not real. Possible seizures. Racing pulse. Irregular heartbeat. These symptoms may appear within 12 to 48 hours after quitting drinking.

- **Level 3) Major Withdrawal:** Delirium. Alcohol-induced hallucinations. Patient generally cannot distinguish hallucination from reality. Profuse sweating. Seizures. Severe blood pressure spikes. Sever tremor. Racing and irregular heartbeat. Fever. Possible death. These symptoms may appear within 48 to 72 hours after quitting drinking and peak in five days.

Popular slang in the United States refers to the shakiness which comes with mild alcohol withdrawal as "D.T.s". This is a rather confusing use of terminology since properly speaking "D.T.s" refers to delirium tremens which is associated with major withdrawal. Real delirium tremens is life-threatening and can kill one in three untreated patients (some sources say one in five). The shakiness associated with minor withdrawal is not life-threatening. Perhaps the best and most accurate description of D.T.s in literature is Mark Twain's description of Pap Finn's attempt to kill his son in the book Huckleberry Finn.

What Causes Alcohol Withdrawal?

Alcohol withdrawal is caused by neurotransmitter rebound. When alcohol suppresses the action of a neurotransmitter system over a long period of time the neurotransmitter system adapts by working harder and harder to overcome the effect of the alcohol and to try and function at normal levels in spite of the presence of the alcohol. When the alcohol is suddenly removed from the body the neurotransmitter system still continues to function far in excess of normal levels. Since the alcohol is no longer present to suppress the effects of this hyperactivity, what we now see are effects which are precisely the opposite of those caused by alcohol. It is much like two people playing tug-of-war who are equally balanced--if one person suddenly lets go of the rope the other goes flying in the opposite direction. When alcohol is suddenly removed from a neurotransmitter system which has been fighting to overcome its effects --the neurotransmitter system goes flying off in the opposite direction.

The main neurotransmitter system involved in alcohol withdrawal is the GABA system. Alcohol's effect on the GABA system leads to relaxation, sleep, calm, and the soothing of panic. When alcohol is suddenly removed from the brain then the neurotransmitter rebound in the GABA system leads to insomnia, nightmares, hallucinations, anxiety, panic, muscle cramps, high blood pressure, racing heart, sweating and seizures. Benzodiazepines affect the GABA system in much the same way as alcohol does and this is why benzodiazepine withdrawal has much the same effect as alcohol withdrawal and is also life-threatening.

Some web sites try to use scare tactics and tell you that very tiny amounts of alcohol will cause withdrawal, that it is impossible to taper off alcohol, or that no one can quit drinking on their own. These things are no more true than the scare tactics of Reefer Madness were true. You do not need a Higher Power to take charge of your drinking. Even people who have had alcohol withdrawal in the past do not need to repeat the experience. It is up to you as an individual to decide if your best bet is safer drinking, reduced drinking, or quitting altogether.

22.2) How to Prevent Alcohol Withdrawal

Alcohol withdrawal occurs when the brain has been exposed to alcohol over long periods of time. There are three sure ways for most people to prevent alcohol withdrawal:

- **Have several abstinence days every week--this will work even if you choose to get intoxicated on some days**

- **Or if you choose to drink every day then do not exceed four standard drinks per day.**

- **Don't mix alcohol with benzodiazepines like Valium or Librium or Klonopin.**

Having several abstinence days every week gives the alcohol a chance to get out of your system completely and this gives your neurotransmitter systems to return to normal. And since the body metabolizes about one standard drink per each hour and a half, if you limit yourself to four standard drinks per day then this gives your neurotransmitter systems many hours each day to return to normal, too. When your neurotransmitter systems have enough time to return to normal this prevents withdrawal from occurring

Both alcohol withdrawal and benzodiazepine withdrawal are a result of their effects on the GABA neurotransmitter system. Mixing the two can increase one's chance of death from benzodiazepine overdose as well as worsen withdrawal symptoms which occur when either one is discontinued.

Even if you have had alcohol withdrawal in the past this does not mean that you ever need to suffer from alcohol withdrawal again in the future as long as you follow the above rules. The one exception to this is people who have undergone KINDLING. Kindling is quite rare these days. Kindling is caused when people are repeatedly withdrawn cold turkey from alcohol with no tapering and no medications. In times past in the United States people were often withdrawn cold turkey from alcohol to "teach them a lesson." This always failed to help anyone quit drinking--all it did was to cause a great deal of human suffering.

People who have undergone kindling will suffer withdrawal after drinking even small quantities of alcohol. There is very little option for people who have undergone kindling besides abstinence from alcohol. Marijuana Maintenance can be a good option for people with kindling. But if you don't have kindling, you can avoid alcohol withdrawal syndrome by following the simple advice in this section.

22.3) The Odds Of Going Through Alcohol Withdrawal

What is the likelihood that you will go through life-threatening alcohol withdrawal if you suddenly stop drinking? The more that you drink per day and the more consecutive days that you drink, the more likely you are to go through alcohol withdrawal. If you never drink two days in a row you will not go through alcohol withdrawal. Drinking every night increases your chances of undergoing withdrawal. And drinking both morning and night every day of the week increases the odds of going through withdrawal even more.

Women are more sensitive to the negative effects of alcohol than are men. If you are a woman of average weight and you have been drinking 6 standard drinks a day every day for a month then you have about a fifty-fifty chance of going through minor withdrawal, but it probably won't be life threatening. On the other hand a woman who has been drinking 11 standard drinks a day for a month has about a fifty-fifty chance of going through major life threatening withdrawal. If you have been drinking a shorter period of time then you will have to have drunk more per day to be in danger of withdrawal. A woman who has 8 standard drinks per day every day for a week has about a fifty-fifty chance of having minor withdrawal whereas a woman who drinks around 15 standard drinks a day everyday for a week has about a fifty-fifty chance of having major withdrawal. This is illustrated graphically in **Figure 22.1**. There is little chance of withdrawal for anyone who has been drinking for less than three days in a row. See above for the distinction between major and minor alcohol withdrawal. Chapter 13 gives the definition of a standard drink. Just for reference, a fifth of whiskey contains 17 standard drinks.

168

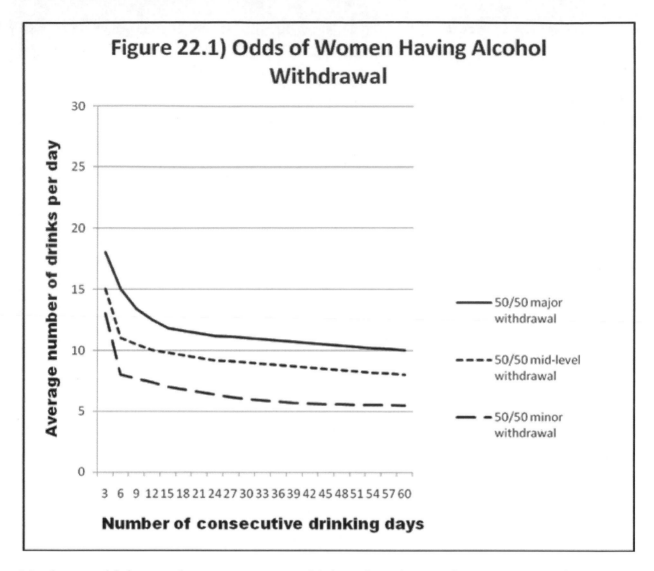

Figure 22.1) Odds of Women Having Alcohol Withdrawal

Men have to drink more than women to get withdrawal syndrome. If you are a man of average weight and you drink 8 standard drinks a day for a month you are in danger of minor withdrawal symptoms. If you drink 13 a day for a month then you have about a fifty-fifty chance of having major life threatening withdrawals. Drinking 10 a day for a week will lead to minor withdrawal and 18 a day for a week to major life-threatening withdrawal as illustrated in **Figure 22.2**.

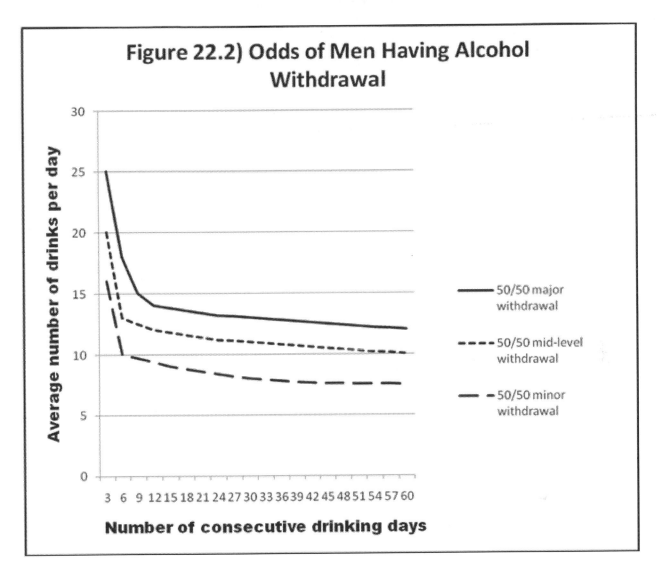

Figure 22.2) Odds of Men Having Alcohol Withdrawal

- 50/50 major withdrawal
- 50/50 mid-level withdrawal
- 50/50 minor withdrawal

If you have any reason at all to believe that you might undergo life-threatening major withdrawal when you quit drinking then it is essential that you either go to a medical detox or that you taper off as discussed in the section on **tapering off alcohol** in Chapter 6. Alcohol withdrawal can kill.

The numbers of drinks in Figure 22.1 and Figure 22.2 are ballpark guesstimates based on my experience with alcohol and with heavy drinkers and with my investigation of the best sources available on the topic. No one has experimentally studied how many drinks per day for a month will lead to life threatening withdrawal in a human being because such experiments could never pass an ethics review board. So in lieu of that we must make a guess based on the best data which is available to us. I believe that the data in Figure 22.1 and Figure 22.2 are definitely within the ballpark.

There are any number of scare web sites out there which deliberately exaggerate the likelihood that you will undergo life-threatening alcohol withdrawal. It is profitable for alcohol treatment centers to use scare tactics and tell you that you will die unless you enter their program. We at HAMS have no reason to scare you or to do anything except to tell you the God's honest truth about alcohol withdrawal.

REFERENCES:

Bayard M, McIntyre J, Hill KR, Woodside J Jr. (2004). Alcohol Withdrawal Syndrome. <u>American Family Physician</u>. 69(6), 1443-50.
PubMed Abstract:
http://www.ncbi.nlm.nih.gov/pubmed/15053409
Free Full Text:
http://www.aafp.org/afp/20040315/1443.html

Blondell RD. (2005). Ambulatory Detoxification of Patients with Alcohol Dependence. <u>American Family Physician</u>. 71(3), 495-502.
PubMed Abstract:
http://www.ncbi.nlm.nih.gov/pubmed/15712624
Free Full Text:
http://www.aafp.org/afp/20050201/495.html

CHAPTER TWENTY THREE: Alcohol Tolerance

23.1   What Is Alcohol Tolerance?
23.2   What Is Reverse Tolerance?

23.1) What Is Alcohol Tolerance?

When the body and the brain are regularly subjected to alcohol over a long period of time certain changes occur which help them adapt to the presence of alcohol. The average human being metabolizes around one standard drink (0.6 oz of ethanol) per each hour and a half. In people who drink large amounts of alcohol on a regular basis the liver adapts to break down the alcohol more rapidly than it does in people who rarely drink. The liver does this by producing larger amounts of the enzymes which break down alcohol. Because the liver has become more efficient at breaking down alcohol, drinkers need to drink more alcohol in order to get the same effect. This is the role that the liver plays in the development of alcohol tolerance.

The brain also has a role in the development of alcohol tolerance. When the neurotransmitter systems in the brain are regularly exposed to large amounts of alcohol they begin to adapt to the presence of alcohol. The alcohol works to suppress the functioning of the neurotransmitter systems. For example alcohol affects the GABA system causing sleepiness and a reduction in anxiety and alertness. With long term exposure to alcohol the GABA system adapts so that the alcohol causes less relaxation, sleepiness, and dulling of alertness. Because of this adaption to the presence of alcohol by the brain heavy drinkers begin to require more alcohol to get the same effect.

Some interesting research has shown that not only are the body and the brain involved in tolerance, but the environment is involved as well. Both human beings and laboratory animals that are given their usual dose of heroin in an unaccustomed environment have been found to frequently suffer from overdose. Tolerance to alcohol or other drugs has been shown to drop significantly in novel environments.

This has important implications for practicing harm reduction. You may be perfectly functional drinking the usual amount of alcohol in your usual watering hole. If you drink the exact same amount of alcohol in a strange environment it may make you very drunk and disabled instead. So always be cautious when drinking in a new environment.

23.2) What Is Reverse Tolerance?

Reverse tolerance results from liver damage which leads to a reduction in the production of liver enzymes. People suffering from reverse tolerance become more intoxicated with small doses of alcohol than do people with normal livers. Heavy drinkers can also reduce their alcohol tolerance by taking a break from alcohol and letting their livers return to normal.

In the average healthy human being alcohol is metabolized by the liver at the rate of about one standard drink (0.6 oz ethanol) per each hour and a half. In people who frequently engage in heavy drinking alcohol tolerance develops. Changes occur in the brain and the liver which work to adapt them to the steady presence of alcohol. When alcohol tolerance develops people need to drink much more alcohol to get the same effect as they used to.

Reverse Tolerance occurs when a heavy drinker develops liver damage and the liver no longer produces as great a quantity of the enzymes needed to break down alcohol in the body as it did before. Since people with a lot of alcoholic liver damage can no longer metabolize alcohol very well, these people can get very intoxicated on small quantities of alcohol--much smaller quantities than are needed to affect the person who rarely drinks. This phenomenon is known as **Reverse Tolerance**. The way that **Reverse Tolerance** can develop over a lifetime is illustrated by the curve in **Figure 23.1**.

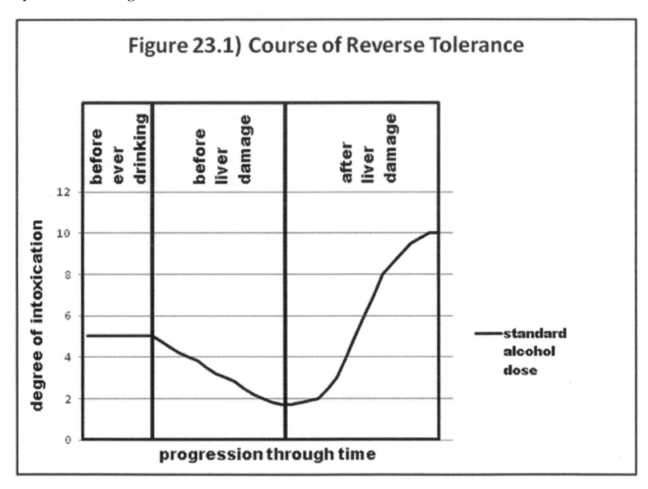

As we can see from **Figure 23.1**, tolerance in an adult who has never had a drink of alcohol in his/her life remains steady. Once a person begins to drink alcohol on a regular basis the dose response goes down--in other words the same dose of alcohol produces less intoxication than it used to. Saying that the dose response to alcohol goes down is exactly the same as saying that alcohol tolerance goes up--and vice versa. Dose response and tolerance are mirror images of each other. As long as a steady consumption of alcohol is maintained, tolerance will tend to increase and dose response will tend to drop. If liver damage begins to occur, however, tolerance will begin to drop once again and dose response will tend to increase. When there is sufficient damage to the liver there will be considerably less tolerance and considerably greater dose response to alcohol than there was before the person ever took their first drink.

173

It is important to note that most heavy drinkers do NOT develop liver damage or Reverse Tolerance. The majority of heavy drinkers will not suffer liver damage and hence will not develop Reverse Tolerance.

One should be very careful not to confuse Reverse Tolerance with the **Healthy Tolerance Reversal** which occurs when a heavy drinker does a period of abstinence from alcohol or a period of moderate drinking. When the amount of alcohol to which the liver is exposed on a daily basis is greatly decreased, liver enzymes begin to return to normal levels and alcohol tolerance (as well as dose response) tends to return to levels similar to those before the subject began drinking heavily.

The essential difference between Reverse Tolerance and Healthy Tolerance Reversal is that Reverse Tolerance is caused by damage to the liver which is often irreversible. In Healthy Tolerance Reversal the liver is actually becoming more healthy than it was during the period of heavy drinking--and the reason why the tolerance is dropping is that the excessive and unhealthy levels of liver enzymes associated with heavy drinking are now returning to normal and healthy levels. In Reverse Tolerance many of the cells needed to produce these enzymes have died and that is the reason why less of the enzymes are produced. In Healthy Tolerance Reversal the liver cells are going back to producing normal levels of these enzymes rather than the excessive levels which they produced during the heavy drinking period--no cells die when Healthy Tolerance Reversal takes place.

A period of abstinence may not necessarily return tolerance to the same level as before the person ever took a drink of alcohol; however, an abstinence period significantly reduces tolerance from the level it was at during the time of heavy drinking. **Figure 23.2** illustrates the course of Healthy Tolerance Reversal in a typical individual.

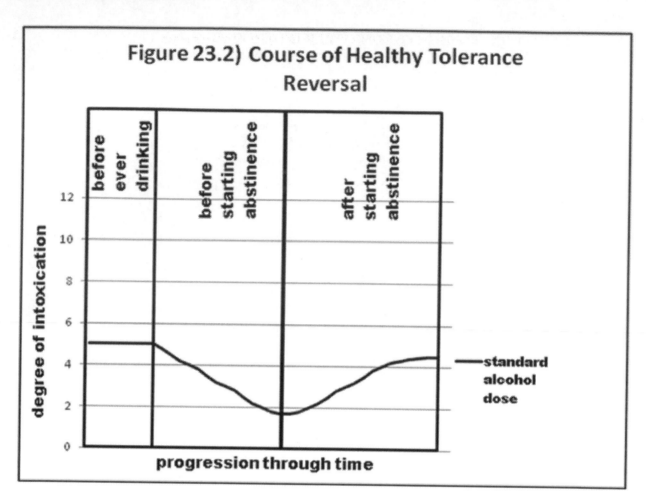

Figure 23.2) Course of Healthy Tolerance Reversal

How much time is needed for Healthy Tolerance Reversal to take place? There is not an exact answer to this. Tolerance will start dropping as soon as heavy drinking ceases, but experts say that it takes a month or two for the full effect of Healthy Tolerance Reversal to take place.

CHAPTER TWENTY FOUR: Hangover

24.1) What Causes Hangover?

Despite the fact that alcohol hangover is omnipresent in throughout the world wherever alcohol is consumed, surprisingly little scientific research has been published on the topic. In their 2009 review of the topic of hangover, Dr. Gemma Prat and her colleagues sum up the state of the knowledge about alcohol hangover in scientific circles today. They note that there is not even a generally agreed upon operational definition of hangover. Only in very recent years have scales been introduced to measure hangover and most of the research published on the topic of hangover has not used any form of standardized scale. We will follow Dr. Prat in defining hangover as a state of distress which occurs after Blood Alcohol Content (BAC) has reached zero.

Not only do we lack an agreed upon definition of what a hangover is, we are also uncertain of mechanism by which heavy alcohol consumption causes hangovers, although there are several hypotheses about what might be happening. If you ever visit a web site which claims to explain to you exactly how a hangover works, then you may assume that the site is less than trustworthy--because we are still far, far from having all the answers to this question.

Hangover Symptoms

Physical symptoms of a hangover include fatigue, headache, increased sensitivity to light and sound, redness of the eyes, muscle aches, and thirst. Signs of increased sympathetic nervous system activity can accompany a hangover, including increased systolic blood pressure, rapid heartbeat (i.e., tachycardia), tremor, and sweating. Mental symptoms include dizziness; a sense of the room spinning (i.e., vertigo); and possible cognitive and mood disturbances, especially depression, anxiety, and irritability.

The Withdrawal Hypothesis

Some researchers have speculated that hangover is a form of minor alcohol withdrawal. There is overlap between some of the symptoms of minor withdrawal and hangover such as nausea, headache, and hypersensitivity to light and sound. However there are also some distinct differences. In particular, during a hangover the brain waves measured on an EEG slow down, whereas during alcohol withdrawal the brain waves speed up.

The Acetaldehyde Hypothesis

When alcohol is metabolized in the body it is first converted into acetaldehyde and then this acetaldehyde is converted into acetic acid which is further broken down into carbon dioxide and water. Acetaldehyde is rather poisonous and can cause vomiting, headache, rapid heartbeat and flushing. Antabuse--the drug which makes people sick if they drink alcohol--works by causing acetaldehyde to build up in the body. It is this acetaldehyde which makes people sick when they drink on antabuse. In severe cases mixing antabuse and alcohol can lead to death.

Acetaldehyde is not present during hangovers; by the time one begins to get hangover symptoms the acetaldehyde has already been metabolized by the body and is gone. Some researchers hypothesize that hangover symptoms are caused by the aftereffects of acetaldehyde on the central nervous system. This hypothesis has yet to be confirmed, although Dr. Yokoyama and his colleagues (2005) have found some evidence that individuals who have difficulty metabolizing acetaldehyde have more severe hangovers than do other people.

The Direct Alcohol Effect Hypothesis

Alcohol causes the following effects both during and after intoxication

- Dehydration and electrolyte imbalance: Alcohol inhibits the production of anti-diuretic hormone. This leads to increased urination and dehydration

- Irritated stomach lining: Alcohol directly irritates the stomach lining and this can lead to nausea, vomiting and diarrhea.

- Low blood sugar: Alcohol causes some lowering of blood sugar in all drinkers because alcohol interferes with the generation of glucose by the liver. In most cases this does not lead to severe low blood sugar; however this can lead to severe low blood sugar in individuals who drink on an empty stomach or those with a tendency towards low blood sugar in the first place. Low blood sugar can be associated with tiredness, crankiness, and dizziness.

- Sleep disturbances: Alcohol disturbs the quality of sleep, leads to less REM sleep, and can lead to early waking. These sleep disturbances might contribute to the tiredness and cognitive dysfunction associated with hangover.

- Dilation of blood vessels: This is a possible cause of hangover headache.

- Increased production of cytokines: Cytokines are like hormones that function at the cellular level. Examples of cytokines are interleukins and interferons. Cytokines are responsible for the inflammation and fever which the body uses to fight infections. Alcohol increases the production of cytokines and cytokines might be a cause of muscle aches, headache or poor memory performance while hungover.

The Congener Hypothesis

Congeners are chemical compounds other than alcohol and water which are found in alcoholic beverages and which contribute to giving them a pleasing color and flavor and smell. Examples of typical congeners are amines, amides, acetones, polyphenols, methanol, and histamine.

In 1970 Dr. LF Chapman did an experiment to see whether congeners increase the likelihood of people having hangovers. Dr. Chapman gave one group of subjects bourbon whiskey, a beverage which is very high in congeners. Another group of subjects were given vodka which is very low in congeners. Both groups were given the same dosage of alcohol (1.5g/kg). 33% of the subjects who received the bourbon reported hangover, whereas only 3% of subjects who received vodka reported hangover.

There are a couple of studies (Woo et al, 2005, Bendtsen et al 1998) which suggest that the congener methanol may be involved in hangover. Methanol is also known as methyl alcohol or wood alcohol and is a highly poisonous compound which can cause blindness or death. The human body breaks methanol down into the toxic components formaldehyde and formic acid. Trace amounts of methanol are found in alcoholic beverages, but they are also found in orange or apple juices.

In order to test the hypothesis that methanol is responsible for hangover it would be necessary to conduct the following experiment: a mixture of pure ethanol and water would need to be compared to a mixture of ethanol and water which contained a trace of methanol and both of these should be compared to water containing a trace of methanol. If such an experiment were conducted it would work to confirm or disconfirm the methanol hypothesis of hangover.

There are several other congeners which are also hypothesized to contribute to hangover, namely: isopentanol, ethylic acetate, ethyl formate, and other amines, amides, acetones, polyphenols, and histamine. The hypothesis that these congeners contribute to hangover could be tested the same as the methanol hypothesis above. Such experiments have yet to be carried out.

The Lactic Acid Hypothesis

Alcohol metabolism produces an excess of NADH which leads to excessive production of lactic acid which in turn leads to lactic acidosis. Lactic acidosis could be responsible for the muscle cramps associated with hangover.

Other Factors Contributing to Hangover

Several researchers have proposed that people with a tendency towards alcohol addiction have a tendency to have more severe hangovers and withdrawal symptoms. This is interesting since it is also proposed that people in active alcohol addiction rarely have hangovers compared to normal drinkers.

In a 1993 study, Dr. E Harburg and his colleagues found that people were likely to have more severe hangovers if they felt guilty about drinking; if they were neurotic; if they were angry or depressed when they drank or if they were drinking in response to negative life events

It is rather surprising that no studies have been carried out at all on the importance of eating well, being well hydrated, and drinking slowly on the severity of hangover. Based on our personal experiences here at HAMS we believe that avoiding blood alcohol spikes is of paramount importance in both preventing blackout and in reducing severity of hangover. We can only hope that these factors are researched in a scientific manner in the future. In the meantime we shall merely say that good nutrition can't hurt.

Conclusions

- **Withdrawal:** It is still a matter of debate as to whether alcohol hangover should be considered a form of minor alcohol withdrawal or an independent entity in its own right.

- **Acetaldehyde:** We need further experimental evidence to determine the extent to which acetaldehyde contributes to hangover--if at all.

- **Ethanol itself:** Some direct effects of alcohol itself quite clearly contribute to hangover. These direct effects of alcohol include dehydration; dilation of blood vessels which can lead to headache; irritation of the stomach lining which can lead to nausea and vomiting; sleep disturbances which can lead to cognitive dysfunction; cytokine effects which can lead to headaches and memory dysfunction; sleep disturbances which can lead to feelings of tiredness and memory dysfunction; and low blood sugar which can lead to mood changes or fatigue and dizziness.

- **Congeners:** We have good evidence that congeners can contribute to the intensity of a hangover but are not yet precisely certain of which congeners do so or the exact mechanism by which this happens.

- **Mood:** You are more likely to get a hangover if you drink when you are in a bad mood than if you drink when you are in a good mood.

24.2) Can You Prevent a Hangover?

If you browse the internet you can find dozens of products purporting to prevent hangovers. Do any of these hangover prevention products actually work? Dr. Max Pittler, MD, PhD asked himself this question and did an exhaustive search of the scientific literature looking for its answer. What he found were three hangover preventatives which showed significantly better results than a placebo in randomized, double blind studies. Another five hangover preventatives failed to perform better than placebo. But the vast majority of hangover prevention products have not yet been tested in randomized, placebo controlled, double blind studies--so it is anyone's guess whether they are really effective or not. A couple of these have shown some promise, but further trials are needed to verify their effectiveness.

The three items which Dr. Pittler found effective for hangover prevention are **borage seed oil**, **tolfenamic acid**, and **a yeast preparation**. The five items which did not work are **artichoke extract** (also called Cynara scolymus), **prickly pear cactus extract** (also called O ficus-indica), **tropisetron** (a serotonin receptor antagonist), **propranolol** (a beta blocker), and **fructose** (a sugar).

The Three That Worked

Borage seed oil - In an unpublished research report Moesgaard and Hansen tell us how a commercial preparation of borage seed oil sold under the name Bio-glandin 25 was tested as a method for preventing hangover. Test subjects consumed 8 or 9 standard US drinks (140 to 160 ml pure ethanol) in a party setting. Subjects were given 8 capsules of Bio-glandin 25 before consuming any alcohol. Subjects were given a questionnaire which they completed and returned the following day. Subjects taking the Bio-glandin 25 reported significantly less hangover than those receiving the placebo ($p < 0.01$). Borage seed oil is sold in the US as a dietary supplement.

Tolfenamic acid - Tolfenamic acid is not approved for sale in the US for either humans or for veterinary purposes. It is approved for use as a pain killer in cats and dogs in Canada. In 1983 Dr. Kaivola and colleagues tested tolfenamic acid as a method for hangover prevention in Finland. Subjects were given 200 mg of tolfenamic acid before they started drinking and another 200 mg immediately after finishing. Exact amounts of alcohol consumed were not reported. Hangover symptoms were evaluated the following day with subjects who took tolfenamic acid reporting significantly fewer symptoms than those who received a placebo ($p < 0.01$).

The Yeast Preparation- In 1999 Dr. Laas evaluated the efficacy of a product called **Morning Fit** which is apparently no longer being manufactured. Morning Fit consisted of 250 mg dried yeast, 0.5 mg thiamine nitrate, 0.5 mg pyridozine hydrochloride and 0.5 mg riboflavin. Test subjects were given 3 tablets of Morning Fit after a 3 hour drinking session where 7 US standard drinks (ethanol 100 g) were consumed in the form of 80 proof vodka. Eight hours later a hangover questionnaire was administered. Subjects receiving Morning Fit reported significantly fewer hangover symptoms than those receiving a placebo ($p < 0.05$).

Dr. Pittler notes that none of the above preventatives completely eliminated hangovers, but that they did lessen the symptoms.

Avenues for Further Research

Dr. Pittler notes that there seems to be some evidence that a Traditional Indian Ayurvedic Preparation called Liv52 might be effective for hangover prevention. Additional research in the form of placebo controlled double blind trials is needed to confirm this. Dr. Pittler also notes that there is reason to do further research on pyritinol and prickly pear (O ficus-indica) extract. And succinic acid--the primary ingredient in the popular hangover cure RU21--has yet to be evaluated in a scientific study.

Should Hangovers Be Cured?

Some researchers have raised an ethical question--do hangovers work as a deterrent to heavy drinking? Would curing hangovers lead to an increase in heavy drinking? Although we cannot answer this with certainty, there is another way to view this question. People are known to take a hair of the dog to cure their hangovers. People without hangovers have no need for a hair of the dog. So this leads us to ask the converse question--could curing hangovers lead to a reduction in heavy drinking?

24.3) Hangover Cures - Fact and Fancy

The after-effects of a night of heavy drinking can include headaches, muscle aches, upset stomach, mental fog, dehydration, tiredness, and low blood sugar. Although only time can eliminate a hangover, there are a number of things which people do to try to alleviate the symptoms--some of which may be helpful, some of which are harmless, and some of which are not medically recommended. Things commonly used as remedies for hangover symptoms include food and liquids, analgesics, vitamins, exercise, stimulants, and depressants. Let's look at these in detail:

Food and liquids:

Rehydration: Alcohol is a diuretic and causes dehydration via increased urination. A lot of the wretchedness associated with hangover is due to dehydration so it is important to rehydrate. Sports drinks such as Gatorade have a balanced electrolyte content so they are a good bet for rehydration. Pedialyte has even more electrolytes. If you prefer to use water to rehydrate then we recommend that you also get some salt intake by eating something like french fries for example.

Warning: drinking a lot of water quickly without getting any electrolytes with it can lead to a condition known as water intoxication which is potentially fatal.

Besides rehydrating people also use food and liquids to settle their upset stomachs and raise their blood sugar back up. The following are some favorites:

Chocolate milk or ice cream: this settles the stomach, rehydrates, and raises blood sugar all at once. Milk is also rich in vitamin D.

Cysteine: cysteine has been shown to neutralize a lethal dose of the alcohol metabolite acetaldehyde in rats. It has not been tested with normal levels of alcohol or acetaldehyde in humans so its efficacy as a hangover remedy remains uncertain. Sources of cysteine include eggs, milk, meat, onions and garlic, many of which are used in traditional hangover cures. For the scientific research on cysteine and acetaldehyde see Sprince et al 1974 and Salaspuro 2007.

Beef bouillon: if you find that you can't eat anything else at least try to get down some beef bouillon. This can help you to rehydrate and restore missing electrolytes while at least getting some nutrition back into your system.

Vegemite on toast: a favorite hangover cure in Australia. Vegemite is made from yeast and is rich in B vitamins and folic acid which are depleted by drinking.

Tomatoes: many traditional folk remedies for hangovers call for tomatoes. Tomatoes are a good source of vitamin A and C, beta-carotene, and the antioxidant lycopene. Tomatoes are clearly a healthy and nutritious thing to eat whether they have any magical powers against hangovers or not.

Bacon, eggs and toast: a good meal to settle the stomach and also replenish blood sugar. Both the eggs and the bacon contain cysteine which we just discussed above. Salt in the bacon replenishes the essential electrolyte sodium.

Ocha-zuke: this is a favorite hangover cure in Japan--a gentle dish often eaten when one has an upset stomach. Ocha-zuke consists of a bowl of rice topped with things like chopped nori seaweed or sesame seeds, powdered miso, etc. A steaming hot cup of green tea is poured over the top of the rice and Japanese style pickles such as salt pickled Chinese cabbage are eaten on the side. The tea provides caffeine with less acid than found in coffee.

Kim chee and rice: in Korea kim chee and rice is the cure for everything. Kim chee is Chinese cabbage pickled in red pepper and garlic. Red pepper dilates blood vessels and increases blood flow. Garlic contains cysteine. Koreans like to drink barley tea or ginseng tea with their kim chee and rice.

Borscht: Russians use borscht as a hangover cure.

Bananas: good for replenishing the electrolyte potassium.

Taurine: there is evidence that the amino acid taurine works to prevent and reverse liver damage and that it may also work to prevent or cure a hangover. Natural sources of taurine include seafood and meat. The energy drink Red Bull also contains taurine. However, Red Bull also contains caffeine and mixed drinks made with Red Bull such as Vodka Red Bull are controversial. Sweden banned Red Bull after two people died after drinking Vodka Red Bull. For the scientific evidence on taurine and the prevention or repair of liver damage see Kerai et al 1998 and Kerai et al 1999. See also BBC News 2005.

Herbal teas: ginger tea, ginseng tea, and peppermint tea are all traditional treatments for hangover symptoms. Ginger is a natural painkiller and antioxidant. Ginger has been shown to reduce nausea and gastrointestinal distress in clinical studies. Peppermint tea is traditionally used to reduce nausea and gastrointestinal distress. For the scientific research on ginger as an anti-nausea agent see Borrelli et al 2005, Ernst and Pittler 2000, Levine et al 2008, and Ozgoli et al 2009.

Honey: honey consists of sugars, minerals and vitamins it is good for replenishing blood sugar in people with hangovers. People who have been on long drinking benders and have depleted thiamine should be careful about ingesting sugars because this can precipitate wet brain.

Warning: a diet consisting of nothing but alcohol and carbohydrates with no vitamins can lead to an irreversible form of brain damage known as Wernicke-Korsakoff syndrome aka wet brain aka beri beri. Always be sure to get your vitamins--particularly B1.

Analgesics:

If a night of heavy drinking has left you with a headache or muscle aches your first impulse might be to reach for a painkiller--but you should be aware that not all painkillers are the same.

Warning: Tylenol is toxic to the liver and we strongly recommend that people who drink alcohol avoid Tylenol at all costs because of the potential for liver failure. Tylenol is also sold in the US under the generic names **acetaminophen** and **paracetamol**. **Anacin-3** is also the same as Tylenol although other types of Anacin are not. Tylenol is also sold under the name **Panadol** in Europe, Asia, Central America, and Australia. For the scientific evidence and counter-evidence about the use of Tylenol with alcohol see Myers et al 2008, Prescott 2000, and Schmidt et al 2002.

Aspirin: Aspirin is safe for your liver but may cause stomach bleeding in some individuals. If you have an upset stomach with your hangover aspirin might make this worse. You might want to avoid aspirin if your stomach is sensitive to it. Buffered aspirin is another option. Try to avoid aspirin for at least six hours before drinking again because it can lead to higher BAC (blood alcohol content).

Ibuprofen: Ibuprofen is gentler on the stomach than aspirin and is safe for the liver, but it can still cause stomach bleeding in some individuals. It is sold under the names **Advil** and **Motrin**. Avoid ibuprofen if you have heart, circulatory or gastro-intestinal problems.

Vitamins:

Some people say that hangover symptoms can be cured by mega-doses of vitamins--particularly vitamins C and the B vitamins. These claims have not yet been tested scientifically so we do not know how much truth there is to them. We do know that drinking leads to vitamin depletion and in particular to the depletion of thiamine aka B1. A shortage of vitamin B1 can lead to permanent brain damage in the form of Wernicke-Korsakoff syndrome aka wet brain aka beri beri. We strongly urge all people who drink alcohol to take adequate doses of vitamins every day--particularly B1. On the average drinkers require more vitamins and minerals than non-drinkers.

Warning: excessive doses of certain vitamins can lead to death by vitamin poisoning. Be careful to avoid exceeding the maximum safe doses of vitamins when mega-dosing.

Exercise:

Mild exercise like yoga stretches or walking can help you to work a hangover out of your system. It is very important to remain adequately hydrated and replenish electrolytes if you are exercising with a hangover since your body is already dehydrated. Be sure to drink sports drinks such as Gatorade. We recommend that you avoid strenuous exercise while hungover because you will be less coordinated when hungover and there is a danger of injury as well as dehydration.

Stimulants:

Caffeine: although no scientific studies on the effectiveness of caffeine for treating hangover symptoms have been carried out, millions of people swear by the effectiveness of a big pot of coffee for dispelling the mental fog and morning-after cobwebs which come after a night of heavy drinking. It also goes great with your bacon and egg breakfast. The downside to coffee is that the acids in it might further upset and already upset stomach. Coffee is also a diuretic and can lead to further dehydration--so if you are treating your hangover with coffee be sure to have lots of water with it to help rehydrate.

Nicotine: a lot of people smoke their heads off when they are hungover. Many people report that nicotine helps to dispel some of the mental fog associated with hangover. But if you don't smoke we don't recommend that you start.

Other stimulants: Coca Cola was originally invented as a hangover cure and contained a good dose of cocaine. Cocaine is apparently quite effective at clearing up the mental fog that goes with a hangover--however, we strongly recommend that you avoid using cocaine. First it is illegal. Second, many people get into a vicious cycle of using alcohol to come down from cocaine and then using cocaine to wake up form alcohol--this is real bad news. We recommend that you stick to a pot of coffee or tea instead.

Depressants:

Alcohol: a lot of people cannot stand even the thought of alcohol when they are hungover; they are the lucky ones. Although "the hair of the dog that bit you last night" can relieve the symptoms of a hangover we strongly recommend against it. Drinking many days in a row can lead to alcohol withdrawal syndrome. Having several abstinence days a week is the best way to avoid withdrawals.

For those who do insist on having a "hair of the dog" on the morning after, some popular ones are: the Bloody Mary (vodka and tomato juice), the Mimosa (champagne and orange juice) and the notorious Prairie Oyster (brandy, angostura bitters, Worcestershire sauce and raw egg). There is also a virgin prairie oyster (1 part olive oil, 1 raw egg yolk, salt and pepper, 1-2 tablespoons of tomato ketchup, a dash of Tabasco and Worcestershire sauce and some lemon juice (or vinegar). Yum yum! Because of the danger of salmonella poisoning it is generally recommended that you avoid eating raw eggs.

Other depressants: other depressants such as cannabis or valium can also relieve hangover symptoms but once again we recommend against them. First of all cannabis is illegal and hence best avoided. Moreover, when you are stoned on pot many activities become undoable. Although valium and other benzodiazepines are legal with a prescription, both alcohol and benzos affect the GABA receptors and prolonged use of alcohol and benzos together can lead to dangerous withdrawal syndrome.

Antihistamine:

Some people say that a dose of Benadryl can help them feel better after a night of heavy drinking.

Note:

Much of the information on these hangover cures is anecdotal or inferential since there has not been much scientific research done on them. I have provided references for those bits of information which have some scientific support. The warnings about what to avoid are based on researched scientific fact.

REFERENCES:

BBC News, Wednesday, 28 December 2005, The ultimate hangover cure? By Becky McCall
http://news.bbc.co.uk/2/hi/uk_news/magazine/4563760.stm

Bendtsen P, Jones W, Helander A. 1998. Urinary excretion of methanol and 5-hydroxytryptophol as biochemical markers of recent drinking in the hangover state. <u>Alcohol Alcohol</u>. 33 (4), 431–438.
PubMed Abstract:
http://www.ncbi.nlm.nih.gov/pubmed/9719404

Borrelli F, Capasso R, Aviello G, Pittler MH, Izzo AA. (2005), Effectiveness and safety of ginger in the treatment of pregnancy-induced nausea and vomiting. Obstet Gynecol. 105(4), 849-56.
PubMed Abstract:
http://www.ncbi.nlm.nih.gov/pubmed/15802416

Chapman LF. (1970). Experimental induction of hangover. Q J Stud Alcohol. Suppl 5, 67–85.
PubMed Abstract:
http://www.ncbi.nlm.nih.gov/pubmed/5450666

Chauhan BL, Kulkarni RD. (1991). Alcohol hangover and Liv.52. European Journal of Clinical Pharmacolology. 40 (2), 187-8.
PubMed Abstract:
http://www.ncbi.nlm.nih.gov/pubmed/2065699

Ernst E, Pittler MH. (2000). Efficacy of ginger for nausea and vomiting: a systematic review of randomized clinical trials. Br J Anaesth. 84(3), 367-71.
PubMed Abstract:
http://www.ncbi.nlm.nih.gov/pubmed/10793599
Free Full Text:
http://bja.oxfordjournals.org/cgi/reprint/84/3/367.pdf

Harburg E, Gunn R, Gleiberman L, DiFranceisco W, Schork A. (1993). Psychosocial factors, alcohol use, and hangover signs among social drinkers: a reappraisal. J Clin Epidemiol. 46 (5), 413–422.
PubMed Abstract:
http://www.ncbi.nlm.nih.gov/pubmed/8501466

Kaivola S, Parantainen J, Osterman T, Timonen H. (1983). Hangover headache and prostaglandins: prophylactic treatment with tolfenamic acid. Cephalalgia. 3(1), 31-6.
PubMed Abstract:
http://www.ncbi.nlm.nih.gov/pubmed/6342813

Kerai MD, Waterfield CJ, Kenyon SH, Asker DS, Timbrell JA. (1998). Taurine: protective properties against ethanol-induced hepatic steatosis and lipid peroxidation during chronic ethanol consumption in rats. Amino Acids. 15(1-2), 53-76.
PubMed Abstract:
http://www.ncbi.nlm.nih.gov/pubmed/9871487

Kerai MD, Waterfield CJ, Kenyon SH, Asker DS, Timbrell JA. (1999). Reversal of ethanol-induced hepatic steatosis and lipid peroxidation by taurine: a study in rats. Alcohol Alcohol. 34(4), 529-41.
PubMed Abstract:
http://www.ncbi.nlm.nih.gov/pubmed/10456581

Laas I. (1999). A double-blind placebo-controlled study on the effects of Morning Fit on hangover symptoms after a high level of alcohol consumption in healthy volunteers. Journal of Clinical Research. 2: 9-15.

Levine ME, Gillis MG, Koch SY, Voss AC, Stern RM, Koch KL. (2008). Protein and ginger for the treatment of chemotherapy-induced delayed nausea. J Altern Complement Med. 14(5), 545-51.
PubMed Abstract:
http://www.ncbi.nlm.nih.gov/pubmed/18537470

MedlinePlus Medical Encyclopedia: Hangover treatment
http://www.nlm.nih.gov/medlineplus/print/ency/article/002041.htm

Myers RP, Shaheen AA, Li B, Dean S, Quan H. (2008). Impact of liver disease, alcohol abuse, and unintentional ingestions on the outcomes of acetaminophen overdose. Clin Gastroenterol Hepatol. 6(8), 918-25.
PubMed Abstract:
http://www.ncbi.nlm.nih.gov/pubmed/18486561

Ophardt, C. (2003). Alcohol Metabolism Effects - Elmhurst College
http://www.elmhurst.edu/~chm/vchembook/642alcoholmet.html

Ozgoli G, Goli M, Simbar M. (2009). Effects of ginger capsules on pregnancy, nausea, and vomiting. J Altern Complement Med. 15(3), 243-6.
PubMed Abstract:
http://www.ncbi.nlm.nih.gov/pubmed/19250006

Pittler MH. (2004). Complementary therapies for alcohol hangovers. Focus on Alternative and Complementary Therapies. 9, 265–8.

Pittler MH, Verster JC, Ernst E. (2005). Interventions for preventing or treating alcohol hangover: systematic review of randomised controlled trials. BMJ. 331(7531), 1515-1518.
PubMed Abstract:
http://www.ncbi.nlm.nih.gov/pubmed/16373736
Free Full Text:
http://www.bmj.com/cgi/reprint/331/7531/1515.pdf

Prat G, Adan A, Sánchez-Turet M. (2009). Alcohol hangover: a critical review of explanatory factors. Hum Psychopharmacol. 24(4), 259-67.
PubMed Abstract:
http://www.ncbi.nlm.nih.gov/pubmed/19347842

Prescott LF. (2000). Paracetamol, alcohol and the liver. Br J Clin Pharmacol. 49(4), 291-301.
PubMed Abstract:
http://www.ncbi.nlm.nih.gov/pubmed/10759684
Free Full Text:
http://www.pubmedcentral.nih.gov/articlerender.fcgi?artid=2014937

Rohsenow DJ, Howland J, Minsky SJ, Greece J, Almeida A, Roehrs TA. (2007). The acute hangover scale: a new measure of immediate hangover symptoms. Addict Behav. 32 (6), 1314–1320.
PubMed Abstract:

http://www.ncbi.nlm.nih.gov/pubmed/17097819

Salaspuro V. (2007). Pharmacological treatments and strategies for reducing oral and intestinal acetaldehyde. Novartis Foundation Symposium. 285, 145-53, discussion 153-7, 198-9.
PubMed Abstract:
http://www.ncbi.nlm.nih.gov/pubmed/17590993

Schmidt LE, Dalhoff K, Poulsen HE. (2002). Acute versus chronic alcohol consumption in acetaminophen-induced hepatotoxicity. Hepatology. 35(4), 876-82.
PubMed Abstract:
http://www.ncbi.nlm.nih.gov/pubmed/11915034

Slutske WS, Piasecki TM, Hunt-Carter E. (2003). Development and initial validation of the hangover symptoms scale: prevalence and correlates of hangover symptoms in college students. Alcohol Clinical and Experimental Research. 27 (9):, 1442–1450.
PubMed Abstract:
http://www.ncbi.nlm.nih.gov/pubmed/14506405

Sprince H, Parker CM, Smith GG, Gonzales LJ. (1974). Protection against acetaldehyde toxicity in the rat by L-cysteine, thiamin and L-2-methylthiazolidine-4-carboxylic acid. Agents Actions. 4(2), 125-30.
PubMed Info:
http://www.ncbi.nlm.nih.gov/pubmed/4842541
Abstract
http://www.springerlink.com/content/w307w62037125v33

Swift R, Davidson D. (1998). Alcohol hangover: mechanisms and mediators. Alcohol Health and Research World. 22(1), 54-60.
PubMed Abstract:
http://www.ncbi.nlm.nih.gov/pubmed/15706734
Free Full Text:
http://pubs.niaaa.nih.gov/publications/arh22-1/54-60.pdf

Woo YS, Yoon SJ, Lee HK, Lee CU, Chae JH, Lee CT. (2005). Concentration changes of methanol in blood samples during an experimentally induced alcohol hangover state. Addict Biol. 10 (4), 351–355.
PubMed Abstract:
http://www.ncbi.nlm.nih.gov/pubmed/16318957

Yokoyama M, Yokoyama A, Yokoyama T, Funazu K, Hamana G, Kondo S, Yamashita T, Nakamura H. (2005). Hangover susceptibility in relation to aldehyde dehydrogenase-2 genotype, alcohol flushing and mean corpuscular volume in Japanese workers. Alcohol Clinical and Experimental Research. 29 (7), 1165–1171.
PubMed Abstract:
http://www.ncbi.nlm.nih.gov/pubmed/16046871

CHAPTER TWENTY FIVE: Preventing Alcoholic Blackouts

"God gave us our memories so that we might have roses in December" --J.M. Barrie

25.1   Alcohol and Memory Blackouts
25.2   How to Prevent Alcoholic Blackouts

25.1) Alcohol and Memory Blackouts

Brain researchers divide memory up into two components: Short Term Memory and Long Term Memory. Alcohol interferes with the process of converting Short Term Memories into Long Term Memories--this is why people often forget new things which they learn while under the influence of alcohol and why they sometimes have full-fledged alcoholic blackouts.

Brain researchers have identified several different types of Long Term Memories which are stored in different parts of the brain. These include

- Memory for abstract ideas such as the fact that $2 + 2 = 4$ or the fact that the Norman Conquest took place in 1066. Researchers often refer to these book-learning-type of facts as semantic memory. Memory for these abstract ideas is stored in the right frontal and temporal lobes.

- Autobiographical memories for events which we have actually experienced such as where you were when you heard about nine-eleven or remembering your high school graduation party. These memories are stored in the temporal lobes.

- Other types of memories such as skills learning (riding a bicycle), conditioned responses, etc. which are stored elsewhere.

Studies of individuals who have suffered brain damage clearly indicate that memories for abstract ideas and memories for autobiographical events are stored in different locations via slightly different though similar means of processing. A part of the brain called the hippocampus is responsible for sending short term memories into long term storage in the cortex as well as for retrieving these memories. This process is illustrated in **Figure 25.1**.

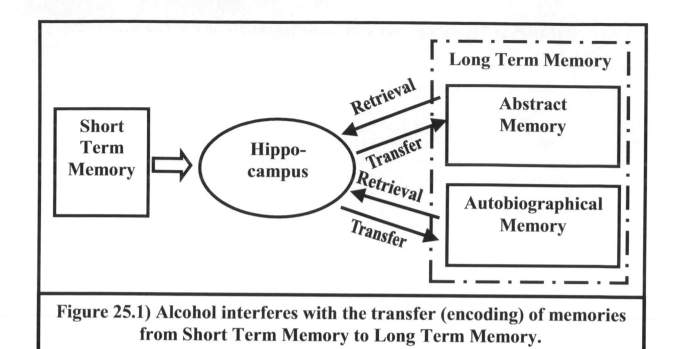

Figure 25.1) Alcohol interferes with the transfer (encoding) of memories from Short Term Memory to Long Term Memory.

Research shows that alcohol intoxication does not interfere greatly with the retrieval of memories from Long Term Memory. It also does not interfere greatly with storage in Short Term Memory so long as the subjects are not distracted during a Short Term Memory task. However, alcohol intoxication interferes in a big way with the transfer of memories from Short Term Memory to Long Term Memory.

At low levels of intoxication--a BAC (Blood Alcohol Concentration--see Chapter 13) of 0.08 to 0.15 for example--alcohol interferes with the formation of Abstract Memories in Long Term Memory. If one learns a new phone number in this moderately intoxicated state, one is unlikely to remember it the following day. At higher levels of intoxication--say from BAC 0.2 to 0.4-- alcohol intoxication may interfere with the formation of Autobiographical Memories in Long Term Memory. Sometimes people form fragmentary memories of events which occur--this is referred to as a **brownout**. Sometimes the memory is lacking entirely--this is a classical **blackout**. We wish to note that having a blackout is not the same as passing out--passing out merely means that you fell asleep while intoxicated. Blacking out refers to a failure to record memories while still conscious. People in a blackout can be walking around and talking and doing things but they are not recording any record of it in Long Term Memory.

A rapid increase in BAC is far more likely to trigger a blackout than a high BAC alone. Let us say that there are two people with a BAC of 0.2. Person A reached the BAC of 0.2 by downing several shots of whiskey in a period of ten minutes and drank on an empty stomach. Person B drank over a period of several hours on a full stomach. Even though they both have an identical BAC of 0.2--person A is far more likely to be in a blackout than person B. A reasonable hypothesis to explain this is that when BAC rises slowly, nerve cells have a chance to adjust to this change. When BAC rises too rapidly the nerve cells do not have sufficient time to adapt.

Research evidence also seems to suggest that there are some people who never have alcoholic blackouts even though they achieve high BACs. However, it seems that everyone suffers from alcohol interfering with the formation of Abstract Memories even though alcohol does not interfere with the formation of Autobiographical Memories for everyone.

Some researchers have hypothesized the existence of state-dependent learning in intoxicated people. This hypothesis proposes that when one learns something while intoxicated, one will be better able to recall it if one becomes intoxicated again. However, experiments have failed to find any evidence which supports the theory of state dependent learning for alcohol intoxication.

On a molecular level, alcohol interferes with the NMDA2 receptor of the neurotransmitter glutamate. The NMDA2 receptor appears to have a major role in the transfer of information from Short Term Memory to Long Term Memory.

It appears that the rapid BAC spikes which cause blackouts also cause impairments in decision-making and impulse control--this is likely the reason for the unpredictable and uncharacteristic behavior of people in an alcoholic blackout. This is just one more good reason to avoid BAC spikes and alcoholic blackouts.

25.2) How to Prevent Alcoholic Blackouts

Alcohol induced blackouts generally tend to occur when the alcohol in your bloodstream spikes too high and too rapidly. This exposes your brain to a sudden spike in BAC (blood alcohol content). Most people can avoid alcohol blackouts fairly easily by following a few simple drinking rules to avoid spiking their BAC. However, some people may have a great deal more difficulty in avoiding alcoholic blackouts than other people do. These include people who have had **gastric bypass surgery**, people with **long histories of severe alcohol abuse and withdrawal**, and people with **genetic irregularities in their alcohol metabolism**.

If you tend to black out very frequently when you drink even if you drink small amounts of alcohol then alcohol abstinence may be your best drinking goal. **Marijuana Maintenance** (discussed in Chapter 6) is a realistic option for people who have too many problems with alcoholic blackouts or with alcohol withdrawal syndrome and who don't wish to abstain from everything.

Strategies to Prevent Blackouts

- **Eat before Drinking:** The stomach has only a few square feet of surface area to use to absorb liquids, but the small intestine has many thousands of square feet for the purpose of absorbing liquids because it is covered with villi. When you eat a meal then you cause the valve between the stomach and the intestine to close for several hours--this greatly slows the influx of alcohol into the bloodstream and prevents BAC spikes.

- **Hydrate:** If you drink a lot of water before you have any alcohol then you will not be thirsty. If you are not thirsty then you will drink more slowly and not spike your BAC so much.

- **Pace Yourself:** Slow down your drinking speed. One way to do this is to alternate non-alcoholic drinks with alcoholic drinks. Another technique is to time your drinks with your watch.

- **Weaker Drinks:** Avoid drinking straight shots of booze if you have blackouts. As a general rule, the weaker the drink the longer it will take to drink it.

- **Strong tasting drinks:** Strong tasting drinks also often take longer to drink than tasteless ones. For example most people will drink a gin martini more slowly than a vodka martini.

- **Rest:** Many people have blackouts if they drink alcohol when they are sleep deprived. Being well rested before you drink will help you to avoid having alcoholic blackouts.

- **Environment:** Drinking in a strange environment can reduce your tolerance to alcohol and increase the likelihood of blackouts. Drinking in a familiar environment is a way to avoid this. See Chapter 30: "Alcohol, Individual and Environment" for a discussion of this phenomenon.

- **Don't Mix Booze and Meds:** Many medications can greatly increase your chance of blackouts if you drink on them. Some can even kill you if you drink on them. Medications which commonly lead to blackouts when mixed with alcohol include narcotic painkillers such as codeine, non-narcotic painkillers like aspirin, and nearly all sleep aids including antihistamines like Benadryl and prescription sleep aids like ambien. For more info on the interactions of medications and alcohol please see Appendix One: "Alcohol-related Drug Interactions".

- **Avoid Drinking Games:** Things like drinking games or beer bongs can spike your BAC very quickly--if you have problems with blackouts then it may be a good idea to stay away from these.

REFERENCES:

Breedlove SM, Rosenzweig MR, Watson NV. (2007). Biological Psychology: An Introduction to Behavioral, Cognitive, and Clinical Neuroscience. Fifth Edition. Sinauer Associates, Inc.

White AM. (2003). What happened? Alcohol, memory blackouts, and the brain. Alcohol Res Health. 27(2), 186-96.
PubMed Abstract:
http://www.ncbi.nlm.nih.gov/pubmed/15303630
Free Full Text:
http://pubs.niaaa.nih.gov/publications/arh27-2/186-196.pdf

CHAPTER TWENTY SIX: Facts and Myths About Cross Addiction and Cross Tolerance

"Every form of addiction is bad, no matter whether the narcotic be alcohol, morphine or idealism." --Carl Jung

If you ever went through any 12 step chemical dependency treatment program you were almost certainly told that you had to abstain from all mood altering substances for the rest of your life because being addicted to one thing meant that you were automatically cross addicted to everything. If you had kicked heroin, for example, you could never have a beer because it would immediately lead you back to heroin. And so forth. Hazelden has even made a video about it.

The simple truth is that cross addiction is a myth with no scientific evidence to back it up. Lots of people who kick heroin or meth or crack go on to become moderate drinkers or even enjoy a bit of recreational alcohol intoxication or marijuana smoking. Why do 12 step treatment programs tell you this lie? Because the only recreational drugs which are allowed at 12 step meetings are caffeine and nicotine. Apparently this is because AA founder Bill Wilson refused to give up coffee or cigarettes. Having a beer now and then is no more likely to make you go back to other drugs than is having a cup of coffee or a cigarette.

If you think that drinking might lead you to a lapse of judgment and a return to a habit that you have kicked then it is reasonable to avoid drinking. However, for some people it is better to drink than to feel deprived of everything. Because when people feel deprived of everything it can often lead to a **Ricochet Effect** of the kind which we described in Chapter 15: "Damage Control: Dealing With Slips, Setbacks, and Ricochets". Substituting a less harmful drug for a more harmful one is a harm reduction strategy which has shown high success rates.

- **CROSS ADDICTION is the myth that if you are addicted to one drug then you are automatically addicted to all drugs including unrelated drugs--except for caffeine and nicotine which are acceptable drug addictions for twelve step members.**

- **CROSS TOLERANCE is the scientifically established fact if you have tolerance and withdrawal for a drug, then other drugs in the same drug family will show similar tolerance and withdrawal effects--but drugs from a different drug family will not.**

For example, heroin, morphine, codeine, methadone, etc. are all opiates and they all affect the brain's opioid receptors. If a person is addicted to heroin then that person can use another opiate such as codeine or methadone to prevent withdrawal because these drugs all belong to the same family and have cross tolerance with each other. However, an opiate like heroin does not have cross tolerance with a benzodiazepine like Valium. The opiates may have a limited cross-tolerance with alcohol which affects many receptors--but if this is the case then it is a rather limited cross-tolerance.

Valium, Librium, Xanax, Ativan and Klonopin are all closely related drugs which belong to the benzodiazepine family of drugs. These drugs all affect the GABA receptors in your brain. If you become addicted to any one of these benzodiazepines then you can substitute any other because there is cross-tolerance. Since alcohol also affects GABA receptors there is quite a bit of cross-tolerance with alcohol but not as much with each other since alcohol affects many different receptors. However you cannot substitute heroin for Valium because heroin does not affect the GABA receptor. There is no cross tolerance between heroin and Valium.

Many other drugs are still under study but it appears that there may be some cross-tolerance between nicotine, caffeine, crystal meth, Ritalin (methylphenidate), and amphetamine.

REFERENCES:

Hazelden. (1999). Cross Addiction The Back Door to Relapse DVD

Holtzman SG. (1987). Discriminative stimulus effects of caffeine: tolerance and cross-tolerance with methylphenidate. Life Sci. 40(4), 381-9.
PubMed Abstract:
http://www.ncbi.nlm.nih.gov/pubmed/3807640

Jain R, Holtzman SG. (2005). Caffeine induces differential cross tolerance to the amphetamine-like discriminative stimulus effects of dopaminergic agonists. Brain Res Bull. 65(5), 415-21.
PubMed Abstract:
http://www.ncbi.nlm.nih.gov/pubmed/15833596

Leith NJ, Barrett RJ. (1981). Self-stimulation and amphetamine: tolerance to d and l isomers and cross tolerance to cocaine and methylphenidate. Psychopharmacology (Berl). 74(1), 23-8.
PubMed Abstract:
http://www.ncbi.nlm.nih.gov/pubmed/6791199

Wooters TE, Neugebauer NM, Rush CR, Bardo MT. (2008). Methylphenidate enhances the abuse-related behavioral effects of nicotine in rats: intravenous self-administration, drug discrimination, and locomotor cross-sensitization. Neuropsychopharmacology. 33(5), 1137-48.
PubMed Abstract:
http://www.ncbi.nlm.nih.gov/pubmed/17581534
Free Full Text:
http://www.nature.com/npp/journal/v33/n5/pdf/1301477a.pdf

PART IV: HARM REDUCTION IN CONTEXT

"Evidence...proves that prohibition only drives drunkenness behind doors and into dark places, and does not cure it or even diminish it." --Mark Twain

CHAPTER TWENTY SEVEN: *Harm Reduction Information for Friends and Family of Drinkers*

"Only the soft overcomes the hard, by yielding, bringing it to peace" --Lao Tze

27.1) How to Change Your Spouse's Drinking

If you have a spouse with a drinking problem then it is likely that you have tried to get your spouse to change before--perhaps with little or no success. You may have tried logical reasoning with your spouse and gotten nowhere. You may have tried confrontation and found that that didn't work. You may have accused your spouse of denial and found that you were talking to a wall. The fact is that research shows that the above mentioned strategies are not only unhelpful, they are counterproductive (Miller and Rollnick 2002). The good news is that there are strategies which will more often than not lead a person to change. In this chapter we are going to introduce you to a psychotherapeutic technique called **Motivational Interviewing** which has applications beyond the psychotherapeutic setting as well,

First it is important for us to note that the husband/wife relationship is a very different one that the client/therapist relationship and therefore **Motivation Interviewing** techniques need to be adapted and combined with some other ideas when used in a spousal relationship. It is important in both the client/therapist relationship and in the husband/wife relationship to set clear-cut boundaries--however the nature of the boundaries will differ greatly between the two. It is essential that the spouse does not "play therapist". Even in the client/therapist relationship **Motivational Interviewing** seeks to minimize the power differential between the client and the therapist--we cannot emphasize enough that this is even more essential in the husband/wife relationship.

The first thing which you should always do as the spouse of a heavy drinker is to protect yourself and your family by practicing the principles of harm reduction for yourself and your family. There are a certain number of heavy drinkers who suffer from comorbid Anti-Social Personality Disorder. These people are extremely unlikely to change their drinking behaviors under any circumstances and it is likely that if your spouse is such a person then the only recourse will be to leave your spouse. However, this case is the exception rather than the rule, and most heavy drinkers are likely to be amenable to making some changes if approached correctly.

Although we use the word "spouse" throughout this chapter for the sake of simplicity, the principle we talk about here can apply to any significant other in any type of relationship.

STEP ONE: Set Boundaries and Practice Harm Reduction for Yourself and Your Children

The standard 12 step view is that the spouse of a drinker must never do anything to protect the drinker--that any such behavior is always "enabling" and that the drinker must be made to suffer until he or she finally decides to join AA and never drink again. This view of things is often unreasonable and unrealistic. Causing a drinker to suffer often causes him/her to drink more, not to quit. Much higher success rates have been demonstrated with **Motivational Interviewing** techniques. Instead of helping your spouse to change for the better, refusing to "enable" your spouse may well lead him/her to change for the worse and to damage yourself and your family in the process.

Patt Denning gives us an excellent concrete example of this in her book <u>Practicing Harm Reduction Psychotherapy</u>. A young woman consults a 12 step addictions counselor because she is concerned about her husband's drinking. The husband is the sole source of household income. The 12 step counselor tells this woman that she must stop "enabling" her husband and that in particular she must not call in sick for her husband if he is passed out drunk and cannot wake up to go to work. The end result of this is that the husband is fired, the family is forced to go on welfare, the husband is still drinking, and everything is far worse than it was before.

The moral of this story is that not all behaviors which are labeled as "enabling" are bad. In a harm reductionist approach to this situation the wife would make an effort to help the husband retain his job and rely on the **Motivational Interviewing** techniques which we discuss below to try and persuade him to change his drinking for the better.

Robert Meyers (1998) points out that if the drinking spouse has any history of domestic violence it is important to make a **Safety Plan** and stick to it if violence threatens. Meyers outlines the following concrete example:

> On some days when the husband returns home from work he is extremely quiet and distant. When the wife asks hem what is wrong he says everything is fine. When she asks how she can help he screams "Get off my back!" Then he gives the wife the "silent treatment" and begins to drink. When she asks again if she can help he screams at her and sometimes shoves her across the room.

A possible **Safety Plan** in this case involves the wife not engaging the husband in conversation at all, but instead informing him that she will be spending the night at her mother's and taking the children and doing so,

It is also essential that one set and stick to some boundaries regarding one's spouse's drinking. Some examples are:

- Informing the spouse that you absolutely refuse to ride in the car when the spouse is driving under the influence.
- Informing the spouse that you will refuse to have sex with the spouse when the spouse is intoxicated.

STEP TWO: Understand That Harm Is Hierarchical

Should you insist that your spouse be totally abstinent or accept small changes in drinking behavior? That is a question which it is impossible for a book to answer. Every situation and every individual is unique and only you can decide what is acceptable for you. We suggest that you use a Decisional Balance Sheet to help you clarify your own thinking and make a decision. A sample sheet on this topic is given at the end of this chapter.

However, as harm reductionists we feel that in most cases it is more important that your spouse eliminates the riskiest aspects of his/her alcohol use than that he/she becomes perfectly abstinent. We strongly suggest that you read Chapter 5 on the hierarchy of harms and keep this information in mind. We feel that any effort that your spouse makes to drink safely is to be encouraged--safe drinking is better than unsafe drinking. Any effort that your spouse makes towards reduced drinking is better than no effort towards reduced drinking. You might wish that your spouse were perfectly abstinent right now and forever, but in most cases this is an unrealistic demand and an attempt to achieve this can often backfire and lead to a spouse whose drinking is far worse than before. It is better to make small steps in a positive direction than to make one giant step forward followed by ten giant steps back.

Always remember that "better is better" and that "perfectionism is the enemy of the good". As Plato said, "Never discourage anyone who continually makes progress, no matter how slow."

STEP THREE: Learn the "Don'ts"

1. **Don't confront.**
2. **Don't engage in logical argumentation.**
3. **Don't work the spouse's program for the spouse.**
4. **Don't play the blame game**
5. **Labels do more harm than good**

1) Don't confront.

Going head to head with your spouse and telling your spouse that his/her drinking is bad and must change immediately or else is the one surefire way to ensure that your spouse's drinking will change for the worse. Miller and Rollnick are the experts on motivational Interviewing and they conducted a scientific study which proved that the more that people were confronted the worse their drinking became (Miller and Rollnick, 2002).

2) Don't engage in logical argumentation.

Logical argument is an excellent tool in its place: such as a peer reviewed journal or a formal debate. It is not a very good tool for convincing someone to make a change. In point of fact using logical argumentation is more likely to change a person's behavior in the opposite direction.

The reason for this is that a logical argument calls forth a counterargument from the person with whom you are arguing. Arguing logically with your spouse against drinking will serve to evoke logical arguments from your spouse in favor of drinking. Logical argumentation is not a good way to bring about change. Usually it only serves to strengthen your spouse's reasons in favor of drinking.

3) Don't work the spouse's program for the spouse.

If your spouse has decided to work on cutting back by charting and drink counting then let him do so himself. Don't count and chart your spouse's drinks for him. And don't confront him for going over. First of all the only way that the spouse can exercise the moderation muscle or the abstinence muscle is by doing it for him/herself. Second, pushing too hard leads the spouse to push back in an equal and opposite direction. Remember that every action has an equal and opposite reaction.

Likewise if the spouse drinks on a planned abstinence day it is not appropriate to pull the bottle out of his/her hand and dump it down the drain. Nor should you confront the spouse the following day about his/her failure. Likely the spouse already feels bad enough about the failure him/herself. If the spouse brings it up then console rather than attack.

4) Don't play the blame game

If you and your spouse spend a lot of time trying to affix blame on each other you will be unlikely to accomplish much in the way of making positive changes. Quite the opposite--the more time spent affixing blame the more likely the drinker is apt to move towards drinking more. If you seek positive change then don't play the blame game.

5) Labels do more harm than good

There is absolutely no way in which calling your spouse an "alcoholic" can be useful or helpful at all and this sort of labeling might actually cause a great deal of harm. If your spouse rejects the label, then your spouse might well just get pissed off at being called a bad name and drink more than ever. And if your spouse accepts the label and starts calling him/herself an alcoholic and believes that he/she is powerless over alcohol this often becomes a self fulfilling prophecy and also leads to increased drinking. Even if you believe that the only possible acceptable goal is for your spouse to not merely abstain but also join AA, calling your spouse an "alcoholic" is unlikely to be the way to achieve that goal. Accusing your spouse of being in "denial" is another label that does more harm than good.

STEP FOUR: Change Your Interactional Style and Practice the "Do's" of Motivational Interviewing

If you are fortunate enough that you can find a couples counselor who understands both **Motivational Interviewing** and **Harm Reduction** and if your spouse is willing to go, then you are the most fortunate of couples and by all means go! If you are fortunate enough to find such a counselor and your spouse is unwilling to go then by all means go by yourself and use what this person has to teach you.

Unfortunately, the vast majority of Americans will be unable to find a couples counselor who is trained in **Harm Reduction** and **Motivational Interviewing** in their area. The 12 steps remain highly popular in spite of research which shows that they are less effective than numerous alternative approaches (Hester and Miller 2003). If you cannot find a counselor who is familiar with **Motivational Interviewing** and **Harm Reduction** then you will have to approach your spouse yourself using a modified variant of **Motivational Interviewing** which we have developed for use by spouses.

The following five items are the essential elements of the approach we advocate for **Motivational Spousal Change**. The first four come from **Motivational Interviewing** and the last item pertains specifically to couples:

1. **EMPATHETIC LISTENING leads to serious thinking**
2. **ELICITED PLANS are motivated plans**
3. **AVOID CONFRONTATIONAL ACTIONS that lead to equal and opposite reactions**
4. **SUPPORT SELF-BELIEF because faith in one's self can move mountains**
5. **EXPRESS CLEAR NEEDS AND GRIPES so that boundaries are clear**

1) EMPATHETIC LISTENING leads to serious thinking

As the spouse of a heavy drinker you may very well see only the down side of your spouse's alcohol use. However, if you want to help your spouse change his/her drinking for the better then it is essential that you understand that the drinking has a positive pay off for your spouse. If it did not then your spouse would not drink. You have to give your spouse a chance to talk about both the pros and the cons of drinking. If you concentrate only on talking about the negative aspects of drinking then you reinforce the positive aspects in the subconscious.

Give your spouse a chance to express ambivalence about drinking. Let your spouse know that you are not necessarily demanding total abstinence but that it is important for you to see some improvement in terms of safer drinking or reduced drinking. If your spouse is still in the precontemplation stage then suggest charting as a good way to start getting a handle on drinking.

2) ELICITED PLANS are motivated plans

A key point about motivational interviewing which makes it different from confrontational approaches is that you elicit change goals from your spouse instead of trying to logically argue him/her into accepting goals which you have chosen or threatening him/her or confronting him/her.

Let us take the following as a scenario. A wife is very concerned about her husband's drinking because he gets drunk several nights a week and always drives home from the bar in a state of intoxication. The wife waits until the husband is sober and in an approachable mood and then lets him know that she is very concerned about his drinking. Particularly the drinking and driving. She loves him very much and does not want to lose him in some stupid auto accident. Is there any way that he can think of to eliminate the drinking and driving? He stops and thinks and volunteers that if he plans his drinking in advance he can always take the subway instead of driving when he plans to go to a bar. That way he will have no recourse but to take the subway or a taxi home.

This is the key point about motivational interviewing--because he thought of and suggested the plan of using the subway both to and from he will be highly motivated to use this plan. If someone had attempted to force him or argue him into using this plan he would be feeling highly resistant to it. The heart of MI is that the person creates/chooses their own plan. The skill of MI lies in eliciting this kind of thinking, and in not using argumentation or confrontation. Eventually you may also want to suggest that your spouse check out the HAMS web site, book, and support groups.

One big difficulty which you may have as a spouse is learning how to change your style of interaction from one that is confrontational to one that is non-confrontational. You probably have some very ingrained habits in the way in which you interact with your spouse. **The Spousal Style CBA (Cost Benefit Analysis)** and the **Spousal Goal CBA** are two exercises which you can use to improve the way that you interact with your spouse on drinking issues. Samples of these follow this section.

3) AVOID CONFRONTATIONAL ACTIONS that lead to equal and opposite reactions

Step Two describes some of the confrontational approaches to avoid. Miller and Rollnick refer to this as Rolling with Resistance. In the case of a spouse it is also important to remember that there can be a time to beat a strategic retreat. If your spouse is not willing to listen now it may be worthwhile to wait until later to approach your spouse about change.

4) SUPPORT SELF-BELIEF because faith in one's self can move mountains

Always let your spouse know that you believe that your spouse has the inner strength to change for the better. Let your spouse know that alcohol is a powerless inanimate object and that your spouse is more powerful than alcohol. Show support for every positive change as a triumph.

Any time your spouse reports making a successful change--no matter how small--be prepared to openly celebrate this with your spouse even if it is by something as silly as doing the Snoopy dance. For example if your spouse has been a daily drinker for a long time and has just achieved his/her first abstinence day then this is a cause for celebration. If it is your spouse's goal to drink less per session and your spouse succeeds at this then this is also a cause for celebration. Etc. etc. remember that nothing succeeds like success; so don't fail to remind your spouse of his/her successes.

If your spouse complains of backsliding and says that he/she feels like a "failure", remind him/her of the old Japanese proverb "fall down seven times get up eight"--as long as you keep on trying you are a success and not a failure. If your spouse expresses a strong desire to change but complains of feeling a lack of ability to change then it may be helpful to remind your spouse of instances in the past when he/she has accomplished something difficult such as passing a test or quitting smoking or what have you.

5) EXPRESS CLEAR NEEDS AND GRIPES so that boundaries are clear

One big difference between the husband/wife relationship and the therapist/client relationship is that husbands and wives have a right and a need to mutually express certain needs and gripes to each other. Since the therapist is the employee of the client the only real gripe the therapist can have is if the therapist is not paid, and the only real gripe the client can express is if the therapist is an incompetent nincompoop.

Husbands and wives on the other hand are a long-term partnership--ideally a lifelong partnership--and very often the raising of children is a central goal of this partnership. Since the only alternative to working together to get along is to divorce--it is important that these partners express needs and gripes clearly to each other so that they can work together to fulfill the central goal of the partnership.

STEP FIVE: Learn To Change Your Thinking or Your Situation

Hopefully the first four steps have worked just fine and your spouse has changed in a way that you are happy with and you have no need for a step five. If not, then your last two choices are to either change your situation or change your thinking or both. The most obvious way to change your situation is to leave your spouse--and if this is necessary then it is necessary. One may also change one's thinking by accepting the fact that it is not always possible to change another person. This is the way of the Stoic and the Buddhist.

STEP SIX: Be Prepared for Change

You might be surprised if your spouse makes a radical change for the better in his/her drinking that you are now feeling less happy with your spouse than you were before the change was made. You had gotten used to the status quo before the change was made and now you feel at sea. Perhaps your husband ignored the kids before the change and now wants to play an active part in rearing them and you feel that your role as the sole arbitrator over the children is being usurped. Feeling this way is natural, but it is not healthy if you want to keep a healthy marriage together. The children may also not be at all used to getting input from dear old dad if he has been lost to them through drinking. You will both need to be flexible and willing to make changes to accept and grow with the new spouse you now have--so be prepared.

****

Do Interventions work?

Groups are powerful--Interventions take advantage of that power to force people into treatment against their will. Does this succeed in getting people to enter treatment? Yes there is some evidence that it has some success. Does it succeed in keeping people abstinent? There is no real evidence for this. Intervention can also lead to resentment. What we see is that other methods show a much higher success rate than intervention does (Meyers et al 1998).

27.2) My Spousal Style CBA

free download at http://hamsnetwork.org/worksheets

Continue to use a confrontational style with my spouse.

Pros	Cons

Use empathetic listening and elicit harm reduction plans instead.

Pros	Cons

27.3) Sample Spousal Style CBA

free download at http://hamsnetwork.org/worksheets

Continue to use a confrontational style with my spouse.

Pros	Cons
1) It is easier to talk to my spouse the same way I always have than to learn a new way 2) I get ego gratification from bawling out my spouse 3) I get revenge by watching my spouse fail when I refuse to enable him/her	1) My spouse may drink more in reaction 2) My spouse might get fed up and leave

Use empathetic listening and elicit harm reduction plans instead.

Pros	Cons
1) Statistics show that this method has a better chance of succeeding 2) A chance at lasting change is worth the effort 3) Reduced harm is always better than increased harm	1) My spouse might not change anyway 2) It is very hard work to change my way of talking to my spouse when I am used to being confrontational

27.4) My Spousal Goal CBA

free download at http://hamsnetwork.org/worksheets

Insist that my spouse become totally abstinent right now

Pros	Cons

Encourage my spouse to take small steps toward harm reduction

Pros	Cons

27.5) Sample Spousal Goal CBA

free download at http://hamsnetwork.org/worksheets

Insist that my spouse become totally abstinent right now

Pros	Cons
1) If my spouse abstains for good then all drinking harms are eliminated for good 2) It makes me feel righteous	1) This might backfire and my spouse might drink more 2) Making my spouse feel bad about him/herself might lead to increased drinking

Encourage my spouse to take small steps toward harm reduction

Pros	Cons
1) It is easier to succeed at a small change than a large one 2) It might be possible to eliminate the biggest alcohol related harms immediately	1) I want change and I want it now! 2) We might continue to suffer alcohol related harms due to my spouse's drinking

27.6) How to Be Supportive Of a Spouse Who Is Practicing Harm Reduction

(Note: For the sake of simplicity we use the words "spouse" and "he"--but everything which we say here applies to spouses, partners, friends and family regardless of sex or sexual preference.)

1) Accept your spouse's harm reduction goal--whether that goal is safer drinking, reduced drinking or quitting

It is important that you be accepting of your spouse's goal vis a vis alcohol--if you try to impose the goal that you think your spouse ought to have upon him you might find that this backfires and your spouse's behavior gets worse than ever. Every action has an equal and opposite reaction. If your spouse has decided that what he wants to work on is safer drinking and you decide that you are going to try and make your spouse quit instead of drinking safely, then you may well find that your spouse's drinking gets worse than ever.

Likewise, if your spouse is choosing to quit then it is not appropriate to tell your spouse that anyone can moderate and that moderate drinking should be the goal--when people choose to change then they generally know what the best change goal is for them at this point in time so it is important to respect it.

2) Don't try to make your spouse run before he can walk

Accept your spouse where he is at and be supportive of the changes which he is choosing to make. If he is choosing a goal of safer drinking then do not try to force him into a goal of moderate drinking right now.

If he chooses to have one alcohol abstinence day a week for the first month then do not try to force him to have six alcohol abstinence days per week for the first month. Slow and steady wins the race.

3) Don't try to work your spouse's program for him

If your spouse has decided to cut back on drinking and measure every drink then your spouse has to do this for himself--if you start measuring his drinks for him then this will backfire and he may want to drink more than ever. Likewise if he is monitoring how much he is buying--he has to do this for himself and you can't do it for him.

If your spouse goes over limits then it is not your place to grab the bottle and dump it down the sink--he will just get another and resent you for it and perhaps stop trying to change at all. Let him decide in the morning that he has made a mistake.

The only exception to this is when safety is involved.

4) ALWAYS BETTER SAFE THAN SORRY--this is the heart of harm reduction.

Never ride with anyone who has been drinking before driving. And if your spouse has given you the car keys before he started to drink--then don't give them back after he is intoxicated.

5) Accept the fact of regression

Prochaska teaches us that slips are the norm when people change their behavior. For example-- only one person in 20 quits smoking cigarettes on the first try. If your spouse is the lucky one who manages to change his behavior on the first try then hurrah!!

But do not become angry or backbiting if your spouse fails to change perfectly on the first try. In particular, if your spouse chooses a goal of safer drinking or reduced drinking then if your spouse slips at some point, do not say "I knew this would never work and the only answer is to send you to AA and make you quit."

If you say nasty things like this your spouse may just up and leave. If he does not leave he may decide to stop working at making any changes at all since the changes which he has made are not appreciated. Remember--if your spouse successfully moderates his drinking nine times out of ten then this is nine time better than if he never moderated his drinking at all.

6) Reward without patronizing.

Telling your spouse that you really like the changes that he has made in his behavior is a good way of rewarding him verbally. Of course food and sex are always good rewards too:-)

27.7) What to Do If Your Spouse Won't Change His/Her Drinking

(Note: For the sake of simplicity we use the words "spouse" and "he"--but everything which we say here applies to spouses, partners, friends and family regardless of sex or sexual preference.)

First off we want to say that if the spouse is making any serious effort at changing drinking-- whether the spouse's goal is safer drinking, reduced drinking, or quitting, then we urge you to try and be supportive even if your spouse F%$#s up sometimes. If your spouse is making a serious effort at a harm reduction goal then it is unreasonable and unrealistic of you to try and set a goal of total abstinence for your spouse. This approach often backfires and winds up making your spouse's drinking worse. Likewise, it is unreasonable to demand that your spouse drink in moderation if your spouse has chosen abstinence as a more achievable goal.

However, it is also unreasonable to stay with a spouse who endangers yourself or your children-- if this is the case then leaving your spouse may be the only viable option. Remember, scientific research shows that alcohol does not turn essentially peaceable people to violence--alcohol only brings out violence in people who are inherently violent to begin with. Research shows us that many people who use a lot of drugs or alcohol have co-occurring Antisocial Personality Disorder. Antisocial Personality Disorder makes people violent whether they drink alcohol or not. Drinking alcohol just makes them more violent. Antisocial Personality Disorder is very resistant to change--so beware.

If your spouse is not underlyingly violent you must still make choices and take steps to reduce potential harms to yourself and your family if your spouse refuses to change his drinking. Alanon may tell you that you need to let your spouse suffer the consequences of his drinking--that you should let your spouse get fired rather than call in sick for him if he is too drunk to go to work. We do not agree with this approach. It is important for you to protect yourself and your family on all levels--physically, emotionally, psychologically, and financially. Getting yourself and your spouse and your family put out on the street because you can't pay your rent is not going to help anyone--and it will likely do nothing to change your spouse's drinking either. Planning for your own safety and planning to reduce all harms--including financial harms--to yourself and your family is what you must do.

Don't ever ride in an automobile with someone who has been drinking. If your spouse can't stop himself from drinking and driving then always make sure that you have transportation for yourself and your family arranged--don't let him pick up the kids if you don't know if he will be driving sober or not. If your spouse has the good sense to give you his car keys before he starts drinking then don't give them back after he is drunk. Alanon might tell you to let him suffer the consequences of his own actions--but do you really want a dead spouse on your conscience?

If it looks like your spouse is financially imperiling you and your family then it may be incumbent upon you to get a job and take care of the family in his stead. Just make sure that your spouse keeps his job and keeps supporting you until you are safe and secure with an income of your own. Once you can pay the bills yourself you can choose to cut him loose if need be or to stay if you wish. With financial freedom you can be your own master.

You may indeed choose to stay with a person whom you live in spite of that person's over-drinking so long as that person is not violent. As long as you choose to continue to live with the spouse then you must protect yourself emotionally and psychologically as much as possible. Here is where practicing Cognitive Behavioral Therapy (CBT) comes in. Learning how to practice CBT will help you to survive difficult emotional times.

In conclusion, if you choose to stay with someone who insists on continuing to engage in destructive drinking them protect yourself, financially, emotionally, and psychologically. But if this person abuses you physically or mentally then it is time to leave. If you need help to leave then get it.

REFERENCES:

Denning, Patt (2000). Practicing Harm Reduction Psychotherapy. Guilford. New York.

Hester R, Miller W. (2003). Handbook of alcoholism treatment approaches (3rd ed). Boston: Pearson, Allyn, & Bacon.

Meyers RJ, Smith JE, Miller EJ. (1998). Working Through the Concerned Significant Other. In W. R. Miller, N. Heather (eds.) Treating Addictive Behaviors, 2nd Edition. Plenum Press. New York.

Miller WR, Rollnick S. (1991, 2002). Motivational Interviewing: Preparing People To Change Addictive Behavior. New York: Guilford Press.

Moeller FG, Dougherty DM. (2001). Antisocial personality disorder, alcohol, and aggression. Alcohol Res Health. 25(1), 5-11.
PubMed Abstract:
http://www.ncbi.nlm.nih.gov/pubmed/11496966

Free Full Text:
http://pubs.niaaa.nih.gov/publications/arh25-1/5-11.pdf

CHAPTER TWENTY EIGHT: *The HAMS Support Group*

Not everyone needs to join a support group to change their drinking--some people just need information of the kind that you are finding in this book. But for other people, joining a support group can be the essential element which spells the difference between succeeding at changing their drinking or not. All HAMS support groups are free-of-charge and lay-led. HAMS offers both live and online support groups. As of this writing live HAMS support groups are only offered in New York City, but HAMS online support groups have members from all over the world.

HAMS support groups encourage independence and self-efficacy. Lifelong membership is not required in HAMS support groups. HAMS groups emphasize information as well as group support. Many people attend one HAMS group--obtain the information which they needed to make changes--change their drinking and do not have to come back. Other people choose to come back on a continuing basis because they enjoy the support and find that declaring their plan in a public place and reporting their successes or failures helps to keep them accountable.

HAMS groups are purely secular in nature--public prayer has no place in HAMS groups.

Cross talk is encouraged in HAMS.

HAMS members generally avoid giving each other advice. We have found that it is generally more helpful to speak using the first person pronoun "I" and to share what has been helpful for us than it is to use the second person pronoun "you" and tell others what they ought to do.

HAMS members respect individual differences--we avoid statements like "we are all alike" and are more likely to say "different strokes for different folks." We also avoid "mind reading"--we do not assume that other people's thoughts reflect our thoughts or that other people's experience reflects our experience--hence we avoid phrases like "I used to be just like you". We recognize that there are many different branches on each individual's road of life.

Meanness and personal attacks are not allowed in HAMS.

HAMS members do not attempt to choose drinking goals for other members--each member chooses a drinking goal for him/herself only.

HAMS support groups find that the following things work and are beneficial to our members:

- A safe supportive environment where members can honestly report successes and failures without being judged
- A safe place to talk about what is working and what is not working and what needs to be change
- An environment which recognizes that different people hold different values about intoxication
- Freedom to choose a goal that the individual considers desirable--ranging from safer drinking to quitting

- Recognition that different people change at different rates using different techniques and pursuing different goals--i.e. different strokes for different folks
- Information including info on tapering and withdrawal
- Humor--laughter can be more intoxicating than alcohol

HAMS support groups have found that people can do without the following--so these things are off limits: lies, bullying, threats, religious coercion, mind reading, and terminal identification-itis.

If you are interested in starting a HAMS support group in your community please contact us:

Tel: 347-678-5671

Email: hams@hamshrn.org

CHAPTER TWENTY NINE: Harm Reduction and the Stages of Change Model

Starting in 1977 and continuing to the present, Dr. James Prochaska and his colleagues have conducted research towards developing a **Stages of Change Model** of behavioral change. Although the Prochaska group has primarily researched people who are quitting smoking, their Stages of Change Model is useful for discussing changes in all sorts of behaviors, ranging from smoking to drinking alcohol to gambling to overly strict religious beliefs to more. The Stages of Change are:

- **Not even thinking about changing - PRECONTEMPLATION**

- **Thinking about making a change - CONTEMPLATION**

- **Getting ready to change - PREPARATION**

- **Taking action for change - ACTION**

- **Maintaining and consolidating the change - MAINTENANCE - a person maintains the change in the behavior through continued effort**

- **Moving on with life - TERMINATION - the change is now ingrained and the person no longer has to make great efforts to maintain the change**

- **Setbacks - RECYCLING - a person returns from any given stage to an earlier stage**

Some people say that these **Stages of Change** make up a **Spiral of Change** as illustrated in **Figure 29.1**.

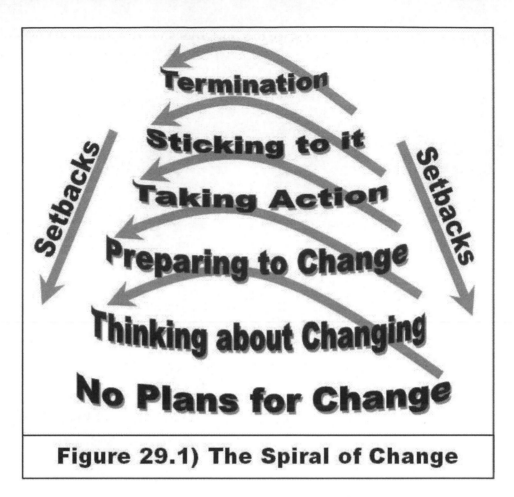

Figure 29.1) The Spiral of Change

Now let's take a closer look at **Precontemplation (not even thinking about changing)**. Some people have no desire to change certain habits. People around them may wish that they would change, but they themselves see no need for change. Perhaps they feel that they have a bad habit that they need to get around to changing one of these days. Or they may not perceive that there is anything wrong with their habits--and indeed who is he to be the judge of what is right for others? Even though person X may call person Y a drunkard, person Y may in return consider person X to be a religious fanatic. A Harm Reductionist approach is nonjudgmental of others and encourages people to make the changes which they choose to make for themselves.

Traditional addictionologists say that precontemplators are "in denial". The Stages of Change Model does not attack people and tell them that they are in denial--rather it recognizes that they are not yet thinking about change. A Harm Reductionist Model goes further and accepts the fact that each individual has the unalienable right to choose which changes he/she wants to make for him/herself.

Next let us look at how the various stages apply in a real person.

The Stages of Change Model applies separately for each individual change that a person is making. For example, if a person both smokes tobacco and gambles, this person might hypothetically be in the **Precontemplation Stage** of changing their tobacco habit, but in the **Action Stage** of changing their gambling habit. This is because people decide to change different habits at different times in their lives. The stage that a person is in with respect to one habit will not necessarily have any effect on the stage that one is in with regard to a different habit.

This has many important ramifications for a harm reduction approach to alcohol. A person may be in **Precontemplation Mode** with regard to the goal of **quitting drinking**, in **Contemplation** with regard to the goal of **reduced drinking**, and in **Action Mode** with regard to the goal of **safer drinking**, all at the same time. Since the drinking goals are essentially independent of each other[6], the Stages of Change for each goal are also independent of each other. Some people may never feel a need or a desire to quit drinking--these people are in Precontemplation Mode with regard to the goal of quitting drinking for their entire lives. Likewise, some people may decide that they never wish to start drinking and may be lifelong teetotalers who never have a drink of alcohol in their entire lives. We can also say that these people are in **Precontemplation Mode** with regard to the goal of **taking up drinking**. There are no inherent moral judgments attached to the Stages of Change Model.

Harm Reduction has a slightly different take on the idea of **Recycling (Setbacks)** than does the standard Prochaskan view. Harm Reduction recognizes that some people who have quit drinking alcohol entirely may at a later date decide to switch their goal from one of alcohol abstinence to one of problem-free drinking instead. In Harm Reduction we do not call this a "slip" or a "relapse" or an instance of "recycling". We recognize each individual's unalienable right to choose his/her own drinking goal and recognize such a conscious decision as an individual's personal choice. This is quite distinct from a slip or a ricochet which occurs in pursuit of the current alcohol goal. We refer you to Chapter 15 for more information on setbacks and how to deal with them.

****

People who decide that they want to start attending a HAMS support group can potentially be in any of the stages of change. However, it is probable that most newcomers to HAMS are either in the Contemplation Stage, the Preparation Stage, or the Action Stage. Different people take different amounts of time to transition from one stage to another. Some people may take a month to transition from Contemplation or Preparation to Action, and some may take six months or even longer. Do not worry; at HAMS no one will push you to run before you can walk. Harm Reduction meets everyone "where they are at" and respects that.

How long a particular Stage of Change lasts varies greatly from individual to individual. Even within the same individual, the stages can last for varying lengths of time depending on which behavior the individual is working on at the moment. So sometimes it may take many months to transition from one stage to the next, at other times it may seem to happen almost instantaneously.

Prochaska found that although some people succeed in making their behavioral change on the first try, it was more common that several attempts we needed before success was achieved, so as the old saying goes, "if at first you don't succeed, try, try again." Prochaska also found that not

---

[6] There is not complete independence, since successfully quitting drinking logically implies reducing alcohol intake to zero.

everyone entered the **Termination Stage** of change where they no longer even thought about the old behavior any more. Some people remained in **Maintenance Mode** for good instead.

REFERENCES:

Prochaska JO, Norcross JC, DiClemente CC. (1994). <u>Changing for good.</u> New York. Morrow.

CHAPTER THIRTY: *Alcohol, Individual, and Environment*

"Alcohol is a very necessary article... It enables Parliament to do things at eleven at night that no sane person would do at eleven in the morning." --George Bernard Shaw

In the 1970s and 80s when Harvard professor Norman Zinberg MD was doing research on the effects of recreational drugs on human beings he found a lot of effects which could not be explained simply by the chemical effects of the drug on the histology and the physiology and the neuro-anatomy of the human subject alone. Dr. Zinberg discovered that in order to understand the effects of a drug on an individual, one also had to look at the mindset and beliefs and many other internal factors of the individual as well as looking at the environment and culture in which the individual used the drug. Dr. Zinberg referred to the beliefs and other internal factors as the "set" (short for mind-set) and he referred to the external factors as the "setting". The book in which Dr, Zinberg published the results of his research is titled <u>Drug, Set, and Setting</u> and is a pioneering work in this field. Dr. Zinberg's research is not just for illegal drugs--it applies to the legal drug alcohol as well--and so does the research of many others who followed Dr. Zinberg. In HAMS we use the terms **Alcohol**, **Individual**, and **Environment**. We illustrate the concept graphically in **Figure 30.1**.

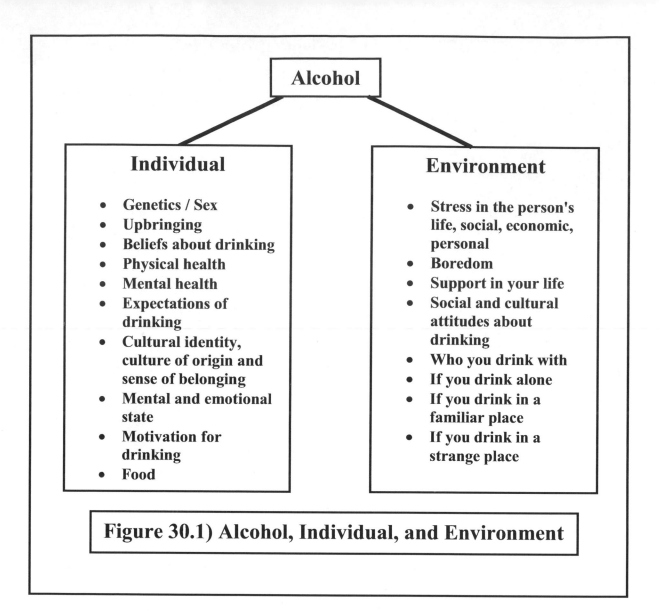

Figure 30.1) Alcohol, Individual, and Environment

INDIVIDUAL

GENETICS / SEX

The single-gene theory of "alcoholism" has been abandoned long ago by all serious researchers as has the term "alcoholism" itself which is now limited to appearing in works of pop psych like AA's "Big Book". Contemporary researchers know that many different genes can have an effect on the way an individual metabolizes alcohol as well as having an influence on an individual's tendency to become a habitual drinker. Contemporary researchers use a diathesis-stress model-- what those big words mean is that both genetics and environment have a contribution to make in a person's drinking habits. At HAMS we find that the concepts of choice and self-efficacy are very helpful, too.

Tolerance

Some people are born with a much higher tolerance to alcohol than others. Men also generally have a higher tolerance to alcohol than women because of genetic factors--women have less of the enzyme which breaks down alcohol in their stomachs.

Asian Flush

When alcohol is metabolized in the human body it is first converted into a poison called acetaldehyde. Acetaldehyde is very rapidly converted into a harmless acetyl radical by an enzyme called acetaldehyde dehydrogenase. In most people the enzyme which breaks down the acetaldehyde is very efficient. However, some Asians have less efficient forms of this enzyme, and this allows the buildup of the poisonous acetaldehyde in their systems. This toxin can cause them to flush bright red after a single drink and to become very ill from drinking alcohol. Antabuse does the same thing--it causes the buildup of acetaldehyde in your body by blocking the action of this enzyme. There are two types of Asian flush syndrome--fast-flushing and slow flushing. The fast flushers have the least efficient form of the enzyme needed to break down the toxin and get the sickest from drinking alcohol. Fast-flushers never become addicted to alcohol-- but this does not mean that they do not sometimes choose to get addicted to other drugs. Slow flushers are less likely to become addicted to alcohol than non-flushers.

Adoption Studies

Goodwin and colleagues studied both adopted sons and adopted daughters of alcoholics into non-alcoholic families in an attempt to find a genetic basis for alcoholism. What they found was that about one in five sons of alcoholics became alcoholics whether they were raised by alcoholic parents or non-alcoholic parents. The prevalence of alcoholism in the general population was assumed to be about one in twenty. On the other hand daughters of alcoholics were no more likely to become alcoholics than daughters of non-alcoholics. The Goodwin studies suggest that both genetic and environmental factors are at work in the development of a drinking habit. This is because we have to explain why four out of five sons of alcoholics do not become alcoholics and also why the daughters show no apparent genetic tendencies. It is most likely that environment is responsible for both of these outcomes.

Rat Park

We discuss Rat Park in detail below. Suffice it to say that the same rats will consume eight times as much morphine in a bad environment as they do in a pleasant environment. This clearly shows that both environment and genetics have a major effect on drug and alcohol use.

The Stress Vulnerability Protective Factors Model

Many researchers today prefer the stress vulnerability protective factors model (formerly called the diathesis-stress model). This model states that some people have a greater genetic vulnerability to developing an alcohol problem than other people. However, environmental factors (called stressors) are also required for an alcohol habit to develop--this is not something which occurs in a vacuum. The environment can also contain protective factors which can help to prevent an alcohol habit from developing.

How many genes are involved in problem drinking?

Very many! In 2008 Ducci and Goldman have published and excellent review of what is known about the genetics of alcohol abuse. Genes which affect alcohol abuse fall into the following categories:

- Genes which predispose people to addictions in general whether the addiction is alcohol or tobacco or some other drug or behavior
- Genes which predispose people specifically towards alcohol abuse - these are genes which cause one to have a low response to the effects of alcohol so that one has to drink a lot to become intoxicated
- Genes which specifically protect one from becoming alcohol addicted--specifically the genes responsible for Asian flush syndrome
- Genes which predispose people towards mental health problems such as Anxiety, Depression, ADHD, or Antisocial Personality Disorder - these disorders make it more likely that one will abuse alcohol

Ducci and Goldman estimate that the heritability of alcohol problems is around 0.5. In contrast the heritability of Anxiety Disorder is around 0.32 and that of Autism around 0.9. This means that alcohol problems are moderately heritable.

RELIGIOUS UPBRINGING

A 2004 article by Galen and Rogers states that there is less problem drinking among college students who are religious than those who are not. Some people cite this as evidence that giving children a religious upbringing will reduce the likelihood of them becoming adult problem drinkers--however, the one does not necessarily follow from the other. Many people with a religious upbringing wind up rebelling against it and doing the exact opposite of what they were told. This is particularly common of the upbringing is strict and repressive. If they are raised as religious teetotalers the rebellion can often come in the form of drug use or heavy drinking. I once conducted an informal survey on an email group for people with alcohol problems and nearly half of the people who responded stated that they had had an oppressive religious upbringing which they had rebelled against. Moreover, drug and alcohol counselors who work with a twelve step model report that it is virtually impossible to get people who have rebelled against their religious upbringing to accept AA's "higher power". It is unfortunate that these people are rarely referred to secular alternatives.

Although the Galen and Rogers study is an interesting first step--it leaves several questions unanswered. Does a religious upbringing lead to more or fewer problem drinkers? Is an upbringing in a liberal religion which allows drinking more likely to give rise to problem drinking than a conservative teetotaler religion or vice versa? Data from Cahalan and Room (1974) shed some interesting light into questions which were not addressed by Galen and Rogers, The data in **Table 30.1** come from Cahalan and Room's 1974 analysis of data collected by the National Institute of Mental Health in 1967 and 1969. This data was collected by interviewing a random sample of 1,561 Americans throughout the United States.

Table 30.1) Drinking Pattern by Religious Affiliation - from Cahalan & Room						
	N	Non-drinker	Problem-Free Drinker	Potential Problems Only	Heavy Drinker No Consequences	High Consequences
Catholic	487	6%	37%	23%	19%	16%
Jewish	40	8%	60%	25%	5%	3%
Liberal Prot.	220	10%	42%	24%	13%	11%
Conservative Prot.	663	24%	37%	19%	6%	14%
No Religion	84	6%	42%	20%	14%	18%
Other	67	15%	28%	25%	19%	12%

This data suggests that cultural factors such as religious affiliation can have a major impact on a person's drinking pattern. It is interesting to note that the Conservative Protestants in this data sample have both high rates of alcohol abstainers and high rates of drinkers who suffer severe consequences from their drinking. We hypothesize that this is a result of black-and-white thinking about alcohol. On the other hand Jews, who traditionally frown on drunkenness and use alcohol in their religious rituals, have high rates of moderate drinkers and few abstainers or problem drinkers.

Now what we can say as harm reductionists? From a harm reductionist point of view you do not need to let your upbringing determine your behavior for your entire life. You can choose to drink in the way that is right for you or to abstain from alcohol. The power is yours--not your upbringing's.

BELIEF

Belief is a factor of overwhelming importance in how one deals with alcohol. If one believes that one is in control and that practicing harm reduction, moderation, or alcohol abstinence is entirely in the power of the individual then one will have a fairly easy time controlling drinking or quitting. If one believes that quitting is easy then it will be easy--Alan Carr's book The Easy Way to Stop Drinking is devoted to convincing people that it is easy to quit. If one believes that it is hard then it is hard. And if one is convinced that it is absolutely impossible to quit without divine intervention then that person will have to wait around until God intervenes--unless of course they choose to change their beliefs. If people believe that alcohol will make them belligerent and cause them to fight then they will become belligerent and fight when they drink. If people believe that alcohol will make them docile and sleepy then they will become docile and sleepy when they drink. In this section we shall look at some famous studies of the effects of belief on drug and alcohol use.

Alan Marlatt Shows the Power of Belief

In 1973 Dr. G. Alan Marlatt and his colleagues published a study which showed that belief has a greater effect than alcohol itself on the behavior of alcoholics. Subjects in this experiment were divided into four groups:

- Group one) Subjects in this group were given tonic only and told truthfully that it was tonic only
- Group two) Subjects in this group were given a five to one mixture of tonic and vodka and told falsely that they were being given tonic only
- Group three) Subjects in this group were given tonic only and told falsely that it was a mixture of vodka and tonic
- Group four) Subjects in this group were given a five to one mixture of tonic and vodka and told truthfully that it was a mixture of vodka and tonic

A pretest of the beverages demonstrated that subjects were unable to distinguish the vodka tonic mixture from the tonic only drink.

The Marlatt experiment studied the effects of belief on both alcoholics and social drinkers. The subjects of this experiment were 32 alcoholics and 32 social drinkers. Care was taken to avoid borderline cases--the alcoholics in the study were people who reported major alcohol related problems and no intention to abstain. The results of the experiment are summarized in **Table 30.2** and illustrated graphically in **Figures 30.2** and **30.3**.

Table 30.2) Ounces of beverage consumed per condition				
Beverage condition	Alcoholics		Social drinkers	
	Told tonic	Told alcohol	Told tonic	Told alcohol
Given tonic	10.94	23.87	9.31	14.62
Given alcohol	10.25	22.13	5.94	14.44

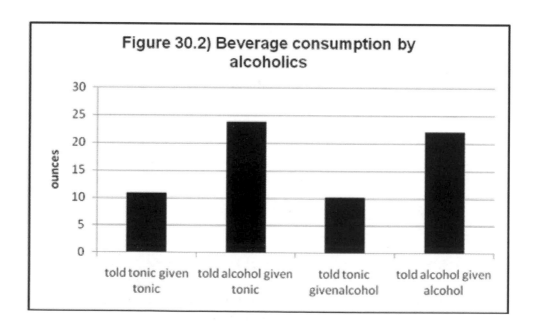

Figure 30.2) Beverage consumption by alcoholics

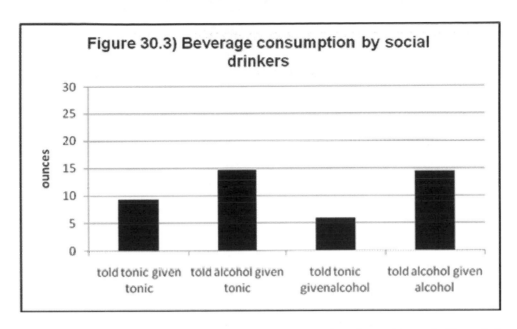

Figure 30.3) Beverage consumption by social drinkers

The only significant factor in the Marlatt experiment was what the subjects believed that they were drinking. The Marlatt experiment demonstrated beyond a shadow of a doubt that alcoholics do not suffer from a loss of control when they consume a single drink of alcohol--in other words the "one drink = one drunk" theory is false. What is essential is belief.

PHYSICAL AND MENTAL HEALTH

Both physical and mental health can have a major effect on the way in which alcohol impacts you. If you have liver damage this can lead to reverse tolerance (Chapter 23). Drinking when you are ill can prolong the physical illness.

Many people abuse alcohol because they are self-medicating a mental health issue. We strongly recommend that you find a good harm reduction therapist to help you deal with any mental health issues.

EXPECTATIONS OF DRINKING

This is strongly tied into both beliefs and cultural expectations. If you believe that drinking makes you fight you will fight when you drink. If you believe that it makes you docile you will become docile. If you believe that it makes you glamorous or rich it probably won't--but these beliefs might make it harder to control or quit.

Cultural Identity (Ethnicity) and Drinking

Harvard Medical School conducted a study of the development of adolescents into adults starting in 1940. This study selected 456 lower class boys from the inner city schools of Boston and followed their development into adulthood. In the mid 1970s Dr. George Vaillant took data on the drinking patterns of 401 of the subjects of this study who were now men in their late 40s. The data in **Table 30.3** is from Dr. Vaillant's 1980 book (revised edition 1995). Dr. Vaillant refers to these subjects as "the Core City Sample".

Table 30.3) Ethnic Identity and Drinking Patterns - from Vaillant 1980					
	N	Abstainers	Problem-Free Drinkers	Alcohol Abuse	Alcohol Dependence
Irish	76	21%	43%	8%	28%
Old American	35	20%	40%	13%	27%
Polish, Russian	17	18%	53%	11%	18%
English, Anglo-Canadian	98	21%	45%	11%	23%
Northern Europe other	20	5%	65%	5%	25%
French Canadian	26	15%	54%	8%	23%
Southern Europe other	23	30%	57%	9%	4%
Italian	99	18%	70%	8%	4%
Jewish	6	50%	33%	17%	0%
Chinese	1	0%	0%	100%	0%

The data from the Core City Sample show a very strong influence of ethnic and cultural identity on drinking patterns. This is particularly striking when we compare the drinking patterns of the Irish (n = 76) with the Italians (n = 99). 70% of the Italians fall into the category of problem-free drinkers and only 4% of them fall into the category of Alcohol Dependence. Whereas only 43% of the Irish in the sample are problem-free drinkers and 28% of them fall into the category of alcohol dependence.

The difference is attributed to the fact that traditionally the Italians teach their children responsible drinking in the home whereas the Irish often view alcohol as the devil's brew. This data clearly demonstrates that cultural factors in one's upbringing can have a major impact on one's pattern of alcohol use.

MENTAL AND EMOTIONAL STATE

Many people report bad effects if they drink when they are angry or depressed.

MOTIVATION FOR DRINKING

Drinking because you are happy and want to celebrate will have a very different effect than drinking because you are sad and trying to kill the pain.

FOOD AND WATER

We cannot emphasize too much how important it is to be well hydrated and to drink on a full stomach to avoid BAC (Blood Alcohol Content) spikes.

ENVIRONMENT

STRESS AND BOREDOM

Rat Park

The Rat Park experiment is an excellent example of the effects of stress and boredom on drug use in animals.

We have all heard the horror stories about monkeys or rats who are able to self-administer drugs like cocaine by pulling a lever and who give themselves fatal overdoses. Anti-drug crusaders use these as cautionary tales about the power of drugs and the powerlessness of the drug taker. However, they are leaving certain crucial factors out of the equation. To wit--the animals are locked in tiny little cages and isolated from their fellows and they are totally bored spitless with absolutely nothing to do except to administer drugs to themselves.

Dr. Bruce Alexander and his colleagues decided to investigate whether animals would become drug addicts in a naturalistic environment or if it was the fact that the animals were locked up in such awful conditions which led to their addiction. This study was published in 1978 and is often referred to as the "Rat Park" study.

Dr. Alexander and colleagues had one group of rats with access to an opiate solution in a naturalistic setting where the rats could run around and play with and have sex with other rats. The other group of rats was in the usual isolated cages. What they found was that the rats who lived in Rat Park consumed only one eighth as much of the opiate solution as did the rats in isolated cages. In other words--addiction is a function of environment.

What this tells us as harm reductionists is that if you live in a bad, sad and miserable environment then it may well drive you to drink. We encourage you to do what you can to better your environment. Even hanging out with the other HAMS members in the HAMS chat room can be a way to get some needed social contact and to help you get away from over-drinking.

SPOUSAL SUPPORT

Very often the worst possible mistake that a person can make in response to a spouse's drinking is to assume that abstinence is the only solution and that the drinking spouse must "hit bottom" to get better. The real truth is that if the drinking spouse is willing to work at harm reduction then this person should be offered support for every positive change. Experience shows that far more people get better through baby steps and small changes than do through dramatic conversions of the AA type. So support every positive change--the marriage you save may be your own.

SOCIAL AND CULTURAL ATTITUDES TOWARD DRINKING

Extreme attitudes can lead to rebellion. Although many children of alcoholics become alcoholic through imitation, many others become teetotalers through rebellion. Many children of teetotalers follow suit and become teetotalers themselves whereas others rebel and become heavy drinkers. But moderation tends to bring about moderation. One can conform to the environment one lives in or one can rebel against it--or one can choose to follow one's own path.

WHO DO YOU DRINK WITH, IF ANYONE?

If you hang out with heavy drinkers when you drink then you will be more likely to drink heavily. If you hang out with moderate drinkers you will be more likely to moderate. Some people choose to drink alone at home for safety reasons. This is not necessarily a problem. However if you drink when alone and when with company this might mean that you drink all the time and this can be a problem.

STRANGE VS. FAMILIAR ENVIRONMENT

Environment Changes Tolerance

If you drink alcohol or take drugs in an unaccustomed setting your tolerance is much lower than if you drink or use drugs in your usual setting. This phenomenon is called **Conditioned Tolerance**. In 1982 Dr. Siegel and colleagues published a study on the effects of morphine and environment on rats. They injected the rats with increasing doses of morphine in the same environment for many days in a row to get the rats to build up tolerance to the morphine. Then one day they gave the rats the same dose of morphine as usual in a totally novel environment. All the rats showed signs of overdose and several of them died. None of the rats had died of overdose in their usual environment. This study proved the existence of conditioned tolerance. Interviews with people who have had drug overdoses confirm the existence of conditioned tolerance

What are the implications of this for people who practice alcohol harm reduction? If you choose to drink alcohol in a strange and new environment rather than your accustomed environment then you should be prepared for the possibility that the alcohol might have a much greater effect than usual and that you may become far more intoxicated than usual. So be prepared and plan ahead!

MORE ON ENVIRONMENT

Cohen et al 1971 demonstrated that alcoholics can control their drinking if they are rewarded by being placed in a positive rather than an impoverished environment.

REFERENCES:

Alexander BK, Coambs RB, Hadaway PF. (1978). The effect of housing and gender on morphine self-administration in rats. Psychopharmacology (Berl). 58(2), 175-9.
PubMed Abstract:
http://www.ncbi.nlm.nih.gov/pubmed/98787

Bigelow, George; Liebson, Ira. (1972). Cost factors controlling alcoholic drinking. The Psychological Record Volume 22.
Abstract:
http://thepsychologicalrecord.siuc.edu/22%20Bigelow%20&%20Liebson%20Abstract.pdf

Cahalan D. Room, R. (1974). Problem drinking among American men. New Brunswick, NJ: Rutgers Center of Alcohol Studies.

Cohen M, Liebson IA, Faillace LA, Allen RP. (1971). Moderate drinking by chronic alcoholics. A schedule-dependent phenomenon. J Nerv Ment Dis. 153(6), 434-44.

PubMed Info:

http://www.ncbi.nlm.nih.gov/pubmed/5123713

Abstract:

http://journals.lww.com/jonmd/Abstract/1971/12000/Moderate_Drinking_By_Chronic_Alcoholics_A.6.aspx

Ducci F, Goldman D. (2008). Genetic approaches to addiction: genes and alcohol. Addiction. 103(9), 1414-28.

PubMed Abstract:

http://www.ncbi.nlm.nih.gov/pubmed/18422824

Free Full Text:

http://www.pubmedcentral.nih.gov/picrender.fcgi?artid=2665791&blobtype=pdf

Galen LW, Rogers WM. (2004). Religiosity, alcohol expectancies, drinking motives and their interaction in the prediction of drinking among college students. J Stud Alcohol. 65(4), 469-76.

PubMed Abstract:

http://www.ncbi.nlm.nih.gov/pubmed/15376822

Gercvich J, Bácskai E, Farkas L, Danics Z. (2005). A case report: Pavlovian conditioning as a risk factor of heroin 'overdose' death. Harm Reduct J. 2, 11.

PubMed Abstract:

http://www.ncbi.nlm.nih.gov/pubmed/16042795

Free Full Text:

http://www.pubmedcentral.nih.gov/picrender.fcgi?artid=1196296&blobtype=pdf

Goodwin DW, Schulsinger F, Moller N, Hermansen L, Winokur G, Guze SB. (1974). Drinking Problems in Adopted and Nonadopted Sons of Alcoholics. Arch Gen Psychiatry. 31(2), 164-169.

PubMed Abstract:

http://www.ncbi.nlm.nih.gov/pubmed/4851437

Abstract:

http://archpsyc.ama-assn.org/cgi/content/abstract/31/2/164

Goodwin DW, Schulsinger F, Knop J, Mednick S, Guze SB. (1977). Alcoholism and Depression in Adopted-Out Daughters of Alcoholics. Arch Gen Psychiatry. 34(7), 751-755.

PubMed Abstract:

http://www.ncbi.nlm.nih.gov/pubmed/879972

Marlatt GA, Demming B, Reid JB. (1973). Loss of control drinking in alcoholics: an experimental analogue. J Abnorm Psychol. 81(3), 233-41.

PubMed Info:

http://www.ncbi.nlm.nih.gov/pubmed/4710045

Abstract:

http://psycnet.apa.org/journals/abn/81/3/233/

Siegel S. (1984). Pavlovian conditioning and heroin overdose: Reports from overdose victims. Bulletin of the Psychonomic Society. 22, 428-430.

Siegel S, Hinson RE, Krank MD, McCully J. (1982). Heroin "overdose" death: contribution of drug-associated environmental cues. <u>Science</u>. 216(4544), 436-7.
PubMed Abstract:
http://www.ncbi.nlm.nih.gov/pubmed/7200260

Vaillant, G E. (1995). <u>The natural history of alcoholism revisited</u> Cambridge, Mass. Harvard University Press.

Wall TL, Peterson CM, Peterson KP, Johnson ML, Thomasson HR, Cole M, Ehlers CL. (1997). Alcohol metabolism in Asian-American men with genetic polymorphisms of aldehyde dehydrogenase. <u>Ann Intern Med</u>. 127(5), 376-9.
PubMed Abstract:
http://www.ncbi.nlm.nih.gov/pubmed/9273829
Free Full Text:
http://www.annals.org/cgi/reprint/127/5/376.pdf

Zinberg, N. (1984). <u>Drug, Set, and Setting: The Basis for Controlled Intoxicant Use</u>. Yale University Press. New Haven, CT.
Excerpts: http://www.druglibrary.org/schaffer/lsd/zinberg.htm

CHAPTER THIRTY ONE: How the Meaning of the Word "Alcoholism" Has Changed

"The intermediate stage between socialism and capitalism is alcoholism." --Norman Brenner

Introduction

In 1972 the National Council on Alcoholism published an article titled "Criteria for the diagnosis of alcoholism". This article was published simultaneously in the <u>Annals of Internal Medicine</u> and the <u>American Journal of Psychiatry</u> and became the official touchstone for the diagnosis of alcoholism by physicians and psychiatrists. In terms of quantity this article stated that a person weighing 220 lbs or more had to drink at least a quart of whiskey (24 standard drinks) per day for at least two days in a row to be classified as "alcoholic". The full criteria for different body weights are given in **Table 31.1** below.

Table 31.1 Drinking Criteria for "Alcoholism"			
Weight lbs	Whiskey qt (43% etoh)	Pure ethanol oz	Standard drinks
220	1.0	13.76	24
200	0.9	12.38	21.5
180	0.8	11.01	19
160	0.7	9.63	17
140	0.6	8.26	14.5
120	0.5	6.88	12

In other words, in 1972 a person could drink a quart of whiskey or even more in a day and as long as they did not drink the following day and did not have other alcohol related problems such as DUI they could not be diagnosed as "alcoholic" or even as having an alcohol problem.

In 1980 with the publication of the DSM-III the American Psychiatric Association officially removed "Alcoholism" as a diagnostic category and replaced it with two new categories: **Alcohol Dependence** and **Alcohol Abuse**. Very simply put, Alcohol Dependence refers to a physical or psychological dependence an alcohol which makes it difficult to quit drinking, whereas Alcohol Abuse refers to a pattern of alcohol use which leads to life problems such as DUIs or problems at work or at school but which is not accompanied by physical or psychological dependence. Alcohol Abuse is NOT considered a precursor or a milder form of Alcohol Dependence--experts today consider them to be two completely separate categories.

The creation of the two categories Alcohol Abuse and Alcohol Dependence was a definite step in the right direction. However, even though it was recognized that there is more than one type of pattern of problematic drinking, there was as yet only one accepted treatment methodology. The 12 steps of AA were prescribed for all alcohol problems in spite of the fact that there were no serious studies of their clinical efficacy.

Another step in the right direction came when recent editions of the DSM decided to introduce the following Course Specifiers--Early and Sustained Full remission and Early and Sustained Partial Remission--to the category of Substance Related Disorders aka Substance Use Disorders. This was the first acknowledgement by the medical and psychiatric community of the very commonly observed fact that many people reduce or otherwise moderate their substance use. This was a vast improvement over the previously held idea that a full year of abstinence was required for an "alcoholic" to be considered "in remission". Even one drink of alcohol per year meant that an alcoholic was classified as "actively alcoholic".

In recent years the NIAAA and SAMHSA have introduced the concept of Binge Drinking as a third form of problematic alcohol use in addition to the already accepted diagnostic categories of Alcohol Dependence and Alcohol Abuse.

SAMHSA defines binge drinking as follows:

- Five or more drinks on the same occasion at least once in the past 30 days

NIAAA defines binge drinking as follows (NIAAA 2004):

- A "binge" is a pattern of drinking alcohol that brings blood alcohol concentration (BAC) to 0.08 gram percent or above. For the typical adult, this pattern corresponds to consuming 5 or more drinks (male), or 4 or more drinks (female), in about 2 hours.

As we can see there has been a tremendous change in the definition of "bad" drinking from 1972 to the current year of 2009. For a 180 lb man in 1972, "bad" drinking meant 19 drinks on a single occasion (and it didn't count if you didn't drink the following day). For a 180 lb man in 2009, "bad" drinking is 5 drinks on one occasion (within 2 hours). This is nearly a 4-fold difference. The 1972 definitions do not speak of BAC--however, if we assume that the drinker consumed his alcohol over an 8 hour period we arrive at a BAC of 0.3--which could be dangerous to a neophyte but which is harmless to a seasoned heavy drinker. We illustrate these differences graphically in **Figure 31.1** and **Figure 31.2**:

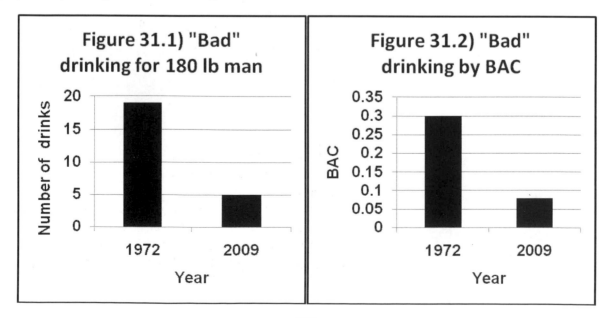

We applaud the current system of discussing problematic drinking in terms of Alcohol Dependence, Alcohol Abuse, and Binge Drinking as being a major improvement over the 1972 system of dichotomously dividing alcohol use into the categories of "Alcoholism" vs. "Non-alcoholism". However, as Harm Reductionists we have certain objections to parts of the classificatory schema as well as the treatments and strategies derived from them.

One of the biggest problems is that absolutely no distinction is made between a binge of 5 drinks in one sitting and a binge of 25 drinks in one sitting. For example, in a 2003 article in the Journal of the American Medical Association, Naimi warns us that "Adverse health effects specifically associated with binge drinking include unintentional injuries (e.g., motor vehicle crashes, falls, drowning, hypothermia, and burns), suicide, sudden infant death syndrome, alcohol poisoning, hypertension, acute myocardial infarction, gastritis, pancreatitis, sexually transmitted diseases, meningitis, and poor control of diabetes." Naimi uses the five drink definition of binge drinking. But five drinks at one sitting does not lead to alcohol poisoning, although 25 can. As harm reductionists we believe that it is essential to make the distinction between recreational intoxication and dangerous binging. This has consequences for all drinkers, but most particularly for young people.

Moreover, as harm reductionists we do not condemn recreational alcohol intoxication as "bad", "immoral", "diseased", or a "mental illness". We accept it as an individual's free right of choice just as we accept that people have a right of free choice to engage in other high risk behaviors such as driving automobiles or male homosexuality. Prohibition does not work. Risk management does.

Binge Drinking and Young People

Our belief is that the single best strategy to prevent harm to youth as a result of alcohol use is to educate youth about safe drinking practices, ways to avoid BAC spikes, and also that there is a tremendous difference between 5 drinks and 25 drinks.

A neo-prohibitionist stance which attempts to scare kids away from engaging in recreational intoxication by lying to them about the dangers of 5 drinks is doomed to fail--just as we have witnessed that attempts to scare youth away from marijuana by using "Reefer Madness" campaigns have failed. Once youth discover that you have lied to them about the effects of marijuana they will no longer believe what you say about the effects of heroin and will soon rush into addiction. Likewise if you lie to youth about the effects of five drinks they will soon rush to drink 25 drinks as a result. The one cardinal sin which we can commit against youth which will guarantee that they will abuse drugs and alcohol is to lie to them about drugs and alcohol.

Moreover we wholeheartedly reject SAMHSA and NIAAA's "gateway" theory of binge drinking which assumes that college age binge drinking must be suppressed because binge drinking in college leads to Alcohol Abuse or Alcohol Dependence later in life. This "gateway" theory of binge drinking is flatly contradicted by the evidence from the CDC report which clearly demonstrates that the vast majority of college age people who drink heavily later "mature out" of this phase when they grow older. This is no more realistic than the theory that marijuana use leads to heroin use or that mothers' milk leads to crack. **Figure 31.6** illustrates the "maturing out" phenomenon graphically.

Moreover, as harm reductionists we see no need to condemn the recreational alteration of consciousness as evil. This need to condemn pleasure as evil seems to hark back to the anhedonic views of our Calvinist forefathers. We do not condemn recreational alcohol intoxication--we are interested in eliminating harms which result from careless or uninformed drug or alcohol use.

We see absolutely nothing inherently evil about attaining a BAC of 0.08 just as we see nothing inherently evil about eating a pork chop. Alcohol and red meat may not serve to prolong the lifespan, but for many people good drink and good meat are worth that price.

Finally, we are concerned that we have seen many binge drinkers treated with the "one size fits all" notion that Alcoholics Anonymous is good for every alcohol problem. In point of fact, we do not know what the effects of AA may be on binge drinkers or Alcohol Abusers. For all we know it might make them drink more.

How Many "Bad" Drinkers Are There?

On page 20-21 of the AA "Big Book" Bill Wilson tells us that even people who have withdrawal symptoms bad enough to require medical attention may not be "true alcoholics". It seems that the kind of drinker that Bill Wilson calls an "alcoholic" in the "Big Book" is the kind of a person who has full blown withdrawal when s/he stops drinking. This is not just minor or moderate alcohol withdrawal where a person may shake or sweat or have rapid pulse or may even hallucinate but yet be aware that the hallucinations are unreal. This is major alcohol withdrawal where the drinker suffers delusions and believes the hallucinations to be real and has seizures and has major blood pressure spikes which can result in heart attack or death. Doctors tell us that this kind of major alcohol withdrawal only shows up in about one out of three hundred Americans. If we are generous we might estimate that one in a hundred Americans fit Bill Wilson's description of an alcoholic in 1939--surely no more than this.

However, the NIAAA tells us that currently 8.5% of the US population suffers from an Alcohol related Disorder, 3.8% suffer from AD and 4.7% suffer from AA. An additional 11.3% of Americans are current binge drinkers according to data from the CDC (2004)--which means that almost 20% of Americans have some sort of a problem with alcohol whether it is Alcohol Abuse, Alcohol Dependence or binge drinking.. This breakdown of types of problematic drinking is illustrated graphically in **Figure 31.3**.

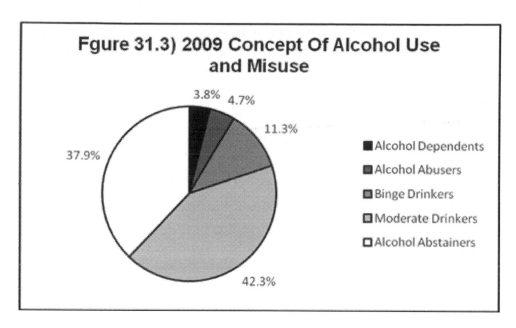

Fgure 31.3) 2009 Concept Of Alcohol Use and Misuse

- Alcohol Dependents
- Alcohol Abusers
- Binge Drinkers
- Moderate Drinkers
- Alcohol Abstainers

Moreover, other data from this same CDC report suggests that 32% of Americans have engaged in binge drinking (five or more drinks) at least once in their life--which we illustrate in **Figure 31.4**.

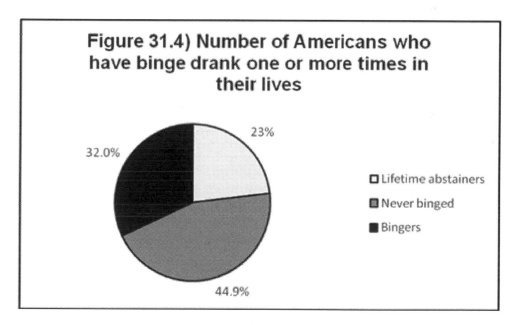

Figure 31.4) Number of Americans who have binge drank one or more times in their lives

- Lifetime abstainers
- Never binged
- Bingers

Note that **Figure 31.3** represents current patterns of use whereas **Figure 31.4** illustrates lifetime patterns of use. We have extrapolated longitudinal data from cross-sectional data to construct **Figure 31.4**, but we should be within the ballpark as there have been no real radical changes in drinking behavior within our lifetimes.

By way of contrast **Figure 31.5** illustrates how problem drinking ("alcoholism") was viewed in 1939 when Bill Wilson published AA's "Big Book".

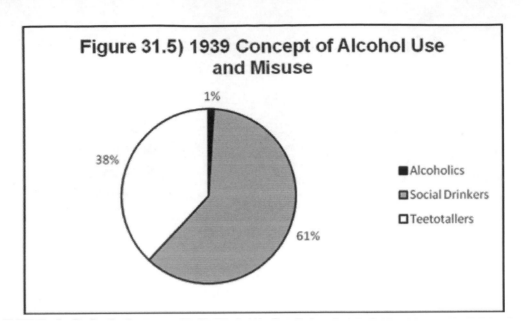

Figure 31.5) 1939 Concept of Alcohol Use and Misuse

1%

38%

61%

■ Alcoholics
▨ Social Drinkers
☐ Teetotallers

Rejecting the Disease Theory

In the final analysis we feel compelled from a Harm Reductionist point of view to reject the disease theory entirely. We feel that the risks and harms associated with alcohol use can only be dealt with rationally and practically if they are considered to be continuous variables rather than the categorical variables which the US government currently uses. The categories of binge drinking, Alcohol Dependence and Alcohol Abuse may at times be useful, but ultimately we believe that they are but useful fictions which can become harmful when misapplied. We see the risks associated with alcohol use as lying on a continuum which we plot on the **Alcohol Risk Chart** and **The Harm Reduction Pyramid** which we presented in Chapter 5.

Are People Drinking More?

No. the evidence shows that there has been a steady decline in alcohol consumption in the United States from the 1980s to the present. According to the NIAAA, Americans consumed 2.76 gallons of ETOH per capita in 1980, whereas in 2005 they consumed only 2.23.

Maturing Out

The data show that the majority of people mature out of drug or alcohol problems on their own without treatment. **Figure 31.6** is from NIAAA 2008.

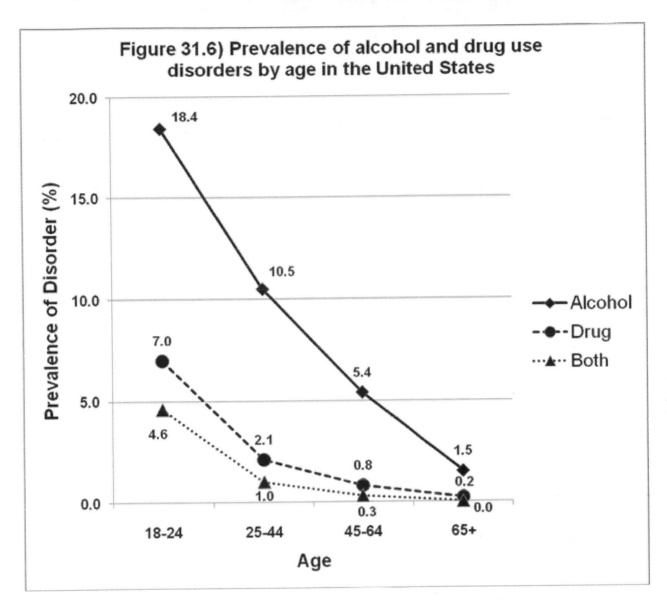

Figure 31.6) Prevalence of alcohol and drug use disorders by age in the United States

According to the NIAAA (NIAAA Five Year Strategic Plan) only 7.1% of people with Alcohol Use Disorders receive treatment, yet nearly all untreated AUDs get better with time.

REFERENCES:

Centers for Disease Control and Prevention. (CDC). (2004). Health Behaviors of Adults: United States, 1999–2001. National Center for Health Statistics. Vital Health Stat 10(219). (Schoenborn CA, Adams PF, Barnes PM, Vickerie JL, Schiller JS.)
PubMed Abstract:
http://www.ncbi.nlm.nih.gov/pubmed/15791896
Free Full Text:
http://www.cdc.gov/nchs/data/series/sr_10/sr10_219.pdf

Delirium Tremens: Overview - eMedicine
http://emedicine.medscape.com/article/166032-overview

Accessed February 1, 2010.

Grant BF, Dawson DA, Stinson FS, Chou SP, Dufour MC, Pickering RP. (2004). The 12-month prevalence and trends in DSM-IV alcohol abuse and dependence: United States, 1991–1992 and 2001–2002. <u>Drug Alcohol Depend</u>. 74(3), 223-34.
PubMed Abstract:
http://www.ncbi.nlm.nih.gov/pubmed/15194200

Naimi TS, Brewer RD, Mokdad A, Clark D, Serdula MK, Marks JS. (2003). Binge drinking among US adults. <u>JAMA</u>. 289(1), 70–75.
PubMed Abstract:
http://www.ncbi.nlm.nih.gov/pubmed/12503979
Free Full Text:
http://jama.ama-assn.org/cgi/reprint/289/1/70.pdf

National Council on Alcoholism. (1972). Criteria for the diagnosis of alcoholism by the Criteria Committee, National Council on Alcoholism. The American Journal of Psychiatry. 129(2), 127-35.
PubMed Info:
http://www.ncbi.nlm.nih.gov/pubmed/5041051
Abstract:
http://ajp.psychiatryonline.org/cgi/content/abstract/129/2/127

National Council on Alcoholism. (1972). Criteria for the diagnosis of alcoholism. Annals of Internal Medicine. 77(2), 249-58.
PubMed Info:
http://www.ncbi.nlm.nih.gov/pubmed/4641659
Abstract:
http://annals.org/content/77/2/249.abstract

National Institute on Alcohol Abuse and Alcoholism. (not dated). Apparent per capita ethanol consumption for the United States, 1850 - 2007.
Free Full Text:
http://www.niaaa.nih.gov/Resources/DatabaseResources/QuickFacts/AlcoholSales/consum01.htm
Accessed February 1, 2010.

National Institute on Alcohol Abuse and Alcoholism. (1995). <u>Alcohol Alert No. 30: Diagnostic Criteria for Alcohol Abuse and Dependence</u>.
Free Full Text:
http://pubs.niaaa.nih.gov/publications/aa30.htm

National Institute of Alcohol Abuse and Alcoholism. (2004). NIAAA council approves definition of binge drinking. NIAAA Newsletter; No. 3, p. 3.
Free Full Text:
http://pubs.niaaa.nih.gov/publications/Newsletter/winter2004/Newsletter_Number3.pdf

National Institute of Alcohol Abuse and Alcoholism. (2004a). Alcohol Abuse Increases, Dependence Declines Across Decade: Young Adult Minorities Emerge As High-Risk Subgroups.
Free Full Text:
 http://www.niaaa.nih.gov/NewsEvents/NewsReleases/NESARCNews.htm

National Institute on Alcohol Abuse and Alcoholism. (2008). Alcohol Alert No. 76: Alcohol And Other Drugs
Free Full Text:
 http://pubs.niaaa.nih.gov/publications/AA76/AA76.htm

Substance Abuse and Mental Health Services Administration (SAMHSA). Results from the 2002 National Survey on Drug Use and Health: National Findings. NHSDA Scrics H–22, DHHS Pub. No. SMA 03–3836. Rockville, MD: SAMHSA, Office of Applied Studies, 2003.
Free Full Text:
http://www.oas.samhsa.gov/nhsda/2k2nsduh/Results/2k2Results.htm.

CHAPTER THIRTY TWO: To the Health Care Professional

"First do no harm" --Hippocrates

Dear Health Care Professional,

If you have a patient who has an allergic reaction to penicillin, you know that the answer is not to give your patient more penicillin; the answer is to find an alternative medication which helps rather than harms your patient.

Many people have found AA and 12 step programs to be a great help in dealing with their alcohol problems; however, research shows us that for the majority of people with alcohol problems the 12 step approach is less helpful than other approaches (Brandsma et al. 1980) in spite of the fact that it is the most frequently prescribed. In point of fact, 12 step programs can actually be harmful for some people and make both their drinking and their mental health issues worse than before. This was my personal experience with the 12 step approach and this same experience has been shared by many friends of mine who have found that the only way to resolve their alcohol and/or mental health issues was to leave AA and seek out a different approach.

If your patient tells you that he/she feels that AA is a bad fit, it is probably the truth. It should not be taken as a sign of denial. Very often this is a case of your patient's innate drive for health objecting to what they perceive to be unhealthy in the 12 step approach and seeking out a healthier approach instead. As a health care provider, the single most important thing that you can do for a patient with an alcohol problem is to ask your patient what sort of steps he/she wishes to take to deal with that problem and to actually listen to your patient's answers.

If your patient expresses a wish to enter a traditional 12 step treatment program then the odds are that this is the best place for this person. If your patient expresses a desire for a secular abstinence-based support group then your patient will most likely benefit from a referral to a group such as SMART Recovery, Seculars On Sobriety (SOS), or Women For Sobriety (WFS). If your patient requests psychotherapy then by all means refer your patient to a psychotherapist. As the Brandsma et al (1980) study shows, psychotherapy can often be more effective than the 12 steps in treating an alcohol problem.

Finally, if your patient is more interested in pursuing a safer drinking plan or a reduced drinking plan rather than in making alcohol abstinence the goal, by all means encourage your patient to follow this path. People who are coerced into 12 step abstinence-based programs against their will often show a Ricochet Effect and they may wind up killing themselves or someone else on the rebound from this program when they drink again (Marlatt and Gordon, 1985).

We wish to encourage you as a health care provider to remember that you have all of the following options when dealing with a patient who has an alcohol problem:

- **A 12 step, abstinence-based, spiritual program**

- **A secular, abstinence-based, program such as SMART, SOS, or WFS**

- **Psychotherapy--preferably with a therapist understanding the principles of harm reduction**

- **A harm reduction-based program for safer or reduced drinking**

One size does not fit all.

Not everyone with a stomach ache needs an appendectomy, some need their stomach pumped instead. Likewise, not everyone who drinks too much needs AA. Some people will do best with a secular approach or with psychotherapy. And some will benefit the most from harm reduction.

Sincerely

Kenneth Anderson, Executive Director, The HAMS Harm Reduction Network, Inc.

REFERENCES:

Brandsma JM, Maultsby MC, Welsh RJ. (1980). Outpatient treatment of alcoholism: A review and comparative study. Baltimore: University Park Press.

Marlatt A, Gordon J. (1985). Relapse Prevention: Maintenance strategies in the treatment of addictive behaviors. New York, Guilford.

APPENDICES

APPENDIX I: Drug and Alcohol Interactions

Drugs.com lists 774 US prescription or OTC (over the counter) drugs which interact with alcohol. This includes 122 drugs which have major interactions with alcohol, 621 with moderate interactions, and 31 with minor interactions. This does not include all interactions with illegal drugs or with drugs which are available by prescription only outside of the US.

Some drug and alcohol interactions are severe and can lead to sudden death or permanent organ damage. Other drug and alcohol interactions are mild and have effects that may actually be sought after in some instances. For example, a person coming off of a drinking bender and trying to get some sleep may choose to mix Benadryl with a few drinks because this person wants the interaction effect of increased drowsiness.

Some people also choose to mix alcohol with recreational drugs to modify their effects. Mixing alcohol and marijuana is quite safe so long as one compensates for the increased impairment. But mixing alcohol with barbiturates like seconal or benzodiazepines like Valium can easily lead to death through respiratory suppression. Bad idea.

Most people have heard of Antabuse (disulfiram)--the drug that makes you sick when you drink alcohol. Sometimes this is portrayed in a comic manner as a drug that makes people vomit when they drink. However, the reality is that the mixture of alcohol and Antabuse causes the buildup of a poison called acetaldehyde in the body, and this poison can lead to permanent organ damage or even death. Some antibiotics as well as certain other drugs which contain sulfur can react with alcohol the same way as Antabuse does. These drugs can cause death when mixed with alcohol.

In this appendix we list some of the most common drug and alcohol interaction you should be aware of. The first listing is by major class, and the second is alphabetical by both generic and brand name.

However, don't assume that it is safe to use a new medication with alcohol simply because it is not listed here. Many medications are sold under a confusing number of different brand names and new drugs are invented every day. If you start a new medication, whether prescription, OTC (over the counter), or herbal, we strongly urge you to check it out for possible interactions with alcohol using a reliable source such as the PDR (Physician's Desk Reference) or drugs.com.

Part I: Drug and Alcohol Interactions by Drug Class: A-Z

Information in this article is restricted to drugs available by in the US and US brand names unless otherwise noted. We refer to drugs by their generic names and include their most common US brand names in parenthesis. Although generic names are the same worldwide, brand names outside the US often differ. Moreover, the same drug may be sold under many different brand names within the US. This listing is not complete, so always check a trusted source such as the PDR or drugs.com before mixing any unknown drug with alcohol.

Useful Definitions:

CNS Depression: CNS depression refers to a slowing down of the Central Nervous System (CNS), which is characterized by slower breathing, lower heart rate, slowed reaction time, and lowered alertness. In extreme cases, CNS depression results in unconsciousness, coma, or death. The term CNS depression should not be confused with depressed mood--which is unrelated.

Psychomotor Impairment: slurred speech, staggering gait, slowed reaction time, impaired coordination, etc.

Acetaminophen

ACETAMINOPHEN (Tylenol, Paracetamol) **MAJOR INTERACTION - POTENTIAL ORGAN DAMAGE**: Mixing acetaminophen with alcohol can cause a shortened lifespan due to liver damage. If you drink alcohol on a regular basis we recommend that you avoid acetaminophen entirely. Always check any prescribed or OTC (over the counter) painkiller or sleep aid to see if it contains acetaminophen. Acetaminophen is sold under a host of brand names too numerous to list in their entirety here. A few common ones include, Tylenol, Excedrin, Anacin-3, Tylenol PM, Excedrin PM. Acetaminophen is the most dangerous OTC painkiller for drinkers.

Anesthetics

Daily drinking can increase the amount of propofol (Diprivan) required to induce loss of consciousness. Daily drinking increases the risk of liver damage that may be caused by the anesthetic gases enflurane (Ethrane) and halothane (Fluothane).

Antabuse

Antabuse (disulfiram) is the drug which makes you sick when you drink alcohol. Antabuse works by blocking the metabolism of acetaldehyde. Acetaldehyde is a poisonous byproduct of alcohol metabolism which is normally eliminated from the body almost as quickly as it is produced. Antabuse blocks the action of the enzyme which breaks down acetaldehyde and allows it to build up in the body.

If a person drinks alcohol after taking Antabuse it causes flushing, throbbing in head and neck, throbbing headache, respiratory difficulty, nausea, copious vomiting, sweating, thirst, chest pain, palpitation, dyspnea, hyperventilation, tachycardia, hypotension, syncope, marked uneasiness, weakness, vertigo, blurred vision, and confusion. In severe reactions, there may be respiratory depression, cardiovascular collapse, arrhythmias, myocardial infarction, acute congestive heart failure, unconsciousness, convulsions, and death. The intensity of the reaction may vary with each individual but is generally proportional to the amount of disulfiram and alcohol ingested. In the sensitive individual, mild reactions may occur when the blood alcohol concentration is increased to as little as 5 to 10 mg/100 ml. At a concentration of 50 mg/100 ml symptoms are usually fully developed, and when the concentration reaches 125 to 150 mg/100 ml unconsciousness may occur.

Because medication compliance is extremely low, Antabuse has not generally been found more effective than a placebo in treating drinking problems. However, there is some evidence that

Antabuse is useful for individuals who are highly motivated to abstain. Antabuse has also proven effective when used with a community reinforcement approach, for example when the Antabuse is administered by a spouse.

Some people have used Antabuse to help them practice harm reduction. In this case the individual takes Antabuse while they are choosing to maintain an abstinence period. When the individual chooses to have a drinking day the individual discontinues the Antabuse and allows about four days for the Antabuse to clear the system. The individual has their drinking day and then returns to Antabuse and abstinence.

CAUTION: Antabuse should not be taken by people with liver damage or heart disease. Antabuse can cause liver damage or failure even in healthy individuals. Antabuse can react with many medications other than alcohol. People who are allergic to Antabuse should not take Antabuse.

Some antibiotic and antidiabetic medications react with alcohol in a manner similar to that of Antabuse.

Antianxiety (anxiolytics)

Benzodiazepines are commonly prescribed for anxiety--however these are not very safe to take with alcohol--see the main article on benzodiazepines below. BuSpar (buspirone) is an alternative antianxiety drug which does not have negative interactions with alcohol and is preferred for people who have difficulty controlling their drinking.

Anticoagulants

Possible **MAJOR INTERACTION**. Anticoagulants such as warfarin (Coumadin) are blood thinners which are used to prevent heart attacks, strokes, and blood clots in veins and arteries. Mixing a large amount of alcohol with warfarin (Coumadin) can greatly increase its activity leading to danger of **DEATH** by hemorrhage. On the other hand, daily drinking can reduce the effectiveness of warfarin (Coumadin). People taking warfarin (Coumadin) are advised to drink moderately or abstain from alcohol.

Antidepressants

Tricyclic antidepressants and MAOIs are older antidepressants which are less used these days because of their toxicity (tricyclics) or their potentially lethal food and drug interactions (MAOIs), although these antidepressants may be used as a last resort with depression which is resistant to the new antidepressants. The best known of the new antidepressants are the Selective serotonin reuptake inhibitors (SSRIs) like Prozac. Other new antidepressants include: Serotonin-norepinephrine reuptake inhibitors (SNRIs), Noradrenergic and specific serotonergic antidepressants (NaSSAs), Norepinephrine (noradrenaline) reuptake inhibitors (NRIs), Norepinephrine-dopamine reuptake inhibitors (NDRIs), Selective serotonin reuptake enhancers (SSREs), and Norepinephrine-dopamine disinhibitors (NDDIs). Other antidepressants include remeron.

The research suggests that at least some antidepressants are effective at reducing depression even if people continue to drink alcohol heavily while taking them. However, these antidepressants may be more effective if people abstain completely from alcohol while taking them. Research also suggests that while antidepressants may reduce alcohol consumption in some heavy drinkers, they may lead to an increase in alcohol consumption in others. See Chapter 10 Section 2.3 for more on this topic. Alcohol may possibly increase the side effects of the new antidepressants such as Prozac and Paxil. Mixing alcohol with any antidepressant may also lead to additive impairment of coordination or other CNS effects. Always use caution with alcohol and antidepressants. If the combination of alcohol and antidepressants appears to be causing you major problems, be prepared to quit one or the other.

MAOIs (Monoamine Oxidase Inhibitors)

Although MAOIs do not react with alcohol itself, MAOIs can have a **SEVERE AND FATAL** interaction with alcoholic beverages which contain tyramine--such as beer or red wine. Alcoholic beverages such as vodka which contain no tyramine are the safest for people taking MAOIs. MAOIs include: phenelzine (Nardil), tranylcypromine (Parnate), isocarboxazid (Marplan), selegiline (Emsam).

Tricyclic Antidepressants

Tricyclic antidepressants can cause CNS depression and impaired psychomotor performance; alcohol can intensify this CNS depression and impaired psychomotor performance. The lethal dose of tricyclics is close to the therapeutic dose which means that there is a high risk of lethal overdose with tricyclics. Alcohol can potentiate **LETHAL TRICYCLIC ANTIDEPRESSANT OVERDOSE**. Tricyclic antidepressants include: amitriptyline (Elavil), amoxapine (Asendin), desipramine (Norpramin), doxepin (Sinequan), imipramine (Tofranil, Tofranil-PM), nortriptyline (Pamelor), protriptyline (Vivactil), trimipramine (Surmontil).

The New Antidepressants

The new antidepressants such as Prozac and Paxil are generally much safer than the old ones; they are much less likely to cause overdose than the tricyclics and have far fewer food and drug interactions than the MAOIs. However, bupropion (Wellbutrin, Zyban) has a **MAJOR INTERACTION** with alcohol. Bupropion (Wellbutrin, Zyban) increases the risk of **seizures** in people who suddenly stop drinking. Heavy drinkers are advised to avoid bupropion (Wellbutrin, Zyban). If you already take bupropion (Wellbutrin, Zyban), be careful to taper off alcohol slowly--**DO NOT** quit cold turkey. There are also anecdotal reports of bupropion (Wellbutrin, Zyban) increasing the risk of blackouts in drinkers.

Although antidepressants may help some people to stop drinking, there is also evidence that they made lead to increased drinking for some people. Alcohol may increase the side effects of antidepressants. If you find that you are having bad effects from mixing antidepressants and alcohol be prepared to quit one or the other. It may be necessary to taper off antidepressants to avoid withdrawal syndrome.

The new antidepressants include the following:

Selective serotonin reuptake inhibitors (SSRIs):

citalopram (Celexa), escitalopram (Lexapro, Cipralex), paroxetine (Paxil, Seroxat), fluoxetine (Prozac), fluvoxamine (Luvox), and sertraline (Zoloft, Lustral)

Serotonin-norepinephrine reuptake inhibitors (SNRIs)

desvenlafaxine (Pristiq), duloxetine (Cymbalta), milnacipran (Ixel, Savella), venlafaxine (Effexor)

Norepinephrine reuptake inhibitors (NRIs)

reboxetine (Edronax) and viloxazine (Vivalan)

Norepinephrine-dopamine reuptake inhibitors (NDRIs)

bupropion (Wellbutrin, Zyban)

Other Antidepressants

Mirtazapine (Remeron, Remeron SolTab) is a tetracyclic antidepressant which is also used as a sleep aid. Mirtazapine (Remeron, Remeron SolTab) causes drowsiness and motor impairment and alcohol can increase these effects.

Antidiabetics

People with diabetes should use caution when drinking alcohol. Large amounts of beer or sweetened wines contain large amounts of carbohydrates and can lead to a dangerous rise in blood sugar and dehydration. Conversely, large amounts of spirits like vodka or whisky can lead to a dangerous drop in blood sugar and dehydration. Drinking on an empty stomach can increase this drop in blood sugar. Extreme high blood sugar or extreme low blood sugar combined with dehydration can lead to **DIABETIC COMA** and **DEATH**.

Some patients taking the antidiabetic chlorpropamide have reported an Antabuse-type reaction (see Antabuse) involving flushing and nausea. People who experience an Antabuse-type reaction when taking chlorpropamide should not drink alcohol with this medication. Antabuse-type reactions can lead to **ORGAN DAMAGE** or **DEATH**. Chlorpropamide is a member of a class of drugs called sulfonylureas. Other antidiabetic sulfonylureas may also result in an Antabuse-type reaction. These drugs include: tolazamide (Tolinase), glimepiride (Amaryl), chlorpropamide (Diabinese), acetohexamide (Dymelor), glipizide (GlipiZIDE XL, Glucotrol, Glucotrol XL), glyburide (DiaBeta, Glycron, Glynase, Glynase PresTab, Micronase), and tolbutamide (Orinase, Tol-Tab).

Patients taking insulin should limit alcohol consumption and avoid drinking on an empty stomach to avoid drops in blood sugar. Patients mixing alcohol with metformin (Fortamet, Glucophage, Glucophage XR, Glumetza, Riomet) may suffer from lactic acidosis.

Antihistamines

First generation antihistamines such as diphenhydramine (Benadryl) and doxylamine (Unisom) cause drowsiness as a side effect and for this reason are often used as OTC sleeping pills. According to drugs.com, diphenhydramine is sold under 86 different brand names for OTC use as a sleep aid or an allergy medicine--some of the more common of these names are Benadryl, Simply Sleep, Sominex, etc. Alcohol can increase the sedating effects of these antihistamines, particularly in the elderly. Alcohol appears to have no interaction with the second generation, non-sedating antihistamines such as cetirizine (Zyrtec), fexofenadine (Allegra), desloratadine (Clarinex), or loratadine (Claritin, Alavert).

Anti-Infectives

Anti-Infective drugs include antibiotic, antiviral, antitubercular, and antifungal drugs. Alcohol doesn't diminish the effectiveness of most anti-infective drugs, although it may increase some side effects such as upset stomach or dizziness. .Some anti-infectives, however, interfere with the metabolism of alcohol and lead to the buildup of the poison acetaldehyde exactly as the drug Antabuse does. Mixing these anti-infectives with alcohol can lead to death.

The following anti-infective drugs show an Antabuse-type interaction (see Antabuse) when mixed with alcohol which could result in **ORGAN DAMAGE OR DEATH**: metronidazole (Flagyl), tinidazole (Tindamax), cefoperazone (Cefobid), cefotetan (Cefotan), moxalactam (Moxam), Ketoconazole (Nizoral), cefamandole (Mandol), and trimethoprim-sulfamethoxazole (Bactrim). Some of these appear to have more severe Antabuse-type interaction than others.

Other Reactions Of Anti-Infectives With Alcohol:

Doxycycline: Alcohol may reduce effectiveness of doxycycline.

Erythromycin: Erythromycin may increase intoxicating effects of alcohol.

Isoniazid: **Moderate Interaction**. May cause liver damage.

Antimanics

Depakote (divalproex sodium) and lithium are antimanic medications. Depakote (divalproex sodium) has been known to cause liver failure--alcohol may increase the chance of liver problems. It is better to abstain or drink moderately when taking lithium. Large amounts of alcohol can lead to dehydration and increase the chance of lithium toxicity. Alcohol may also cause drowsiness and CNS depression when mixed with lithium.

Antipsychotics

Some antipsychotic drugs show **Moderate** to **Minor Interactions** with alcohol. Mixing alcohol with antipsychotics may lead to increased CNS depression and impaired psychomotor performance. With some antipsychotics there may be increased risk of neurotoxicity. Mixing alcohol with antipsychotics may increase some side effects of the antipsychotics, such as repetitive, involuntary, and purposeless body or facial movements. Antipsychotics which interact with alcohol include: chlorpromazine (Thorazine), haloperidol (Haldol), fluphenazine, prochlorperazine, quetiapine (Seroquel), aripiprazole (Abilify) , olanzapine (Zyprexa), risperidone (Risperdal), ziprasidone (Geodon), paliperidone (Invega), clozapine (Clozaril).

Atypical Benzodiazepines

Atypical benzodiazepines such as Ambien are used as prescription sleep aids. People mixing alcohol with atypical benzodiazepines have reported blackouts, sleepwalking, sleep-eating, etc. Alcohol can increase CNS depression and psychomotor impairment caused by atypical benzodiazepines. Atypical benzodiazepines include: eszopiclone (Lunesta), zaleplon (Sonata), zolpidem (Ambien), and zopiclone.

Barbiturates

Barbiturates have a **MAJOR INTERACTION** with alcohol frequently leading to coma or **DEATH**. Barbiturates include: secobarbital (Seconal), phenobarbital (Luminal, Solfoton), mephobarbital (Mebaral), butabarbital (Butisol Sodium), and pentobarbital (Nembutal). Barbiturates are one of the most dangerous drugs to mix with alcohol--even worse than benzodiazepines or atypical benzodiazepines. Because of the danger of overdose death barbiturates have been largely replaced by benzodiazepines or atypical benzodiazepines. We recommend avoiding alcohol altogether if you are taking barbiturates.

Benzodiazepines

All benzodiazepines show a **MAJOR INTERACTION** with alcohol; potential **DEATH** caused by respiratory depression. Benzodiazepines include: alprazolam (Xanax), chlordiazepoxide (Librium, Librax), clonazepam (Klonopin), clorazepate (Tranxene), quazepam (Doral), estazolam (Prosom), flurazepam (Dalmane), oxazepam, diazepam (Valium), lorazepam (Ativan), midazolam, triazolam (Halcion), temazepam (Restoril), halazepam (Paxipam)

Both alcohol and benzodiazepines act on the GABA system in the brain and when combined in large doses their effect on this system can cause death due to respiratory depression. In lower doses benzodiazepines can greatly increase the effects of alcohol leading to severe drunkenness including frequent accidental injury or death. Both benzodiazepine withdrawal and alcohol withdrawal involve the GABA system. People who have been taking benzodiazepines for a long time should not stop suddenly because sudden withdrawal can lead to death. People who have been drinking alcohol and taking benzodiazepines together for a long period of time may suffer even greater withdrawal from sudden discontinuation or either alcohol or benzodiazepines--a tapering off schedule is necessary to safely discontinue these drugs.

Cardiovascular medications

These include both high blood pressure medications (antihypertensives) and heart medications such as nitroglycerin. The following cardiovascular medications can cause dizziness and fainting when combined with alcohol: nitroglycerin, reserpine, methyldopa (Aldomet), hydralazine (Apresoline, etc.), and guanethidine (Ismelin, etc). Mixing alcohol with high blood pressure medications can also lead to an increased drop in blood pressure. This is particularly the case with alpha-1-adrenergic blockers such as prazosin which can lead to an even greater drop in blood pressure for people with aldehyde dehydrogenase deficiencies (primarily Asians). The antihypertensive verapamil (Calan, etc) can increase the effects of alcohol leading to an unexpected degree of intoxication.

Date Rape Drugs

Rohypnol and GHB. **MAJOR INTERACTION**. Rohypnol and GHB (Gamma-Hydroxybutyric acid, Xyrem, Sodium Oxybate) are both used in conjunction with alcohol as date rape drugs. When combined with alcohol these drugs can cause amnesia, unconsciousness and **DEATH**. Rohypnol is also known as "roofies". Rohypnol is not and never has been legal in the United States but is frequently smuggled in from abroad. GHB is on both Schedule One and Schedule Three in the United States--it is much less frequently prescribed here than it used to be.

Chloral hydrate. "Knockout drops" or a "Mickey Finn" consists of chloral hydrate mixed with alcohol. In 1903 in Chicago, bartender Michael "Mickey" Finn was accused of using knockout drops to rob his customers. This drug is also notorious for being used to shanghai sailors and, of course, has been implicated in date rape since its discovery.

Miscellaneous Drugs

Acitretin (Soriatane) **MAJOR INTERACTION**. Acitretin is a retinoid, which is a form of vitamin A. Acitretin is used to treat severe psoriasis. Acitretin can cause **BIRTH DEFECTS** when mixed with alcohol.

Cimetidine (Tagamet). This antiulcer medication can interfere with alcohol metabolism leading to higher than expected alcohol concentrations. Use caution to avoid unexpected drunkenness, blackouts, etc.

Methotrexate (Rheumatrex) **MAJOR INTERACTION**. Methotrexate (Rheumatrex) is an immunosuppressive which can cause liver damage. Alcohol increases the chance of liver damage and **DEATH** by liver failure.

Metoclopramide (Reglan; Canada: Maxeran). Metoclopramide is used short-term to treat heartburn caused by gastroesophageal reflux. Drinking alcohol while taking metoclopramide can lead to increased drowsiness, CNS depression, and psychomotor impairment.

Phenytoin (Dilantin) is an anti-epileptic drug (also called an anticonvulsant or antiseizure). Daily drinking can lead to a reduction in the effectiveness of this medication and the return of seizures. Binge drinking may increase Dilantin side effects such as psychomotor impairment.

Procarbazine (Matulane). **MAJOR INTERACTION**. Procarbazine is a cancer (antineoplastic) medication. May produce Antabuse-type reaction (see Antabuse).

Tramadol (Tramal, Ultram). Possible **MAJOR INTERACTION**, Tramadol is a narcotic-like pain reliever. Mixing alcohol with tramadol can lead to CNS depression, psychomotor impairment, **DANGEROUS RESPIRATORY DEPRESSION** and **DEATH**.

NSAID Painkillers

NSAID PAINKILLERS (ibuprofen, aspirin, naproxen) show a **Moderate Interaction**: potential gastric bleeding and ulcers. NSAID Painkillers include ibuprofen (Advil, Motrin), aspirin and naproxen (Aleve). Aspirin can interfere with the function of alcohol dehydrogenase. If you take aspirin before drinking alcohol you may become more intoxicated than usual on the same dose of alcohol.

Opiates

MAJOR to Moderate Interaction. When alcohol is mixed with opiate drugs such as morphine or codeine this can lead to increased alcohol intoxication and complete loss of control as well as increased CNS depression, impaired judgment, and psychomotor impairment. In severe cases there can be respiratory depression and **DEATH**. Opiate drugs include: heroin, morphine, codeine, methadone (Dolophinc), oxycodonc (OxyContin), Vicodin, hydrocodone, Percocet, Percodan, Suboxone, buprenorphine, oxymorphone (Opana), levorphanol, fentanyl, propoxyphene (Darvon), Darvocet, Anexsia, Lortab, Lorcet, Roxicet, Tylox, hydromorphone (Dilaudid), meperidine (Demerol), alfentanil (Alfenta), and Wygesic.

Extended Release Opiate Painkillers: Possible **MAJOR INTERACTION**: ALL the precautions which apply to regular opiate painkillers also apply to extended release (long acting) opiate painkillers. In addition to these, there have been reports of alcohol interfering with the extended release mechanism of long acting opiates, leading to a sudden opiate dump and opiate overdose resulting in **DEATH**. Extended Release Opiate Painkillers include long-acting morphine (Kadian, Avinza) and long-acting oxymorphone (Opana ER).

In summary, it may be safe enough to have a glass or two of wine while taking a regular opiate pain reliever, however, mixing large amounts of opiates and alcohol can lead to dangerously out of control drunken behavior and even death from respiratory depression. With long acting opiates it is advisable to forgo alcohol completely because of the possibility of a sudden opiate dump and overdose death.

Other Sedative Drugs

Ramelteon (Rozerem) is a melatonin receptor agonist used for insomnia. Alcohol may increase the sedating effects of ramelteon, leading to increased CNS depression and psychomotor impairment.

Meprobamate (Miltown) is a sedative-hypnotic. Alcohol may increase the sedating effects of meprobamate, leading to increased CNS depression and psychomotor impairment.

Stimulants

Stimulant drugs are commonly prescribed for ADD/ADHD, obesity, or narcolepsy. Some people who use alcohol to come down from stimulants like cocaine or amphetamine and who also use stimulants to come up from alcohol intoxication may be in danger of developing a cyclical dual addiction. Cocaine and alcohol combine inside the human body to form cocaethylene. The stimulant pemoline (Cylert) has been withdrawn by the FDA because it causes **liver damage**--

this drug should never be mixed with alcohol. Alcohol is involved in most Ecstasy-related **DEATHS**--avoid mixing the two.

Stimulants include: cocaine, dexmethylphenidate (Focalin), methylphenidate (Ritalin, Concerta), amphetamine (Adderall), dextroamphetamine (Dexedrine), methamphetamine (dextromethamphetamine, Desoxyn), lisdexamfetamine (Vyvanse), diethylpropion (Tenuate), phentermine (Adipex-P, Oby-Cap, T-Diet, Zantryl), phendimetrazine (Adipost, Anorex-SR, Appecon, Bontril PDM, Bontril Slow Release, Melfiat, Obezine, Phendiet, Plegine, Prelu-2, Statobex), Meridia (sibutramine), modafinil (Provigil), pemoline (Cylert), benzphetamine (Didrex), caffeine (NoDoz, Vivarin, Cafcit, etc), armodafinil (Nuvigil), atomoxetine (Strattera), doxapram (Dopram), mazindol (Mazanor, Sanorex), MDMA ("Ecstasy"), nicotine, yohimbine.

Part II: Drug and Alcohol Interactions by Drug Name: A-Z

Here you we list alphabetically the brand and generic names of some of the most common drugs which interact with alcohol and we reference where they are discussed in detail in part one. **DO NOT** assume that a drug is safe because it is not listed here--this listing is not complete. Always check a reliable source such as the PDR or drugs.com for possible interaction of any drug not listed here.

Abilify (aripiprazole) - see Antipsychotics
acetaminophen (Tylenol, Paracetamol, etc.) - see Acetaminophen
acetohexamide (Dymelor) - see Antidiabetics
acitretin (Soriatane) - see Miscellaneous Drugs: acitretin
Adderall (amphetamine) - see Stimulants
Adipex-P (phentermine) - see Stimulants
Adipost (phendimetrazine) - see Stimulants
Advil (ibuprofen) - see NSAIDs
Alavert (loratadine) - see Antihistamines
Aldomet (methyldopa) - see Cardiovascular Medications
Aleve (naproxen) - see NSAIDs
Alfenta (alfentanil) - see Opiates
alfentanil (Alfenta) - see Opiates
Allegra (fexofenadine) - see Antihistamines
alpha-1-adrenergic blockers - see Cardiovascular Medications
alprazolam (Xanax) - see Benzodiazepines
Amaryl (glimepiride) - see Antidiabetics
amitriptyline (Elavil) - see Antidepressants: Tricyclic Antidepressants
amoxapine (Asendin) - see Antidepressants: Tricyclic Antidepressants
amphetamine (Adderall) - see Stimulants
Anacin-3 (acetaminophen) - see Acetaminophen
Anesthetics - see Anesthetics
Anexsia (acetaminophen and hydrocodone) - see Acetaminophen and see Opiates
Anorex-SR (phendimetrazine) - see Stimulants
Antabuse (disulfiram) - see Antabuse
antianxiety - see antianxiety

antibiotics - see Anti-Infectives
Anticoagulants - see Anticoagulants
antidiabetics - see Antidiabetics
antifungals - see Anti-Infectives
antihistamines - see Antihistamines
antihypertensives - see Cardiovascular Medications
anti-infectives - see Anti-Infectives
antimanics - see Antimanics
antipsychotics - see Antipsychotics
antituberculars - see Anti-Infectives
antivirals - see Anti-Infectives
anxiolytics - see antianxiety
Appecon (phendimetrazine) - see Stimulants
Apresoline (hydralazine) - see Cardiovascular Medications
aripiprazole (Abilify) - see Antipsychotics
armodafinil (Nuvigil) - see Stimulants
Asendin (amoxapine) - see Antidepressants: Tricyclic Antidepressants
aspirin - see NSAIDs
Ativan (lorazepam) - see Benzodiazepines
atomoxetine (Strattera) - see Stimulants
atypical benzodiazepines - see Atypical Benzodiazepines
Avinza (long-acting morphine) - see Opiates
Bactrim (trimethoprim-sulfamethoxazole) - see Anti-Infectives
barbiturates - see Barbiturates
Benadryl (diphenhydramine) - see Antihistamines
benzodiazepines - see Benzodiazepines
benzphetamine (Didrex) - see Stimulants
Bontril (phendimetrazine) - see Stimulants
buprenorphine - see Opiates
bupropion (Wellbutrin, Zyban) - see Antidepressants: The New Antidepressants
BuSpar (buspirone) - see antianxiety
butabarbital (Butisol Sodium) - see Barbiturates
Butisol Sodium (butabarbital) - see Barbiturates
Cafcit (caffeine) - see Stimulants
caffeine (NoDoz, Vivarin, Cafcit, etc) - see Stimulants
Calan (verapamil) - see Cardiovascular Medications
Cardiovascular Medications - see Cardiovascular Medications
cefamandole (Mandol) - see Anti-Infectives
Cefobid (cefoperazone) - see Anti-Infectives
cefoperazone (Cefobid) - see Anti-Infectives
Cefotan (cefotetan) - see Anti-Infectives
cefotetan (Cefotan) - see Anti-Infectives
Celexa (citalopram) - see Antidepressants: The New Antidepressants
cetirizine (Zyrtec) - see Antihistamines
chloral hydrate- see Date Rape Drugs
chlordiazepoxide (Librium, Librax) - see Benzodiazepines

chlorpromazine (Thorazine) - see Antipsychotics

chlorpropamide (Diabinese) - see Antidiabetics

cimetidine (Tagamet) - see Miscellaneous Drugs: cimetidine

Cipralex (escitalopram) - see Antidepressants: The New Antidepressants

citalopram (Celexa) - see Antidepressants: The New Antidepressants

Clarinex (desloratadine) - see Antihistamines

Claritin (loratadine) - see Antihistamines

clonazepam (Klonopin) - see Benzodiazepines

clorazepate (Tranxene) - see Benzodiazepines

clozapine (Clozaril) - see Antipsychotics

Clozaril (clozapine) - see Antipsychotics

cocaine- see Stimulants

Concerta (methylphenidate) - see Stimulants

Coumadin (warfarin) - see Anticoagulants

Cylert (pemoline) - see Stimulants

Cymbalta (duloxetine) - see Antidepressants: The New Antidepressants

Dalmane (flurazepam) - see Benzodiazepines

Darvocet-N (propoxyphene) - see Opiates

Darvon (propoxyphene) - see Opiates

Date Rape Drugs - see Date Rape Drugs

Demerol (meperidine) - see Opiates

Depakote (divalproex sodium) - see Antimanics

desipramine (Norpramin) - see Antidepressants: Tricyclic Antidepressants

desloratadine (Clarinex) - see Antihistamines

Desoxyn (methamphetamine) - see Stimulants

desvenlafaxine (Pristiq) - see Antidepressants: The New Antidepressants

Dexedrine (dextroamphetamine) - see Stimulants

dexmethylphenidate (Focalin) - see Stimulants

dextroamphetamine (Dexedrine) - see Stimulants

dextromethamphetamine (methamphetamine) - see Stimulants

DiaBeta (glyburide) - see Antidiabetics

Diabinese (chlorpropamide) - see Antidiabetics

diazepam (Valium) - see Benzodiazepines

Didrex (benzphetamine) - see Stimulants

diethylpropion (Tenuate) - see Stimulants

Dilantin (phenytoin) - see Miscellaneous Drugs: phenytoin

Dilaudid (hydromorphone) - see Opiates

diphenhydramine (Benadryl, Simply Sleep, Sominex, etc.) - see Antihistamines

Diprivan (propofol) - see Anesthetics

disulfiram (Antabuse) - see Antabuse

divalproex sodium (Depakote) - see Antimanics

Dolophine (methadone) - see Opiates

Dopram (doxapram) - see Stimulants

Doral (quazepam) - see Benzodiazepines

doxapram (Dopram) - see Stimulants

doxepin (Sinequan) - see Antidepressants: Tricyclic Antidepressants doxycycline - see Anti-Infectives

doxylamine (Unisom) - see Antihistamines

duloxetine (Cymbalta) - see Antidepressants: The New Antidepressants

Dymelor (acetohexamide) - see Antidiabetics

Ecstasy (MDMA) - see Stimulants

Edronax (reboxetine) - see Antidepressants: The New Antidepressants

Effexor (venlafaxine) - see Antidepressants: The New Antidepressants

Elavil (amitriptyline) - see Antidepressants: Tricyclic Antidepressants

Emsam (selegiline) - see Antidepressants: MAOIs

enflurane (Ethrane) - see Anesthetics

erythromycin - see Anti-Infectives

escitalopram (Lexapro, Cipralex) - see Antidepressants: The New Antidepressants

estazolam (Prosom) - see Benzodiazepines

eszopiclone (Lunesta) - see Atypical Benzodiazepines

Ethrane (enflurane) - see Anesthetics

Excedrin (acetaminophen) - see Acetaminophen

Excedrin PM (acetaminophen, diphenhydramine) - see Acetaminophen and see Antihistamines

fentanyl - see Opiates

fexofenadine (Allegra) - see Antihistamines

Flagyl (metronidazole) - see Anti-Infectives

flunitrazepam (Rohypnol) - see Date Rape Drugs

Fluothane (halothane) - see Anesthetics

fluoxetine (Prozac) - see Antidepressants: The New Antidepressants

fluphenazine - see Antipsychotics

flurazepam (Dalmane) - see Benzodiazepines

fluvoxamine (Luvox) - see Antidepressants: The New Antidepressants

Focalin (dexmethylphenidate) - see Stimulants

Fortamet (metformin) - see Antidiabetics

gamma hydroxybutyrate (GHB) - see Date Rape Drugs

Geodon (ziprasidone) - see Antipsychotics

GHB (Xyrem, sodium oxybate, gamma hydroxybutyrate) - see Date Rape Drugs

glimepiride (Amaryl) - see Antidiabetics

glipizide (GlipiZIDE XL, Glucotrol, Glucotrol XL) - see Antidiabetics

GlipiZIDE XL (glipizide) - see Antidiabetics

Glucophage (metformin) - see Antidiabetics

Glucophage XR (metformin) - see Antidiabetics

Glucotrol (glipizide) - see Antidiabetics

Glucotrol XL (glipizide) - see Antidiabetics

Glumetza (metformin) - see Antidiabetics

glyburide (DiaBeta, Glycron, Glynase, Glynase PresTab, Micronase) - see Antidiabetics

Glycron (glyburide) - see Antidiabetics

Glynase (glyburide) - see Antidiabetics

Glynase PresTab (glyburide) - see Antidiabetics

guanethidine (Ismelin, etc) - see Cardiovascular Medications

halazepam (Paxipam) - see Benzodiazepines

Halcion (triazolam) - see Benzodiazepines

Haldol (haloperidol) - see Antipsychotics
haloperidol (Haldol) - see Antipsychotics
halothane (Fluothane). - see Anesthetics
heart medications - see Cardiovascular Medications
high blood pressure medications - see Cardiovascular Medications
hydralazine (Apresoline, etc) - see Cardiovascular Medications
hydrocodone - see Opiates
hydromorphone (Dilaudid) - see Opiates
ibuprofen (Advil, Motrin) - see NSAIDs
imipramine (Tofranil, Tofranil-PM) - see Antidepressants: Tricyclic Antidepressants
insulin - see Antidiabetics
Invega (paliperidone) - see Antipsychotics
Ismelin (guanethidine) - see Cardiovascular Medications
isocarboxazid (Marplan) - see Antidepressants: MAOIs
isocarboxazid (Marplan) - see Opiates
isoniazid - see Anti-Infectives
Ixel (milnacipran) - see Antidepressants: The New Antidepressants
Kadian (long-acting morphine) - see Opiates
ketoconazole (Nizoral) - see Anti-Infectives
Klonopin (clonazepam) - see Benzodiazepines
knockout drops (chloral hydrate and alcohol) - see Date Rape Drugs
levorphanol - see Opiates
Lexapro (escitalopram) - see Antidepressants: The New Antidepressants
Librax (chlordiazepoxide) - see Benzodiazepines
Librium (chlordiazepoxide) - see Benzodiazepines
lisdexamfetamine (Vyvanse) - see Stimulants
lithium - see Antimanics
long-acting morphine (Kadian, Avinza) - see Opiates
long-acting oxymorphone (Opana ER) - see Opiates
loratadine (Claritin, Alavert) - see Antihistamines
lorazepam (Ativan) - see Benzodiazepines
Lorcet (acetaminophen and hydrocodone) - see Acetaminophen and see Opiates
Lortab (acetaminophen and hydrocodone) - see Acetaminophen and see Opiates
Luminal (phenobarbital) - see Barbiturates
Lustral (sertraline) - see Antidepressants: The New Antidepressants
Luvox (fluvoxamine) - see Antidepressants: The New Antidepressants
Mandol (cefamandole) - see Anti-Infectives
MAOIs - see Antidepressants: MAOIs
Marplan (isocarboxazid) - see Antidepressants: MAOIs
Matulane (procarbazine) - see Miscellaneous Drugs: procarbazine
Maxeran (metoclopramide) - see Miscellaneous Drugs: metoclopramide
Mazanor (mazindol) - see Stimulants
mazindol (Mazanor, Sanorex) - see Stimulants
MDMA ("Ecstasy")- see Stimulants
Mebaral (mephobarbital) - see Barbiturates
Melfiat (phendimetrazine) - see Stimulants

meperidine (Demerol) - see Opiates

mephobarbital (Mebaral) - see Barbiturates

meprobamate (Miltown) - see Other Sedative Drugs: meprobamate

Meridia (sibutramine) - see Stimulants

metformin (Fortamet, Glucophage, Glucophage XR, Glumetza, Riomet) - see Antidiabetics

methadone (Dolophine) - see Opiates

methamphetamine (dextromethamphctamine, Desoxyn) - see Stimulants

methotrexate (Rheumatrex) - see Miscellaneous Drugs: methotrexate

methyldopa (Aldomet) - see Cardiovascular Medications

methylphenidate (Ritalin, Concerta) - see Stimulants

metoclopramide (Reglan,Maxeran) - see Miscellaneous Drugs: metoclopramide

metronidazole (Flagyl) - see Anti-Infectives

Mickey Finn (chloral hydrate and alcohol) - see Datc Rapc Drugs

Micronase (glyburide) - see Antidiabetics

midazolam - see Benzodiazepines

milnacipran (Ixel, Savella) - see Antidepressants: The New Antidepressants

Miltown (meprobamate) - see Other Sedative Drugs: meprobamate

mirtazapine (Remeron, Remeron SolTab) - see Antidepressants: Other Antidepressants

modafinil (Provigil) - see Stimulants

Monoamine Oxidase Inhibitors - see Antidepressants: MAOIs

Motrin (ibuprofen) - see NSAIDs

moxalactam (Moxam) - see Anti-Infectives

Moxam (moxalactam) - see Anti-Infectives

naproxen (Aleve) - see NSAIDs

Nardil (phenelzine) - see Antidepressants: MAOIs

NDRIs - see Antidcpressants: The New Antidepressants

Nembutal (pentobarbital) - see Barbiturates

nicotine- see Stimulants

nitroglycerin - see Cardiovascular Medications

Nizoral (ketoconazole) - see Anti-Infectives

NoDoz (caffeine) - see Stimulants

Norepinephrine reuptake inhibitors - see Antidepressants: The New Antidepressants

Norepinephrine-dopamine reuptake inhibitors - see Antidepressants: The New Antidepressants

Norpramin (desipramine) - see Antidepressants: Tricyclic Antidepressants

nortriptyline (Pamelor) - see Antidepressants: Tricyclic Antidepressants

NRIs - see Antidepressants: The Ncw Antidcprcssants

NSAIDs - see NSAIDs

Nuvigil (armodafinil) - see Stimulants

Obezine (phendimetrazine) - see Stimulants

Oby-Cap (phentermine) - see Stimulants

olanzapine (Zyprexa) - see Antipsychotics

Opana (oxymorphone) - see Opiates

Opana ER (long-acting oxymorphone) - see Opiates

Opiates - see Opiates

Orinase (tolbutamide) - see Antidiabetics

oxazepam - see Benzodiazepines

oxycodone (OxyContin) - see Opiates
OxyContin (oxycodone) - see Opiates
oxymorphone (Opana) - see Opiates
paliperidone (Invega) - see Antipsychotics
Pamelor (nortriptyline) - see Antidepressants: Tricyclic Antidepressants
Paracetamol (acetaminophen) - see Acetaminophen
Parnate (tranylcypromine) - see Antidepressants: MAOIs
paroxetine (Paxil, Seroxat) - see Antidepressants: The New Antidepressants
Paxil (paroxetine) - see Antidepressants: The New Antidepressants
Paxipam (halazepam) - see Benzodiazepines
pemoline (Cylert) - see Stimulants
pentobarbital (Nembutal) - see Barbiturates
Percocet (acetaminophen/oxycodone) - see Acetaminophen and see Opiates
Percodan (aspirin/oxycodone) - see Opiates and see NSAIDs
Phendiet (phendimetrazine) - see Stimulants
phendimetrazine (Adipost, Anorex-SR, Appecon, Bontril PDM, Bontril Slow Release, Melfiat, Obezine, Phendiet, Plegine, Prelu-2, Statobex) - see Stimulants
phenelzine (Nardil) - see Antidepressants: MAOIs
phenelzine (Nardil), - see Opiates
phenobarbital (Luminal, Solfoton) - see Barbiturates
phentermine (Adipex-P, Oby-Cap, T-Diet, Zantryl) - see Stimulants
phenytoin (Dilantin) - see Miscellaneous Drugs: phenytoin
Plegine (phendimetrazine) - see Stimulants
prazosin - see Cardiovascular Medications
Prelu-2 (phendimetrazine) - see Stimulants
Pristiq (desvenlafaxine) - see Antidepressants: The New Antidepressants
procarbazine (Matulane) - see Miscellaneous Drugs: procarbazine
prochlorperazine - see Antipsychotics
propofol (Diprivan) - see Anesthetics
propoxyphene (Darvocet-N) - see Opiates
propoxyphene (Darvon) - see Opiates
Prosom (estazolam) - see Benzodiazepines
protriptyline (Vivactil) - see Antidepressants: Tricyclic Antidepressants
Provigil (modafinil) - see Stimulants
Prozac (fluoxetine) - see Antidepressants: The New Antidepressants
quazepam (Doral) - see Benzodiazepines
quetiapine (Seroquel) - see Antipsychotics
ramelteon (Rozerem) - see Other Sedative Drugs: ramelteon
reboxetine (Edronax) - see Antidepressants: The New Antidepressants
Reglan (metoclopramide) - see Miscellaneous Drugs: metoclopramide
Remeron (mirtazapine) - see Antidepressants: Other Antidepressants
Remeron SolTab (mirtazapine) - see Antidepressants: Other Antidepressants
reserpine - see Cardiovascular Medications
Restoril (temazepam) - see Benzodiazepines
Rheumatrex (methotrexate) - see Miscellaneous Drugs: methotrexate
Riomet (metformin) - see Antidiabetics

Risperdal (risperidone) - see Antipsychotics
risperidone (Risperdal) - see Antipsychotics
Ritalin (methylphenidate) - see Stimulants
Rohypnol (flunitrazepam) - see Date Rape Drugs
roofies (Rohypnol, flunitrazepam) - see Date Rape Drugs
Roxicet (acetaminophen/oxycodone) - see Acetaminophen and see Opiates
Rozerem (ramelteon) - see Other Sedative Drugs: ramelteon
Sanorex (mazindol) - see Stimulants
Savella (milnacipran) - see Antidepressants: The New Antidepressants
secobarbital (Seconal) - see Barbiturates
Seconal (secobarbital) - see Barbiturates
Selective Serotonin Reuptake Inhibitors - see Antidepressants: The New Antidepressants
selegiline (Emsam) - see Antidepressants: MAOIs
Seroquel (quetiapine) - see Antipsychotics
Serotonin-norepinephrine reuptake inhibitors - see Antidepressants: The New Antidepressants
Seroxat (paroxetine) - see Antidepressants: The New Antidepressants
sertraline (Zoloft, Lustral) - see Antidepressants: The New Antidepressants
sibutramine (Meridia) - see Stimulants
Simply Sleep (diphenhydramine) - see Antihistamines
Sinequan (doxepin) - see Antidepressants: Tricyclic Antidepressants
SNRIs - see Antidepressants: The New Antidepressants
sodium oxybate (GHB) - see Date Rape Drugs
Solfoton (phenobarbital) - see Barbiturates
Sominex (diphenhydramine) - see Antihistamines
Soriatane (acitretin) - see Miscellaneous Drugs: acitretin
SSRIs - see Antidepressants: The New Antidepressants
Statobex (phendimetrazine) - see Stimulants
Stimulants - see Stimulants
Strattera (atomoxetine) - see Stimulants
Suboxone (buprenorphine/naloxone) - see Opiates
sulfonylureas - see Antidiabetics
Surmontil (trimipramine) - see Antidepressants: Tricyclic Antidepressants
Tagamet (cimetidine) - see Miscellaneous Drugs: cimetidine
T-Diet (phentermine) - see Stimulants
temazepam (Restoril) - see Benzodiazepines
Tenuate (diethylpropion) - see Stimulants
Tetracyclic Antidepressants- see Antidepressants: Other Antidepressants
Thorazine (chlorpromazine) - see Antipsychotics
Tindamax (tinidazole) - see Anti-Infectives
tinidazole (Tindamax) - see Anti-Infectives
Tofranil (imipramine) - see Antidepressants: Tricyclic Antidepressants
tolazamide (Tolinase) - see Antidiabetics
tolbutamide (Orinase, Tol-Tab) - see Antidiabetics
Tolinase (tolazamide) - see Antidiabetics
Tol-Tab (tolbutamide) - see Antidiabetics
tramadol (Tramal, Ultram) - see Miscellaneous Drugs: tramadol

Tramal (tramadol) - see Miscellaneous Drugs: tramadol
Tranxene (clorazepate) - see Benzodiazepines
tranylcypromine (Parnate) - see Antidepressants: MAOIs
tranylcypromine (Parnate) - see Opiates
triazolam (Halcion) - see Benzodiazepines
Tricyclic Antidepressants - see Antidepressants: Tricyclic Antidepressants
trimethoprim-sulfamethoxazole (Bactrim) - see Anti-Infectives
trimipramine (Surmontil) - see Antidepressants: Tricyclic Antidepressants
Tylenol (acetaminophen) - see Acetaminophen
Tylenol PM (acetaminophen, diphenhydramine) - see Acetaminophen and see Antihistamines
Tylox (acetaminophen/oxycodone) - see Acetaminophen and see Opiates
Ultram (tramadol) - see Miscellaneous Drugs: tramadol
Unisom (doxylamine) - see Antihistamines
Valium (diazepam) - see Benzodiazepines
venlafaxine (Effexor) - see Antidepressants: The New Antidepressants
verapamil (Calan, etc) - see Cardiovascular Medications
Vicodin (acetaminophen/hydrocodone) - see Acetaminophen and see Opiates
viloxazine (Vivalan) - see Antidepressants: The New Antidepressants
Vivactil (protriptyline) - see Antidepressants: Tricyclic Antidepressants
Vivalan (viloxazine) - see Antidepressants: The New Antidepressants
Vivarin (caffeine) - see Stimulants
Vyvanse (lisdexamfetamine) - see Stimulants
warfarin (Coumadin) - see Anticoagulants
Wellbutrin (bupropion) - see Antidepressants: The New Antidepressants
Wygesic (propoxyphene acetaminophen) - see Acetaminophen and see Opiates
Xanax (alprazolam) - see Benzodiazepines
Xyrem (GHB) - see Date Rape Drugs
yohimbine- see Stimulants
zaleplon (Sonata) - see Atypical Benzodiazepines
Zantryl (phentermine) - see Stimulants
ziprasidone (Geodon) - see Antipsychotics
Zoloft (sertraline) - see Antidepressants: The New Antidepressants
zolpidem (Ambien) - see Atypical Benzodiazepines
zopiclone. - see Atypical Benzodiazepines
Zyban (bupropion) - see Antidepressants: The New Antidepressants
Zyprexa (olanzapine) - see Antipsychotics
Zyrtec (cetirizine) - see Antihistamines

REFERENCES:

Alcohol-Medication Interactions - Alcohol Alert No. 27-1995

Alcohol-related drug interactions. Pharmacist's Letter/Prescriber's Letter, 2008; 24(1):240106.

drugs.com

Physicians' desk reference: PDR. Medical Economics Co. Oradell, N.J.

APPENDIX II: Blood Alcohol Concentration (BAC) Charts

These charts are to be taken only as approximations. Other factors such as the presence or absence of food in the stomach significantly affect BAC levels, as do certain medications such as aspirin.

	Men								
	Approximate Blood Alcohol Percentage								
Drinks	Body Weight in Pounds								
	100	120	140	160	180	200	220	240	
0	.00	.00	.00	.00	.00	.00	.00	.00	The only safe driving limit
1	.04	.03	.03	.02	.02	.02	.02	.02	Driving Skills Significantly Affected
2	.08	.06	.05	.05	.04	.04	.03	.03	
3	.11	.09	.08	.07	.06	.06	.05	.05	-----------------
4	.15	.12	.11	.09	.08	.08	.07	.06	Possible Criminal Penalties
5	.19	.16	.13	.12	.11	.09	.09	.08	
6	.23	.19	.16	.14	.13	.11	.10	.09	Legally Intoxicated
7	.26	.22	.19	.16	.15	.13	.12	.11	
8	.30	.25	.21	.19	.17	.15	.14	.13	-----------------
9	.34	.28	.24	.21	.19	.17	.15	.14	Criminal Penalties
10	.38	.31	.27	.23	.21	.19	.17	.16	Death Possible

Subtract .01% for every forty minutes elapsed since starting drinking
One drink = 1.5 oz 80 proof liquor, 5 oz table wine, or 12 oz beer

	Women									
	Approximate Blood Alcohol Percentage									
Drinks	Body Weight in Pounds									
	90	100	120	140	160	180	200	220	240	
0	.00	.00	.00	.00	.00	.00	.00	.00	.00	The Only Safe Driving Limit
1	.05	.05	.04	.03	.03	.03	.02	.02	.02	Driving Skills Significantly Affected
2	.10	.09	.08	.07	.06	.05	.05	.04	.04	
3	.15	.14	.11	.10	.09	.08	.07	.06	.06	-----------------
4	.20	.18	.15	.13	.11	.10	.09	.08	.08	Possible Criminal Penalties
5	.25	.23	.19	.16	.14	.13	.11	.10	.09	
6	.30	.27	.23	.19	.17	.15	.14	.12	.11	Legally Intoxicated
7	.35	.32	.27	.23	.20	.18	.16	.14	.13	
8	.40	.36	.30	.26	.23	.20	.18	.17	.15	-----------------
9	.45	.41	.34	.29	.26	.23	.20	.19	.17	Criminal Penalties
10	.51	.45	.38	.32	.28	.25	.23	.21	.19	Death Possible

Subtract .01% for every forty minutes elapsed since starting drinking
One drink = 1.5 oz 80 proof liquor, 5 oz table wine, or 12 oz beer

APPENDIX III: Naltrexone, and the Magic of Pharmacological Extinction

Introduction

The drug naltrexone has been approved by the FDA for the treatment of opiate addiction since 1984 and for the treatment of alcohol problems since 1994. Although many doctors have prescribed naltrexone for alcohol problems since it was approved by the FDA, naltrexone has not proven very effective when prescribed according to the FDA's recommendation to take it daily while abstaining from alcohol.

However, David Sinclair PhD, a research scientist working in Finland, has discovered a different way of prescribing naltrexone which has shown an 80% success rate with patients who are prescribed naltrexone and a 90% success rate with patients who take the naltrexone as directed. This method of prescribing naltrexone has come to be referred to as The Sinclair Method. 90% of patients who take naltrexone according to The Sinclair Method either quit drinking or become moderate drinkers in the space of three months (note: some individuals may require six months to a year for The Sinclair Method to take effect). No inpatient treatment is required and naltrexone is available in a cheap generic form which makes this not only a highly effective treatment for alcohol problems, but a one of the least expensive as well.

What is The Sinclair Method?

According to the Sinclair Method patients should only take naltrexone when they intend to drink alcohol and should never take naltrexone when they intend to abstain from alcohol. This is in sharp contrast with the FDA's recommendation that naltrexone should only be given to patients who promise to abstain from alcohol and that it should be administered daily. Moreover, when naltrexone is taken according to the recommendations of the FDA it is only slightly more effective than a placebo--a sharp contrast with the 90% success rate of The Sinclair Method of using naltrexone. In addition, some research suggests that the only patients who benefit by taking naltrexone as prescribed by FDA guidelines are those who cheat and drink on the naltrexone, and that those who abstain while taking the naltrexone not only have greater alcohol cravings than those who get a placebo--but are also more likely to relapse into severe drinking problems in the long term.

The Sinclair Method says to take 50 mg of naltrexone one hour before drinking every time that you drink for the rest of your life. Naltrexone taken according to The Sinclair Method is safe even for drinkers who are heavily physically dependent on alcohol since the naltrexone causes them to gradually drink less and less per day and thus taper off of the alcohol with no withdrawal symptoms whatsoever.

How does The Sinclair Method work?

According to David Sinclair, alcohol addiction is a conditioned response. People become conditioned to drink alcohol because of alcohol's actions in the brain in much the same way that Pavlov's dogs became conditioned to salivate at the sound of a bell. This is because every time that one drinks alcohol, endorphins are released in the brain. Endorphins are chemicals which are responsible for learning new conditioned responses. Normally this is a good thing because the conditioned responses which we learn help us to survive. However, in the case of alcohol addiction, the conditioned response leads people to perpetuate a bad habit. The endorphins which are released into the brain when people drink alcohol reinforce the drinking behavior, and this can lead to addiction to alcohol.

Naltrexone totally blocks the effects of endorphins in the brain. If you take naltrexone before drinking alcohol then the drinking behavior will not be reinforced. When a behavior is not reinforced it eventually disappears. Psychologists refer to this process as "extinction". Since naltrexone is a pharmaceutical, using naltrexone to extinguish drinking behavior is referred to as "pharmacological extinction". Pharmacological extinction of problem drinking by using naltrexone is The Sinclair Method.

When we understand that problem drinking is a conditioned response and that this conditioned response can be extinguished by using naltrexone according to The Sinclair Method, it becomes very obvious why the FDA's method of using naltrexone is not effective. If a person takes naltrexone every day then the naltrexone will tend to extinguish every pleasurable behavior which results in the release of endorphins, not just drinking behavior. This includes everything pleasurable from reading to jogging to sex. Moreover, if one abstains while taking the naltrexone, then drinking will be the only behavior which is NOT extinguished by the naltrexone.

Why Isn't The Sinclair Method Popular In The United States?

Since The Sinclair Method has shown a great deal of success in Finland, why hasn't it been generally adopted in the United States? There are a couple of reasons that this may be the case. Since naltrexone is now available as a generic, the pharmaceutical companies will not make any major profits by promoting it. Moreover, American addictionologists seem to generally shy away from anything which does not involve complete abstinence and surrender to a "Higher Power". Fortunately there are a few professionals in the United States who are now promoting The Sinclair method. We can only hope that this grass roots movement will grow and that more and more people we become familiar with The Sinclair Method and put it into practice to help eliminate the alcohol problems which continue to plague the United States.

REFERENCES:

Anton RF, O'Malley SS, Ciraulo DA, Cisler RA, Couper D, Donovan DM, Gastfriend DR, Hosking JD, Johnson BA, LoCastro JS, Longabaugh R, Mason BJ, Mattson ME, Miller WR, Pettinati HM, Randall CL, Swift R, Weiss RD, Williams LD, Zweben A; COMBINE Study Research Group. (2006). Combined pharmacotherapies and behavioral interventions for alcohol dependence: the COMBINE study: a randomized controlled trial. JAMA. 295(17), 2003-17. PubMed Abstract:
http://www.ncbi.nlm.nih.gov/pubmed/16670409
Free Full Text:
http://jama.ama-assn.org/cgi/reprint/295/17/2003.pdf

Eskapa, R (2008). <u>The Cure for Alcoholism: Drink Your Way Sober Without Willpower, Abstinence or Discomfort</u>. Benbella Books. Dallas, TX.

Heinälä P, Alho H, Kiianmaa K, Lönnqvist J, Kuoppasalmi K, Sinclair JD. (2001). Targeted use of naltrexone without prior detoxification in the treatment of alcohol dependence: a factorial double-blind, placebo-controlled trial. <u>Journal of Clinical Psychopharmacology</u>. 21(3), 287-92.
PubMed Abstract:
http://www.ncbi.nlm.nih.gov/pubmed/11386491

Medical Economics Co. (2009), <u>Physicians' desk reference: PDR</u>. Medical Economics Co., Oradell, N.J.

Sinclair JD. (2001). Evidence about the use of naltrexone and for different ways of using it in the treatment of alcoholism. <u>Alcohol and Alcoholism</u>. 36(1), 2-10.
PubMed Abstract:
http://www.ncbi.nlm.nih.gov/pubmed/11139409
Free Full Text:
http://alcalc.oxfordjournals.org/cgi/reprint/36/1/2.pdf

APPENDIX IV: How Effective Is AA and 12 Step Treatment?

INTRODUCTION

How effective are twelve step programs? Although AA has been around for more than 75 years, the real answer to this question is that no one knows. Studies which have compared AA with a control group have shown mixed results. This article reviews the essential studies of the effectiveness of AA and concludes that although some people find that AA is a useful aid to abstinence from alcohol, others find AA to be damaging and detrimental and to lead to increased drinking rather than abstinence. Hence we recommend that those who find AA to be unhelpful or harmful should find another path such as HAMS, SMART, SOS, WFS, RR, etc. We should also bear in mind that many people who get over an alcohol problem do so on their own without the help of any support group at all.

AA'S RETENTION RATE

A number of researchers have made the claim that 95% of new AA members leave within the first year--that only 5% of new members remain. This claim is based on an AA internal document called <u>Comments On A.A.'S Triennial Surveys</u>. This is a very confusingly written document which appears to be written by someone who is unfamiliar with statistics since there seem to be some elementary analytical errors. However, on a close reading the number 5% quite clearly refers to who are in their twelfth month of AA atteendence, not those who have attended 12 months or more. The document does not tell us how many newcomers remain for more than a year, although it suggests that the number is quite substantial. It would be very interesting if AA ever made the raw data in its triennial surveys available to outside researchers; however, AA steadfastly refuses to do so.

There is, however, one very major problem with AA's triennial surveys, even if the raw data from them were available. That is the fact that only officially recognized AA meetings which are registered with the AA General Service Office (GSO) are polled by these surveys. However, the vast majority of AA newcomers are introduced to AA by "in house" AA meetings which are held by halfway houses or treatment centers. None of these "in house" AA meetings are recognized by AA as "official" AA meetings. This is because halfway houses and treatment centers charge insurance companies money for offering these "in house" meetings and these meetings are closed to outsiders--both violations of AA rules.

When I resided at a halfway house everyone in the house relapsed either during their stay there or immediately after graduation. The success rate for this "in house" AA meting was zero percent. From what I have heard this is quite typical for "in house" AA meetings held at halfway houses. These meetings are generally entirely composed of newcomers and, as mentioned, are never counted in AA's trienial surveys.

12 STEP TREATMENT PROGRAMS

Harvard psychiatry professor George E. Vaillant is a strong supporter of Alcoholics Anonymous who has served as a trustee on AA's General Service Board. Dr. Vaillant conducted an eight year long follow-up of 100 people who had undergone 12 step treatment for alcoholism at Cambridge hospital. When Dr. Vaillant compared the treated group with an untreated control group he got some rather surprising results. He found that people with a diagnosis of alcohol dependence who had never been treated were just as likely to quit drinking as those who went through the 12 step treatment program. In fact, the only significant difference that Dr. Vaillant found between the treated and untreated groups was that people who had gone through the 12 step treatment program were more likely afterwards to attend 12 step AA meetings. They were not more likely to abstain from alcohol however. Vaillant also reports that in the group which quit drinking without attending a 12 step treatment program, three fourths quit on their own without AA attendance either.

Figure IV.1 contrasts Vaillant's 12 step treated sample with an untreated sample of alcoholics at two year follow up. As we can see just as many treated alcoholics are abusing alcohol at the end of two years as are the untreated sample. Moreover, just as many got better on their own as did as a result of treatment.

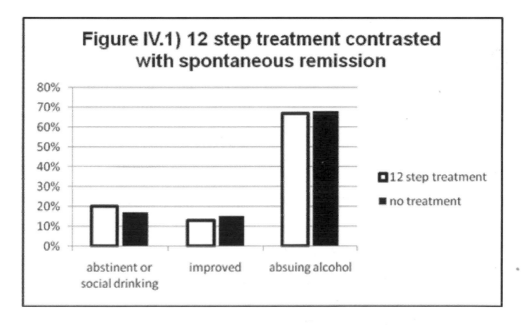

THE BRANDSMA STUDY: PROJECT SHARP

DESIGN

In 1980 Dr Jeffrey Brandsma and colleagues published a large scale controlled study of the effect of alcoholism treatment on alcoholics. 197 patients who met the NCA 1972 criteria for a diagnosis of alcoholism were randomly assigned to one of four treatment groups or to a control group as shown in **Table IV.1**.

Table IV.1) Subjects beginning and completing treatment					
	AA	Insight	Lay-RBT	Pro-RBT	Control	Total
Start	38	38	42	48	31	197
End	12	22	25	26	19	104

Roughly one third of the subjects in this study were self-referred. Roughly two thirds were court ordered to treatment. Treatment was outpatient. The four types of treatment were: Alcoholics Anonymous (AA) meetings, Psychoanalytically-based Insight therapy, Lay-led Rational Behavioral Therapy and Professionally-led Rational Behavioral Therapy.

Subjects were tested for therapeutic outcome at the end of therapy. Follow-up testing was also done 3, 6, 9, and 12 months after the termination of therapy.

RESULTS:

The Eysenck Effect

As early as 1952 Dr. Hans Eysenck noted that that it was always essential to compare mental health treatments to an untreated control group because BOTH treated mental health patients and untreated mental health patients show SIGNIFICANT improvement over time. The effectiveness of a mental health treatment can only be demonstrated if there is a control group. I call this improvement (or "spontaneous remission") in the untreated control group "the Eysenck effect". In 1980 the US Congress published a massive study of the effectiveness of psychotherapy. The upshot of this was that even though psychotherapy is more helpful than no psychotherapy-- untreated patients still show significant improvement over time.

In the Brandsma study 50% of the untreated control group reported an overall reduction in their drinking at the end of the treatment period. 88% of treated subjects reported an overall reduction in drinking at the end of the treatment period. This was a statistically significant difference. There were no significant differences between the four types of treatment on this measure.

Dropout Rates

The AA group had significantly more dropouts than any of the other groups including the control group. 68% of the AA group dropped out. Only 42% of the others dropped out. **Figure IV.2** illustrates the dropout rates graphically.

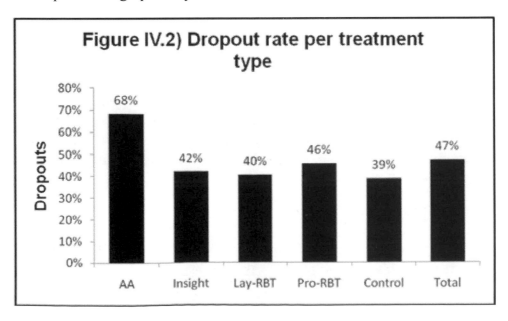

Binge Drinking

The AA group showed a significantly greater number of episodes of binge drinking at the 6 month follow-up period than any other group including the untreated control group. However, this variable was not significantly different at any of the other outcome periods (3, 9 or 12 month) nor was it significant at termination of treatment. A binge was defined as seven or more drinks at one occasion.

Abstinence Days

The Insight group and the Professionally-led RBT group both had significantly more abstinence days than the control group. There was no significant difference between the control group and the AA and the Lay-RBT groups in number of abstinence days.

MMPI Scores

Scores on the addiction scale increased for the AA group during follow-up. Scores on the hysteria scale increased for the AA group during both treatment and follow-up.

Legal

All treated subjects appeared to have fewer legal difficulties than the control group although a confound made an exact comparison impossible.

Total Abstinence

Almost none of the subjects remained totally abstinent after treatment. There were no significant differences between groups on this variable.

Reduced drinking

All groups including the control group showed a significant reduction in drinking compared to pre-treatment levels. All treated groups showed significantly more reduction in drinking than the control group.

12 Month Follow-up Outcomes

At the follow-up 12 months after the conclusion of treatment only the Insight and the Professionally-led RBT group did better than the control group on the measure of drinking days. There were no other significant results of treatment at 12 month follow-up. The AA and Lay-RBT group were not significantly better than the untreated control group on any variable at the 12 month follow-up.

Conclusions from the Brandsma Study

From this study we conclude that whereas AA may be a good and comfortable fit for a few people who have a problem with alcohol, the majority of people with alcohol problems appear to do better with a different approach. We would love to see a study of why so many people dropped out of AA. We hypothesize that this may be due to the fact that AA's theological notions of the powerlessness of humanity and of the need for a rescuing God are unpalatable not only to many atheists and agnostics but to almost all theists who are not Calvinists as well. Unfortunately, no attempt has ever been made to study the best way to match individuals with alcohol treatment which took these theological variables into account.

It may also be the case that the AA philosophy of "powerlessness" over alcohol and slogans such as "one drink, one drunk", "one is too many and a thousand is never enough" and "alcohol is cunning, baffling, and powerful" actually set people up to binge drink rather than to practice damage control when they slip up and fail to abstain as intended. More data on this topic is definitely needed.

PROJECT MATCH

1997's Project MATCH is a rather flawed study which cost the taxpayers 35 million dollars and proved little of any meaningful value. One would hope that a study with this name would attempt to find which treatments were the most effective with which patients--but since the above mentioned theological variables were not taken into account this study did nothing of the sort.

Project MATCH compared three modes of treatment with each other: motivational enhancement; cognitive behavioral coping skills therapy; and "12-step facilitation" therapy. Project MATCH claimed to have demonstrated that all three forms of therapy were equally effective. Actually Project MATCH failed to demonstrate that any of these forms of therapy was effective since there was no control group.

Another problem with Project MATCH is that all the therapies were done in one-on-one sessions with a counselor--however AA meetings and 12 step treatments in real treatment centers are never done one-on-one.

The final objection to Project MATCH is that the treatment sample was pre-selected to be composed of only highly motivated subjects rather than the typical treatment resistant coerced subjects,

In the final analysis we learned little if anything from Project MATCH.

ANECDOTAL EVIDENCE

My personal experience with AA was that it increased my drinking to dangerous and harmful levels which almost killed me and that I only got better after leaving AA. I have met many people with identical experiences who were only able to moderate their drinking or to successfully abstain from alcohol after leaving AA.

DEPENDANT PERSONALITY DISORDER AND AA

In 1988 Poldrugo and, Forti published a study of the relation of personality disorder to alcoholism treatment outcome. Poldrugo and, Forti studied 404 subjects who were undergoing treatment for Alcohol Use Disorders. One quarter of these subjects had personality disorders. What Poldrugo and, Forti found was that alcoholism treatment was far more effective for people suffering from Dependent Personality Disorder (DPD) than for any other group including those with no personality disorder. 75% of individuals suffering from Dependent Personality Disorder completed the course of treatment and remained abstinent for a year. Only 33% of the non-dependent subjects did the same.

The DSM-IV-TR criteria for Dependent Personality Disorder are as follows:

A pervasive and excessive need to be taken care of that leads to submissive and clinging behavior and fears of separation, beginning by early adulthood and present in a variety of contexts, as indicated by five (or more) of the following:

(1) Has difficulty making everyday decisions without an excessive amount of advice and reassurance from others

(2) Needs others to assume responsibility for most major areas of his or her life

(3) Has difficulty expressing disagreement with others because of fear of loss of support or approval.
Note: Do not include realistic fears of retribution.

(4) Has difficulty initiating projects or doing things on his or her own (because of a lack of self-confidence in judgment or abilities rather than a lack of motivation or energy)

(5) Goes to excessive lengths to obtain nurturance and support from others, to the point of volunteering to do things that are unpleasant

(6) Feels uncomfortable or helpless when alone because of exaggerated fears of being unable to care for himself or herself

(7) Urgently seeks another relationship as a source of care and support when a close relationship ends

(8) Is unrealistically preoccupied with fears of being left to take care of himself or herself

To me this suggests that 12 step alcoholism treatment is simply the wrong approach to take with the majority of people who have problems with alcohol. A far better approach to take would be a harm reduction based approach where individuals were treated as responsible adults rather than diseased and powerless puppets of baffling and cunning alcohol. A harm reduction based approach teaches people to take responsibility for working to reduce or eliminate harms associated with alcohol use and is probably far more applicable to the majority of people with alcohol problems than the "powerless" model,

CONCLUSIONS

AA, NA, or other 12 step groups are probably only a good fit for a minority of people with a drug or alcohol problem. The vast majority of people with a drug or alcohol problem will probably do better with either a secularly oriented treatment approach such as is found in SMART Recovery or Rational Recovery or with a harm reduction based approach such as is found in HAMS. Support groups or professional treatment are helpful to some individuals whereas others just need an instruction manual on how to "do-it-yourself".

Some people might find AA unhelpful because it does not fit their personality whereas others may find it a bad fit because of its theology. Baekeland characterizes the average AA member as follows: "He is not highly symptomatic, and is a socially dependant and guilt-prone person with obsessive-compulsive and authoritarian personality features, prone to use rationalization and reaction formation." Moreover there seems to be considerable evidence that AA can cause at least some individuals to drink more than before.

If AA is working for you then fine--keep right on doing it.

However, if you are finding that AA is unhelpful to you or harmful to you in terms of either increasing your drinking or causing psychic distress we advise you to run--do not walk--in the other direction. Do not let anyone coerce you into going to AA meetings against your will, not a spouse or an employer or a doctor or a therapist or a judge--not anyone. The life you save may be your own

As of this writing (September 2009) Federal Circuit Court rulings make it illegal in 16 States for courts to mandate someone to attend AA without offering them a non-religious alternative because of the religious content of AA meetings. Court ordered AA attendance is a violation of separation of church and state as established by the first amendment of the constitution of the United States.

It seems that the research allows us to draw the following conclusions about AA and 12 step treatment

- AA is a good fit for a small number of people with alcohol problems and helps them to abstain.

- AA is a poor fit for the majority of people with alcohol problems and can make some people worse.

- AA is better at creating "true believers" than it is at eliminating problem drinking.

- Whether or not AA is a good fit for a person has little if anything to do with how much a person drinks or the number of alcohol-related problems that a person has--the essential factor is personality type.

- AA is a good fit for black-and-white thinkers who accept proof by authority.

- AA is a poor fit for people who think in shades of gray and demand empirical evidence and scientific proof.

REFERENCES:

269

AA General Service Office (2007). AA Pamphlet P-48 Alcoholics Anonymous 2007 Membership Survey.
http://www.aa.org/pdf/products/p-48_07survey.pdf

Baekeland, F., Lundwall, L., & Kissin, B. (1975). Methods for the treatment of chronic alcoholism: A critical appraisal. In R. J. Gibbons, Y. Israel, H. Kalant, R. E. Popham, W. Schmidt, & R. G. Smart (Eds.), Research advances in alcohol and drug problems (Vol. 2, pp. 247-327). New York: Wiley.

Brandsma JM, Maultsby MC, Welsh RJ. (1980). Outpatient treatment of alcoholism: A review and comparative study. Baltimore: University Park Press.

Bufe C. (1998). AA: Cult or Cure, 2nd ed. Tucson, AZ: See Sharp Press.
Free Full Text:
http://www.morerevealed.com/library/coc/

Eysenck HJ. (1952). The effects of psychotherapy: an evaluation. J Consult Psychol. 16(5), 319-24.
PubMed Info:
http://www.ncbi.nlm.nih.gov/pubmed/13000035

National Council on Alcoholism (NCA). (1972). Criteria for the diagnosis of alcoholism by the Criteria Committee, National Council on Alcoholism. The American Journal of Psychiatry. 129(2):127-35.
PubMed Info:
http://www.ncbi.nlm.nih.gov/pubmed/5041051
Abstract:
http://ajp.psychiatryonline.org/cgi/content/abstract/129/2/127

Peele S, Bufe C, Brodsky A. (2000). Resisting 12-Step Coercion: How to Fight Forced Participation in AA, NA, or 12-Step Treatment. Tucson, AZ: See Sharp Press
Free Full Text:
http://www.morerevealed.com/library/resist/

Poldrugo F, Forti B. (1988). Personality disorders and alcoholism treatment outcome. Drug Alcohol Depend. 21(3):171-6.
PubMed Info:
http://www.ncbi.nlm.nih.gov/pubmed/3168759

United States. Congress. Office of Technology Assessment. (1980). The Efficacy and cost effectiveness of psychotherapy. Washington, D.C. : Congress of the United States, Office of Technology Assessment

Vaillant, G E. (1995). The natural history of alcoholism revisited Cambridge, Mass. Harvard University Press.

APPENDIX V: Carbs, Sugar, and Alcohol Content of Various Drinks

Table V.1) carbs, sugar, calories, and alcohol

beverage	quantity	quantity	calories	carbohydrates	sugars	alcohol
cola	12 oz	1 can	136	35 gm	33 gm	0 gm
beer	12 oz	1 standard drink	153	13 gm	0 gm	14 gm
red wine	5 oz	1 standard drink	125	4 gm	1 gm	16 gm
white wine	5 oz	1 standard drink	122	4 gm	1.5 gm	15 gm
red wine	750 ml	1 standard bottle	625	20 gm	5 gm	80 gm
white wine	750 ml	1 standard bottle	610	20 gm	7.5 gm	75 gm
80 proof spirits	1.5 oz	1 standard drink	97	0 gm	0 gm	14 gm
80 proof spirits	750 ml	1 "fifth"	1623	0 gm	0 gm	236 gm
80 proof spirits	1000 ml	1 liter	2164	0 gm	0 gm	314 gm

To get the same number of carbs contained in one 12 oz can of coca cola one would need to roughly two 750 ml bottles of wine or almost three 12 oz cans of beer. To get the same amount of sugar contained in one 12 oz can of coca cola one would need to drink roughly 6 bottles of red wine or 4 bottles of white wine. It can't be done with beer, as beer normally has no sugar content.

REFERENCES:

USDA Nutrient Data Laboratory Search
http://www.nal.usda.gov/fnic/foodcomp/search

Made in the USA
Lexington, KY
26 July 2012

"In the world of one-size-fits-all treatment programs for alcohol problems, Kenneth Anderson's book is unique in offering a veritable smorgasbord of choices--everything from safe drinking strategies to cognitive and behavior therapies to naltrexone and The Sinclair Method and more. Mr. Anderson is to be applauded for making a host of options available to people who have been failed by more conventional treatment approaches. Because of its wide scope, I believe that this book should be required reading for psychologists, nurses, medical students, families, 'alcoholics' and substance abuse therapists, family practitioners, and law enforcement officials."

--**Roy Eskapa, Ph.D.**
Author of The Cure for Alcoholism
http://thecureforalcoholism.com

"Ken Anderson's book is an excellent and refreshing resource for those wishing to successfully modify their drinking and/or avoid the life-killing programs that now pass for 'treatment' in the U.S. Not only does the material reflect the actual research, but it also debunks the AA/12 Step myths that have dominated our culture to the extent that intelligent people have nowhere to turn for help. I am happy to recommend this book to anyone looking to educate and inform themselves, spouses, family members and friends."

--**Edward W. Wilson, Ph.D.**
Program Director
Non 12-Step
http://www.non12step.com

"Finally! A comprehensive, user friendly, intelligent look at reducing the risks associated with alcohol use from a Harm Reduction perspective. Every aspect, including history, myths and facts, physical/emotional manifestations of alcohol use, and of course, harm reduction theory and action steps toward minimizing negative effects, recovery and beyond. Take your time…this 'manual' reads like a work book and can be one of your most important references on this topic. This has also become mandatory reading for all of our direct services staff and a reference for participant discussion. Well worth adding it to your library."

--**Raquel Algarin, Executive Director**
Lower East Side Harm Reduction Center
http://www.leshrc.org

"HAMS is a person-to-person, grass roots effort to translate into ground-level reality the often abstract claims made by what has become the major reform movement in drug (less so alcohol) policy and (less often) treatment - harm reduction. The truth is that people struggle over their lifetimes to reduce problems associated with substance use and abuse; that few human beings abstain completely and permanently (even among those claiming to do so under the auspices of AA and rehab); yet nonetheless most make improvements in their lives and substance use. NOTHING WE CAN DO by passing laws, trying to herd every substance abuser into treatment, or admonishing high school students never to drink or to take drugs can change this larger human reality. In fact, the reverse is true, and the need to recognize the extent of substance use and abuse in our society increases rapidly, and more people require realistic, harm reduction oriented help. This is not a popular - even an acceptable - truism in the United States, despite ample evidence every day that our larger political and public health policies are meaningless, or worse, counterproductive.

"HAMS is for the large majority of substance users who have problems who remain unserved by our current Alice In Wonderland approaches. The often unacknowledged, majority."

--Stanton Peele, Ph.D., J.D.
Author of <u>The Diseasing of America</u>
http://www.peele.net
http://www.stgregoryctr.com

"Harm reduction programs:

- meet people "where they are" with their drinking,
- don't label people as addicted, diseased or alcoholic,
- empower people to choose their own goals, which can be safer drinking, reduced drinking or abstinence, and
- help people achieve the drinking goals they have chosen.

"<u>How to Change Your Drinking</u> presents 17 elements (not steps) from which readers can choose to use in their program of harm reduction. The many supporting chapters are short and reader-friendly but based on solid research.

"This handbook is pragmatic and excellent."

--David J. Hanson, Ph.D.
Professor Emeritus of Sociology, SUNY, Potsdam.
Web site - Alcohol: Problems & Solutions
http://www2.potsdam.edu/hansondj